£12

1st EDN

2002

D1426718

The Medieval Sea

For Anyusha, Ruby and Tushara

The Medieval Sea

SUSAN ROSE

**hambledon
continuum**

Continuum
The Tower Building, 11 York Road, London SE1 7NX
Suite 704, 80 Maiden Lane, New York NY 10038

British Library Cataloguing-in-Publication Data
A catalogue record for this book is available from the British Library.

ISBN: HB: 1-8528-5563-0

Library of Congress Cataloging-in-Publication Data
A catalog record for this book is available from the Library of Congress.

Typeset by Kenneth Burnley, Wirral, Cheshire
Printed and bound in Great Britain by MPG Books, Cornwall

Contents

Illustrations

Maps and Tables

Abbreviations

ASV   Archivio di Stato di Venezia

PRO   Public Record Office

TNA   The National Archives, Kew

Introduction

The idea of writing a book about all aspects of life at sea in the medieval period was put to me by Tony Morris during a convivial lunch at a pub on the edge of Hampstead Heath. I hope some of the freshness of the sea informs the result.

I should also thank all those I have met at conferences and lectures on maritime subjects whose enthusiasm and knowledge has contributed to this book. I would particularly like to thank Robin Ward for his help with rutters and matters of navigation in general. Both John Dotson and Will Sawyer have been extremely helpful over the location of articles and the gift of offprints. I am responsible of course for any errors of fact or judgement.

I have also received endless support and help from my husband and my family and it is true to say that without this the book would never have been finished. It is dedicated to my three oldest granddaughters. The little ones will have to wait for me to finish another.

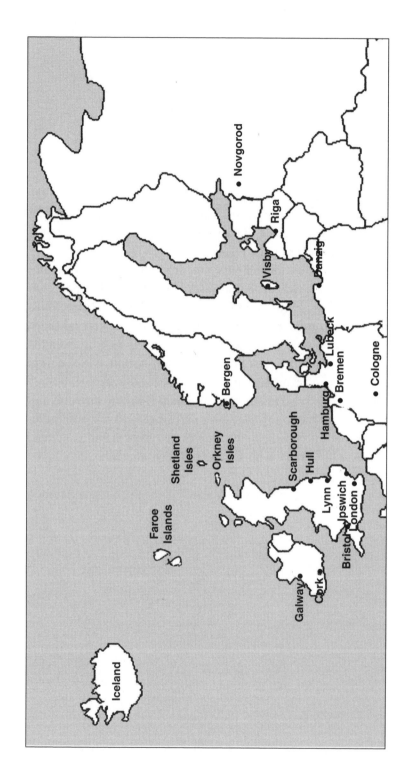

1. Northern waters including Iceland and Greenland

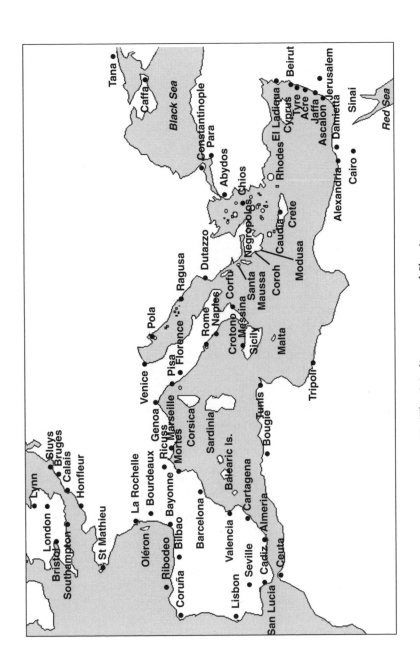

2. The Mediterranean and Iberia

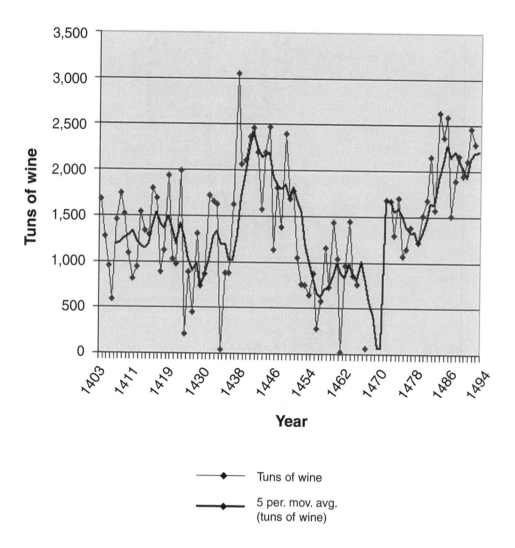

3. Wine imports into Bristol in the fifteenth century

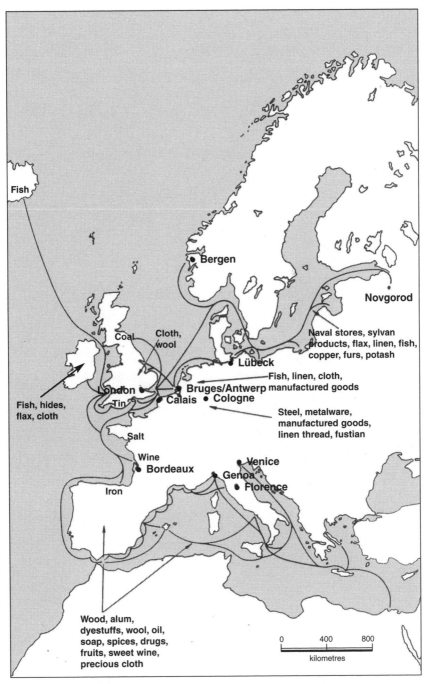

Fish

Coal

Cloth,
wool

Bergen

Novgorod

Naval stores, sylvan
products, flax, linen, fish,
copper, furs, potash

Lübeck

London

Calais

Fish, hides,
flax, cloth

Tin

Bruges/Antwerp

Cologne

Fish, linen, cloth,
manufactured goods

Steel, metalware,
manufactured goods,
linen thread, fustian

Salt

Wine
Bordeaux

Iron

Venice

Genoa
Florence

0   400   800

kilometres

Wood, alum,
dyestuffs, wool, oil,
soap, spices, drugs,
fruits, sweet wine,
precious cloth

4. The principal commodities and routes of sea-borne trade in
Western Europe in the later middle ages

1

Image and Reality

Shortly before his death in 1072 Bishop Leofric of Exeter gave his cathedral library a large book of poems in Old English. It can still be found in the same library. Its pages give us a lively understanding of the place of the sea in the mental world of the Anglo-Saxons. One poem in particular, *The Seafarer*, paints an unforgettable picture of the call of the sea. At one moment the seafarer is tormented by anxiety. He feels the:

> Dreadful tossing of the waves, where the anxious night-watch
> Often held me at the prow of the boat
> When it crashes beside the cliffs. Afflicted by cold
> Were my feet frost-bound by cold fetters.

But despite the loneliness of the sea, hearing 'the seagull singing instead of the laughter of men', when the spring comes:

> The world quickens:
> All of this urges those eager of spirit
> The spirit to the journey, to him who is so inclined
> To venture far out on the paths of the sea.

The seafarer's spirit 'roams beyond the enclosure of the heart' and:

> Along with the sea-flood,
> Travels widely over the whale's haunt,
> Over the world's expanse; it comes again to me
> Eager and greedy; the solitary flier yells,
> Incites the spirit irresistibly on the whale's path
> Over the sea's expanse.[1]

The sea is cold and unforgiving, but it is the path to new lands, to new adventures, with an attraction which cannot be denied.

The same ideas fill the best known of all Anglo-Saxon poems, *Beowulf*. The poem opens with the death of King Scyld and his burial at sea:

> There in the harbour stood the ring-prowed ship,
> The prince's vessel, icy, eager to sail;
> And then they laid their dear lord,
> The giver of rings, deep within the ship
> By the mast in majesty.[2]

Later in the poem, when Beowulf has triumphed over the monster, Grendel's mother, (a fight to the death under water) and is returning home to the land of his people, the Geats, there is another sea-picture of great power.

> The ship surged forward,
> Butted the waves in deep waters;
> It drew away from the shores of the Scyldings.
> Then a sail, a great sea-garment, was fastened
> With guys to the mast; the timbers groaned;
> The boat was not blown off its course
> By the stiff sea-breezes. The ship swept
> Over the waves; foaming at the bows,
> The boat with its well-wrought prow sped
> Over the waves, until at last the Geats
> Set eyes on the cliffs of their own country,
> The familiar headlands; the vessel pressed forward
> Pursued by the wind – it ran up onto dry land.[3]

All this seems set in a heroic mould, but the Exeter Book also contains some realistic yet tender lines which reflect an unselfconscious intimacy with the ways of mariners.

> The ship must be nailed
> The shield framed
> From the light linden.

But how loving the welcome
Of the Frisian wife
    When floats offshore
The keel come home again!
    She calls him within walls,
Her own husband
    – Hull's at anchor! –
Washes salt-stains
    From his stiff shirt
Brings out clothes
    Clean and fresh
For her lord on land again.
    Love's need is met.[4]

It has, in fact, been suggested that there is hardly a single poem written in Anglo-Saxon which is not full of images of the sea. The language used is inventive and expressive with at least twenty-four different single words used as synonyms for the sea and an even greater number of compound phrases like the 'whale's haunt'. In general the images are not those of a calm sea or a summer voyage but ideas of power, of immeasurable strength, of violence and of cold, linked with snow, hail and icy rain.[5] All this closely mirrors the imagery used in poems in Old Norse, where even more inventive descriptive phrases may be found, like 'home of the sea mews' or 'encircler of islands'.[6] Equally in Norse, in inscriptions and verses, the terms, which relate to ships and the sea, are linked to precise meanings, although often used metaphorically. This evidence has been used to understand both Norse society and the technical aspects of Norse ships.[7] For both Anglo-Saxons and Norsemen, particularly in the tenth and eleventh centuries, the sea was a powerful source of inspiration. This could reflect both its everyday importance in their lives and its usefulness as a metaphor for all manner of challenges, dangers and uncertainties.

This pre-eminence, however, was not maintained throughout the Middle Ages in the literature of the British Isles. Nor can sea images be found so deeply embedded in the imaginations of other Europeans. By the fourteenth and fifteenth centuries, in English writing, the sea no longer permeates the imagery in literature on all kinds of topics but is treated on its own as a discrete subject. In other languages it never had so prominent a position. In French the use of the image seems much more conventional and schematic; writers seem to have little personal experience of the sea itself or of sea voyages. It is more a useful metaphor for an unstable changing world than an ever-present element in the lives of many.[8] Where it is used, the sea can appear as calm and peaceful but is also seen as fearful, with sea voyages the source of extreme danger. One French poet compared the force of a storm to the charge of an infuriated wild boar, but what is most striking in most works of the period is the use of what have been called 'tired, conventional images'.[9] Even so, the medieval texts which provide the most vivid descriptions of the sea and voyages are those coming from Norman or Celtic sources. Normandy was the dukedom most influenced by the Norsemen, and Brittany by the seafaring Cornishmen. Both were areas dependent on the sea for a living. Good examples of this kind of writing are Wace's *Le Roman de Brut* or the Breton version of the legend of Tristan.

In Castilian literature, in the same way, the sea was principally a source of inspiration for the writers of romances, and of effective metaphors for theologians for the uncertainties of human existence, until the mid-fourteenth century. After this date, when Castile had gained control of the Straits of Gibraltar and personal experience of seafaring had become more common, it has been suggested that while the old style of writing did not entirely vanish, the sea became for other writers (and in the minds of many Castilians) a place of boundless adventure and a possible source of wealth and power not in a romantic but in a concrete manner.[10] With the success of voyages to the New World at the very end of the century, this trend became even more evident.

In contrast, by tradition Moslems, especially Arabs from the desert, had an aversion to the sea. The general 'Amr described it thus to the second caliph 'Umar, in the late seventh century:

The sea is a boundless expanse, whereon great ships look tiny specks, nought but the heavens above and the waters beneath; when calm, the sailor's heart is broken; when tempestuous, his senses reel. Trust it little, fear it much. Man at sea is an insect on a splinter, now engulfed, now scared to death.[11]

Yet it would be wrong to lay too much emphasis on this early opinion and deduce from it that all Moslem peoples were reluctant seafarers in the Middle Ages. This was far from the truth. It is perhaps the case, however, that the sheer exhilaration to be found sailing over the sea, expressed in some of the sources from northern Europe, is absent in writings in Arabic whether from the eastern or western Mediterranean. The twelfth-century geographer al-Idrisi, from Ceuta, differentiated between the known, the Mediterranean and the Atlantic within easy reach of the coast of North Africa and Iberia; and the unknown sea, the further expanse of the Atlantic. This unknown sea was fearful, full of shadows, tempests, mountainous waves and monstrous beasts.[12]

A thirteenth-century conversation, reported by Ibn Wasil, between Louis IX of France, when a prisoner in Moslem hands, and his guard, Amir Husam al-Din, neatly summarises conventional Moslem antipathy to sea travel. The amir is supposed to have said to his prisoner:

> How could it have come into the mind of a man as perspicacious and judicious as the king to entrust himself thus to the sea on a fragile piece of wood, to launch [himself] into a Moslem country defended by numerous armies and expose himself and his troops to an almost certain death.[13]

To these writers dry land was infinitely preferable to the dangers of the sea.

Some of the most effective and evocative sea poetry of the early Middle Ages does, however, come from a source deeply imbued with Moorish culture. The Jewish poet Judah Halevi grew up in Granada but later in his life travelled to Egypt and other places in North Africa. One of his poems poignantly yet realistically describes both the perils and the beauties of the sea.

> Let not your heart tremble in the heart of the sea, when you see mountains trembling and heaving, and sailors' hands as limp as rags and soothsayers struck dumb . . . The sails quiver and shake, the beams creak and shudder. The hand of the wind toys with the waves like reapers at the threshing: now it flattens them out, now

it stacks them up. When the waves gather strength they are like lions; when they weaken they are like snakes, who then pursue the lions – like vipers they cannot be charmed.

Night then falls and the poet is awestruck by the beauty of the scene:

The stars are astray in the heart of the sea, like strangers expelled from their homes. And in the heart of the sea they cast a light in their image and likeness that glows like fire . . . The sea is the colour of the sky – they are two seas bound together.[14]

Whether the sea had potent attractions, whether it was a fearful place or whether it was a stimulant for symbolism and imagination, it had a strong hold on the minds of many people in medieval times. Despite its dangers it was, or could be, a source of wealth. Sea routes increased trade and allowed commodities of all kinds to be transported over long distances. Contacts could be made by these routes between peoples and cultures. Political advantages might be gained by the domination of coasts and ports. The sea also offered a way in which those with determination and persistence could seek a wider world.

Our basic concern is with the whole of western Europe, including both the northern European and southern African shores of the Mediterranean in the years between about AD 1000 and 1500. During this period the realms in Europe and North Africa changed a great deal; borders shifted, the powers of rulers waxed and waned. In the British Isles, the dominant kingdom of England moved decisively into the orbit of French and Latin culture after the conquest by William of Normandy. Ireland became divided between the east of the country, which was in effect an English colony, and the Celtic west. Scotland remained independent while France saw the monarchy strengthen considerably, so that by 1500 it was arguably the most powerful state in Europe. The Empire's fortunes fluctuated while in the Baltic and neighbouring lands, from the mid-fourteenth century, the Hanseatic League of merchant cities acted in its own best interests, ignoring the demands of other rulers and princes. In the Low Countries the power of cities like Bruges and Ghent was eventually restrained by that of the dukes of Burgundy until the collapse of the dukedom in 1472. In Iberia the rule of the Moslem invaders from the Maghreb, which had reached its apogee in the eighth century, was gradually reduced by the successful assaults of the Christian princes so that by 1500 the peninsula was divided between the kingdoms of Castile and Aragon, united in the persons of their married rulers, Ferdinand and Isabella, and Portugal, with no Moslem realm remaining to the north of the Straits of Gibraltar.

Italy, a geographical not a political label, was a tapestry of different states, some ruled by dukes, princes or the church, others, most notably Venice and Genoa, being republics. The Papal States occupied the centre of the country while to the south was the kingdom of Naples. In the eastern Mediterranean, the advent of the crusades in 1095, leading to the establishment of the kingdom of Jerusalem, had added a new factor to the confrontation of the Byzantine empire and the Moslem states and emirates centred on Damascus and Cairo. By 1500 the kingdom of Jerusalem had long been defeated, but the power structure of the whole area had been changed by the extension of Ottoman rule over most of the Balkans and Anatolia, Egypt and Syria, and the final defeat of Byzantium in 1453.

Beneath this shifting political structure, the physical features of the region, something which could not be ignored by those who wished to venture out upon the sea, were of great importance. We are inclined to think of geographical features as unchanging, but this has never been the case, particularly in the North Sea and Channel and the adjacent coasts. There are considerable differences between the coastline of Kent near Rye and Winchelsea, and in the Rother valley, nowadays and in the medieval period. In particular, great storms in the thirteenth century breached the gravel bank which had protected the area, and caused the complete destruction of Old Winchelsea.[15] The same is true of the east coast from around Orford to the north of Southwold. This can be said with even greater emphasis of the coast of Flanders, the islands in the mouth of the Scheldt and the lands of the Low Countries northwards towards the Elbe. Some changes have been due to the silting of rivers and the action of tides and storms causing erosion and flooding of very low-lying lands. Others were due to the activities of the inhabitants, especially in the Low Countries, who, throughout the period, built dikes, drained the land and cut canals, sometimes to ensure their own safety from storm surges, sometimes to improve communications and reclaim good land.

Further to the east, in the Baltic, an excavation of the medieval harbour at Puck near Danzig has revealed clear evidence of a rise in sea level since the Middle Ages of at least a metre, a consequence of a general subsidence of the land in the area.[16] In the Mediterranean such changes were not common or widespread, but differences in sea level have occurred since the Classical period. The ancient harbours of both Alexandria and Caesarea, for example, are now under water. There is also evidence of changes due to earthquakes and the consequent sea surges, particularly in the eastern Mediterranean.

There were also changes in the climate. In general the years from about 1000 to about 1300 are thought to have been warmer than the periods both before and after. This 'warm' period brought a rise in sea level due to the melting of the Polar ice caps. There is plausible evidence for this in contemporary descriptions of the Fenlands of East Anglia. There seems, for example, to have been a navigable sea inlet which reached as far inland as Norwich. Evidence from the Low Countries points to much more serious consequences of this rise in sea level. Between 1250 and 1287 the sea flooded into the area later known as the Zuyder Zee. The subsequent cooling of the climate in the seventeenth century, and a lowering of sea levels, may have been the cause of the loss of sea channels like that in North Jutland, via the Limfjord, which afforded a link between the North Sea and the Baltic avoiding the Skagerrak and the difficult passage round the Skaw, the northern point of Jutland. Certainly the 'warm' years greatly assisted the settling of Greenland by Vikings and also the prosperity of the Iceland settlements; conversely the 'cold' period beginning about 1300 has been directly blamed for the eventual extinction of the Norse villages in Greenland, the end coming around 1350.

Detailed study of the changing landscape of the Netherlands has shown the economic and political importance of these changes. In fact it has been claimed that, in Groningen, 'the early medieval landscape of the area was destroyed by the waters. That of the present day dates only from the sixteenth and later centuries'.[17] What seems to have happened is that between 950 and 1130 the rise in sea level that had been underway since late Roman times stabilised, allowing an increase in land reclamation and the building of dikes. After 1130 the renewed rise re-enforced the need for dikes to protect inhabited areas and for them to be interlinked. This system largely failed under the storm

surges of the fourteenth and fifteenth centuries, when a series of cata-
strophic floods permanently altered the landscape, waterways and the
fortunes of ports. The worst of all was probably that which occurred
on St Elizabeth's Day in November 1421, when the area known as the
Grote Waard near Dordrecht was completely inundated. According
to contemporaries, seventy-two villages were lost and a hundred
thousand people drowned. The Almere (as the Zuyder Zee was previously known) had earlier ceased to be a fresh water lake and
become an arm of the sea with its new name being first used in the
mid-fourteenth century.

Equally important changes occurred to the rivers Rhine, Maas
(Meuse) and Scheldt. All had entered the North Sea until about 1000
through an area of peat bogs behind coastal dunes. As sea levels rose,
islands like Cadzand and Wulpen emerged, only themselves to be at
least partially overwhelmed in the fifteenth century. The shipping
lanes through these shifting waterways, clearly of great importance to
the trading communities which grew up in the area, were themselves
subject to changes which could be abrupt. The town of Sluys, founded
in 1280–90, was successful as a port because the waterways of the
Ooster Scheldt and the Houte became deeper and wider, and therefore
more suitable for larger ships as water levels rose. Middelburg, on the
other hand, suffered badly as its access to the sea silted up in the
fifteenth century. Kampen owed its prosperity and its prominence in
trade with the Baltic to the fact that it had access to the sea via the
Zuyder Zee from the thirteenth century. By 1441 it was a member of
the Hanseatic League and traded not only with the Baltic but with
Brittany for salt and with the Gironde for wine. Less than a hundred
years later the silting of the River Ijssel made access to the town quays
difficult and this and other factors pushed the town into a precipitate
decline.

Changes in the coastline itself and in channels and waterways were
not the only aspects of the natural environment which were of importance to man's encounter with the sea in medieval times. The patterns
of winds and currents could also greatly affect the ease and routes of
voyages. In northern waters, winds followed no clear seasonal pattern.
The prevailing westerly winds off the Atlantic might be interrupted by
periods of easterlies both in summer and in winter. It is generally
believed that medieval seamen avoided winter voyages to northern

Europe, but the evidence is not conclusive. In the reign of Henry V of England, when regular patrols were sent out to 'keep the seas', these expeditions were put together in the spring and were usually back in harbour by October. On the other hand, an analysis of merchant shipping using the port of Southampton covering several years in the fifteenth century revealed that the busiest months for ships entering and leaving the port were December and January, with the summer months of July and August being the quietest.[18] The Hanseatic League banned ships from leaving port between 11 November and 22 February, but this prohibition was probably as much concerned with the icing up of Baltic ports as bad weather in general.[19] Experienced seamen would, of course, learn to read the patterns of the clouds and winds so that, for example, the signs of an advancing Atlantic cold front and the coming storm were known and acted upon.

In the Mediterranean, it was usually much easier to see the effects of the seasonal pattern of winds on shipping routes. There is a constant counter-clockwise current in the Mediterranean caused mainly by the Atlantic waters flowing in at the Straits of Gibraltar and then along the North African coast, to replenish the waters lost by evaporation in the summer. The speed of this current can reach as much as six knots in the straits, a considerable obstacle to oar-powered or sailing vessels trying to make a passage westward to the Atlantic. Away from the coasts, where sea breezes will blow off shore for most of the day, winds in summer tend to blow steadily from the north west in the western Mediterranean and from the north to north east, the *meltemi*, in the eastern Mediterranean. In winter the direction is more to the north west in the west and more easterly in the Levant. Smaller ships could, to some extent, escape from the effect of these wind systems by hugging the coast as well as by using the force of the current to make progress in a northerly direction. Larger vessels followed well-defined routes usually avoiding the winter months, although this became less noticeable in the later Middle Ages as the design of ships and their sea-keeping qualities improved. Voyages from north to south and from west to east were always faster and less hazardous than those in the reverse directions, because of the prevailing winds. Sailing into the teeth of the *meltemi*, necessary if travelling from Rhodes or Crete to Constantinople, must have been an unwelcome prospect for medieval seafarers. This wind can blow steadily for days at a time in July and August in eastern Mediterranean ports such as Rhodes and Alexandria.[20] A ship might be delayed for long periods waiting for a favourable wind or, if a galley, be faced with an exhausting journey with frequent stops to rest the crew and take on water and other provisions.

The major sailing routes, which can be mapped out from references in contemporary documents, were undeniably supported by the configuration of the land mass, winds and currents. A ship making its way northwards from Alexandria would find it advantageous to set out first for Tyre or Beirut, then to make for Cyprus, Rhodes, the southern coast of Crete and across the Ionian Sea to Cephalonia. At that point some vessels might set a course for the Adriatic, others for the Tyrrhenian Sea and yet others for the Balearics. We must, however, be careful not to overstate the unfriendliness of the southern shores of the Mediterranean to mariners. Even if it was often a lee shore when the *meltemi* was blowing, and had many sandy coasts with few easily identifiable landmarks so that navigation could be tricky, the southern routes were well used by Arab and Jewish traders in the early medieval period,[21] while later many of the ports of Tunisia and the Maghreb were notoriously the haunts of corsairs. The little ships of small traders with local knowledge could follow a myriad of less frequented ways so that, in effect, the whole coastline of the Mediterranean was alive with maritime traffic linking peoples and places together.

This constant traffic was one of the nurseries for the development of almost a common 'language of the sea', elements of which can be traced in both northern waters and the Mediterranean. The word for the second mast added to northern ships sometime in the late fourteenth or early fifteenth century is 'mizzen' in English and something very similar in Dutch, German and the Scandinavian languages. This mast, carried aft of the main mast, also has the same name in Spanish, Portuguese and Italian. In a most surprising way, however, the French word 'misaine' is used for the fore mast (added somewhat later in the fifteenth century). Jal, the author of the pioneering and authoritative *Glossaire Nautique*, published in Paris in 1848, was only able to confess that he had no idea how the French term had acquired so different a meaning. Sandahl writing in the late 1950s attributed it to the way in which the sail plan of galleys was adapted for round ships.[22] We can note the wide distribution of this technical term and what this must imply regarding links between seafaring communities and their sharing of technical information. Other examples abound. Words for different kinds of timber in English, like 'wainscot' and 'deal', usually have a Dutch or Baltic origin. Others like 'poop' are Mediterranean words which came into English via French. The term 'Channel word' has in fact been suggested for terms which can be found in a clearly related form in all the languages of northern seafarers; these mostly concern rigging and include terms like 'bowline', 'halier' (halyard) and 'sheet', and also such common words as 'helm'.[23]

Even the maritime vocabulary of the Ottoman Turks was heavily influenced by both Greek and Italian. Since the Ottomans did not become a naval power until the late fourteenth and fifteenth centuries, the process by which these loan words entered Turkish is plainer and more easily linked to events in the region than in the north. Before 1400 only a few Arabic or Slav maritime words can be found in Turkish, including the word for corsair. In the fourteenth century words of Greek origin appear as the first Ottoman navy was built and manned by Greeks. During the fifteenth century, as Ottoman power advanced into the Balkans and the Aegean, more and more words of both Greek and Italian origin can be found; these include the Turkish words for 'harbour', 'light house', 'biscuit' (the indispensable 'fuel' of galley crews), 'captain' and the mariner's 'compass'.[24]

Not all coastal peoples, therefore, responded to the adventure and challenge of the sea as deeply as tenth-century Anglo-Saxon or late medieval Castilian poets and writers. To some it was more a means to a living; to others simply a realm of darkness. For all, however, it affected their way of life and way of earning a living. Sometimes it was a way of linking people and ideas together, sometimes a barrier to communication. Few embarked on a sea voyage without a degree of apprehension. It did mean entering a world with its own technical language, its own laws and customs. It was, however, also a way to new experiences and possible riches and, it is fair to say, became less feared and more accepted as part of the normal pattern of life by many. This may have lessened the depth of passion and poetic imagination found in the sea poems of the Viking world but also pointed to the social and economic importance of the sea and the activities associated with it at the end of the fifteenth century.

The Shipwright's Craft

By AD 1000 the building of ships had become one of the most complex operations undertaken by either rulers or individuals. Yet it was carried on very widely, both inland on rivers and lakes, and on the coast, in any suitable bay or inlet. Shipwrights were early acknowledged to have special skills and must have had a long and carefully supervised training. Very little is known about this, especially in northern waters. There was a London guild of shipwrights, but its early records were largely destroyed in a fire leaving little except a set of ordinances drawn up in 1426 and amended in 1483.[1] Designing a vessel, an even more skilled occupation, was expected of the most experienced of these craftsmen. Equally bringing together all the supplies needed, timber for the hull of various kinds, cordage, sails, spars, ironwork, and the preservatives, rosin and pitch, and all sorts of miscellaneous items like brass pots (to heat up the pitch), sheepskin mops (to apply the pitch) and shovels (to dig out mud berths and shift sand ballast), required drive, energy and what would now be called management skills. We do not have enough detailed and precise evidence to be sure exactly how all this was achieved, but we can establish some broad parameters.[2]

The evidence is of three kinds, all of which have limitations. Visual evidence from work in both two and three dimensions abounds. All kinds of pictures of vessels can be found, from roughly scratched graffiti on church walls to delicate manuscript illuminations and large-scale and elaborate paintings. In three dimensions, the main sources are seals and medals. With both pictures and items such as seals, the artistic conventions of the time, governing how an object should be represented, pose severe problems if the aim is to use the image to gain technical information about ship construction. Seals and medals are almost uniformly round. On a seal like that of John Holland, lord admiral, 1435–42, to what extent has the ship image been distorted to fit into a circular space? What about the lack of perspective in an image like that of a sea battle from a version at Cambridge of Vegetius' *De Re Militari*? In manuscript illuminations human figures, as the most important elements in the picture (often because of the accompanying narrative), are usually shown as grotesquely big compared with the size of the ship. Among the many extant examples is that of a picture of Henry I returning to England from the *Chronicle of John of Worcester*. Would it ever be practical to expect to deduce accurately the details of rigging from a tiny image from a seal or on the border of a manuscript? A decretal of Pope Pius II from 1464, issued in connection with a hoped-for crusade against the Turks, has a border showing a full range of contemporary shipping, galleys, carracks, single-masted cogs and others, but the details are grossly simplified at best. It was shown in a description of ships at Bordeaux, based on similar representations, that the requirements of the medium falsified a vessel's dimensions and that this kind of image could not be taken as a true image of a trading vessel in use at any particular period.[3]

Images in works on a larger scale, sometimes by well-known artists of the later medieval period, may seem to be more convincing, but the artist's level of knowledge of maritime matters and his access to up-to-date information is unascertainable. The very skill with which the image has been drawn, in a style much more familiar to modern eyes than that of earlier artist-craftsmen, may be misleading. The most familiar and frequently reproduced image of a carrack, the large sailing vessels which dominated both fifteenth-century commerce and naval warfare, is an engraving bearing the initials WA or W and the title *Kraek*. It has recently been argued, however, that this is not a picture of any existing ship but a plan for those making decorations for the floats in a festive procession in Burgundy in 1468. The same image was certainly used by the weavers of a tapestry of much the same date.[4] A careful study has been made of the images of ships appearing in Venetian paintings and sculptures.[5] This makes clear how wary we must be of using such sources. One series of images on the life of St Ursula, dating from 1335, has a panel with the title, 'St Ursula Teaching the Virgins to Sail'. One wonders how effective the lesson was when we realise that the artist (Paolo Veneziano) has left out the mizzen mast, which appears on the image of the ship in earlier panels of the same series on the exploits of this saint.[6] The altar-piece known as the Virgin of the Navigators by Fernandez Alejo, painted between 1531 and 1536 in Seville, shows the Virgin sheltering under her cloak many of the early Spanish travellers to the New World, with a collection of vessels of various types in the foreground. Seville was the centre of Spanish contacts with America and it might be thought that Alejo would have been able to depict ships with access to plentiful models. Just like most earlier paintings, however, it is hard to make reliable deductions about the details of ship construction from these examples.

It might be thought that many of these problems could be resolved by the use of archaeological evidence, from wrecks and sunken vessels and from the objects found on quaysides and riverbanks and sites apparently used for shipbuilding. Here we are certainly much luckier than earlier maritime historians. The advances made by underwater archaeology, in particular in recent times, have greatly increased our knowledge of ancient vessels from the classical to the medieval period. The evidence, however, is very unevenly spread both in date and in location. Wrecks are, to some extent, naturally clustered in dangerous waters or off rocky headlands, but it is also the case that some waters have been much more extensively searched by archaeologists than others.[7] There are also exceptional circumstances like the discovery of the group of scuttled vessels from the eleventh century, blocking the mouth of Roskilde Fjord in Denmark, known as the Skuldelev ships, and the wrecks found when some parts of the Zuyder Zee were reclaimed as polders in the 1940s and 1950s. All these excavated ships are damaged, not only by their initial loss but by the action of wind and water since. Only some materials can survive prolonged immersion, and items such as rigging or sails are very unlikely to be found. Nevertheless some wrecks and other survivals have provided very important evidence of changes in the design and building of ships during the period. The sheer beauty of a Viking ship of the late ninth century is amply demonstrated by the first sight of the Gokstad ship in its specially built exhibition hall in Oslo. Its companion, the Oseberg ship, is equally handsome and still has its high curving prow decorated with elaborate carvings. These two were found in ship burial mounds and were remarkably complete, though 'flattened' by the pressure of the earth heaped over them. With Viking ships the techniques of 'experimental archaeology' – the building of accurate replicas – have also been successfully employed to allow the sailing abilities of these ships to be explored. The Roskilde Museum's replicas of the Skuldelev ships and a two-thirds replica of the Gokstad ship, *Odin's Raven*, have all sailed successfully.

Another vessel of great importance in providing evidence of ship design and construction is the Bremen cog. This wreck was found in the River Weser in Germany in 1962. It was probably lost in a flood while it was being built, since the superstructure had not yet been installed and the only objects found were shipwrights' tools, a barrel of tar and a shoe.[8] Its importance comes from the fact that it is a remarkably well-preserved example of a ship type which held a dominant position in northern waters from the later thirteenth century into the fifteenth century. This was the workhorse of late medieval maritime nations. It was used as a cargo ship, to carry passengers and as a warship, and, far from being an 'unseaworthy box' as some have claimed,[9] it performed well under sail. This has again been demonstrated by the creation of a sea-going replica at Kiel.

In the Mediterranean, fewer medieval ships have as yet been excavated, with divers and archaeologists concentrating more on vessels from an earlier period. Of especial importance, however, is a vessel, which sank in about 1025, excavated in 1977–79 at Serçe Limani in southern Anatolia in Turkey. This small two-masted ship probably went down when its anchor shank broke under the strain of a sudden gust of wind. It was carrying a large cargo of glassware. Its timbers provide valuable evidence of hull construction at this date and are preserved in the museum at Bodrum. The timbers from the wreck of the early fourteenth-century sailing ship, probably a small coasting vessel,[10] found in 1898 south of Venice at Contarina, have been destroyed, but photographs taken at the time clearly show details of her construction. Apart from a Venetian galley dating from the time of the war against Milan in 1509, found at Lazise on Lake Garda, this and two further wrecks from Porto Fuori near Ravenna and Lido di Spina near Ferrara are the only ones so far recorded of the many hundreds of ships which plied the Adriatic and neighbouring coasts in the Middle Ages.[11]

For Venetian shipping and ship construction the documentary evidence is much more copious. This includes not only administrative and general evidence relating to the building and use of ships, including the state fleets of trading and war galleys constructed in the Arsenale, the shipyard of the Venetian Republic, but also technical notes which may be based on manuals for shipwrights. The best known until recently was the manuscript in the Cotton collection of the British Library, part of a notebook compiled by Giorgio Timbotta or Trombetta, a Venetian merchant from Modon in the Peloponnese. A very similar notebook by Michael of Rhodes, a Venetian galley man of Greek origin, written about 1434, came to light in an auction in 2000, but full details of its contents are not yet available.[12] Timbotta's work includes, among notes about music and the uses of the herb rosemary, material about sailmaking, rigging and shipbuilding. It seems to have been written between 1440 and 1444 and gives many technical details for two ship types, a *galia sottil* with twenty-nine banks of oars and a smaller *fusta* with twenty-six. Not only do the notes give precise measurements, they also include some small rough diagrams, unfortunately not to scale. There are also a few notes, some diagrams and a rough sketch of the whole vessel relating to a *galia grossa*. Smaller vessels, ships, boats and sailing ships of various sizes are discussed briefly, with measurements and some general rules for their construction, including rules of thumb such as, 'mast of a ship 3.5 times the beam'. The somewhat quirky nature of the manuscript as a whole is well illustrated by the inclusion of a solution to the problem of how long it would take a mariner to scale a mast if he slipped back a certain amount every night. The answer given (fortunately not based on experience) is two years and nine months.[13]

The sections on rigging and sailmaking begin with the observation that nobody 'can rig any ship or lateener if first the man does not know the measurements of the ship', a plea perhaps for an end to trusting to estimates or the eye of an experienced craftsman. Measurements and directions are given for no fewer than eleven different types of lateen sail. These are assigned to the appropriate vessels, including not only Venetian round ships and galleys but also what are called *zerbe* from both Alexandria and Damietta.[14] There is no similar document for shipbuilding in England until the sixteenth century, when Matthew Baker, a shipwright who worked for the crown from 1572 until his death in 1613, compiled a collection of papers setting out formulae and technical drawings for the design of vessels now known as the *Fragments of Ancient English Shipwrightry*. These papers came into the possession of Samuel Pepys and were originally intended to be one of the sources for his (never written) history of the English navy. It is perhaps an echo of the many medieval illuminations of Noah at work on his ship that even this highly technical work begins with an illustration of Noah's Ark (in this instance shown as a sort of oblong box), with the appropriate quotation from Genesis.[15]

Administrative documents and accounts relating to shipbuilding and ship operations exist not only for Venice but also for Genoa. There are records relating to the building of galleys for the Angevins in the South of France and in Sicily, and for the crown of Aragon, especially in Barcelona. In northern waters the richest archive of this kind of material is probably that for England. This is found mainly in the accounts of the royal exchequer, with the earliest material dating from the reign of King John. It becomes most copious in periods when wars, usually against France, were being actively pursued and culminates in the series of accounts kept by the keepers or clerks of the king's ships (both titles are used). These relate mainly to the reigns of Henry V and Henry VI. They stop in 1452 but then recommence in the reign of Henry VII.[16] The establishment of what is usually called the Navy Board, the point at which England gained a permanent naval administration, did not occur before 1545. Those records that relate to shipbuilding normally give the costs of materials and labour but tend to include few measurements or other technical details, apart from the tunnage (estimated hull capacity measured in tuns or wine barrels) of vessels under construction or repair. This is particularly problematic with regard to rigging, where the only details are the names of the various ropes and cables and their weight, with no indication of how they might have been set up. There are a few similar records from the French royal archives mostly relating to the *Clos des galées*, a yard established by Philip IV to build galleys for the French crown at Rouen in 1294, burnt by the English in 1417.[17] There are virtually no records relating to shipbuilding for commercial or private purposes. Any descriptions of northern ships from our period therefore include a degree of speculation.

One thing is immediately clear. The tradition in southern waters was radically different from that in the Channel and northern waters; only at the end of the Middle Ages did the two begin to come together, producing something much nearer to a common European approach to the building and design of ships.

Perhaps the best known of all early vessels in the northern tradition of shipbuilding are the longships of the Vikings. Their seaworthiness and the courage of their crews are amply demonstrated by the number and extent of their voyages in the often dangerous and stormy waters of the North Atlantic, with the settlement of Greenland and the discovery of Vinland as the most notable of their achievements. The design and construction of their ships is well known from those excavated in Scandinavia and from descriptions of their use in the sagas or poetry. The *Heimskringla* or *History of the Norse Kings* by Snorre Sturlason, written in the early years of the thirteenth century, contains many accounts of naval battles. Although there were differences in design caused by differences in intended use (of the Skuldelev ships, two were cargo vessels, two were warships and one may have been a fishing boat), all were clinker built. This means that the bottom of each plank making up the vessel's sides overlapped the top of the one beneath. The planks were nailed together through the overlap using a system of clench nails. These were iron nails driven from the outside inwards; the shanks of the nails protruded from the planking inside and were hammered over against a square iron rove or metal plate. Unlike in modern clinker building (a technique now used only for rowing boats and similar vessels), caulking was inserted between the planks to prevent leaks due to the unevenness of the planks (usually split not sawn from the timber). Such caulking, made of a mixture of animal hair, moss and tar but often called oakum, has been found at various excavations including one in Newcastle.[18] This style of shipbuilding is also called 'shell first', since the shape of the vessel's hull was built up gradually from the keel or base timber, usually without the use of drawings or prepared measurements. It is hard for a modern shipbuilder to grasp how such a method could work successfully not only for small boats but also, in the fifteenth century, for large ships like the *Gracedieu*. The surviving remains make abundantly clear, however, that this was a viable method of ship construction. It seems that the idea of 'building by eye' is not quite as simple as the phrase might imply. Often the available supply of timber determined basic measurements like the length of the keel. There were also 'rules of thumb' (remembered in rhyming mnemonics) handed on from master to apprentice regarding the proportions of a vessel. These can still be found in the building of special regional craft such as the Somerset turf boats or the Wexford 'cots' even in modern times. It is also the case that on the large hollow stem post of the ship known as Skuldelev 3 there are lines cut on each side corresponding to the strakes or planks of the completed ship and so positioned that these strakes would join the stem at the correct angle. This seems like evidence of a prior design.[19] It is possible, at least by the later medieval period, that measuring sticks were used, probably similar to the 'boat ell' of nineteenth-century Norway.[20]

Viking ships, which were mainly intended for use in war or for personal transport, were propelled by oars but also usually had square sails on a single mast. Early versions seem to have had no decks, though the Gokstad ship had a tent which could be fixed to the vessel's sides for shelter in bad weather and perhaps also at night. Cargo ships were intended normally to proceed under sail and only used oars in harbour or, for example, to beach against the wind. They had a higher freeboard than warships but otherwise were constructed in much the same way. Both types had side rudders so well balanced that little physical effort was needed to hold the vessel on course in fine weather. The larger of the two Skuldelev cargo ships is an example of a *knarr*, the vessel used on long voyages to Iceland or even Greenland laden with colonists, their cattle and their possessions. There were small half decks at the bow and stern but no other protection for passengers and crew; long voyages in bad weather must have required great fortitude.[21]

Ships in the remainder of northern Europe in the eleventh and twelfth centuries probably had many similarities to these vessels. The ships depicted in the Bayeux Tapestry show very similar side rudders, clinker planking and hull shape. All are sailing ships with what may be rather better rigging than that of their predecessors. They could clearly be used to transport horses, although no indication is given of how these were embarked and disembarked; more importantly, the frames in the tapestry showing the building of William I's invasion fleet have good pictures of shipbuilding tools.[22] One shipwright is shown boring holes for treenails or spikes using a breast auger; others are using axes to trim and split timber. Another tool shown may be an early form of bevel gauge.[23] This would have been used to check that the strakes would meet at the correct angle. Documents from about the early twelfth century increasingly refer to vessels known as keels, cogs or hulks. The difference between these is largely conjectural or based on the interpretation of the kind of pictures mentioned above. It has been suggested that the term 'keel' relates to a vessel like those in the Bayeux Tapestry; but modern ship archaeologists are perhaps more responsible for tying the word to one particular ship type than contemporaries, for whom it seems often to have been a synonym for 'ship' or 'boat'. The word 'hulk' is also hard to confine to a clearly differentiated ship type; the one clear piece of evidence is the seal of New Shoreham. This shows a ship with a distinctive 'banana' shaped hull, with the planking coming up beneath the fore and after castles, held together by a large wooden block or even with ropes rather than joined to stem and stern posts. The inscription on the seal reads '*hoc hulci segno vocor os sic nomine digno*' (by the sign of a hulk I am called Mouth which is a worthy name); this becomes meaningful when it is realised that New Shoreham was also known as Hulksmouth.[24] There are other pictures of similar vessels from the same date, the thirteenth century, but the seaworthiness of such a design does seem in doubt. Leeway might pose a great problem and the vessels, as depicted, seem to lack stability.

Much more is known about the cog. This was the workhorse of medieval shipping in northern waters. Cogs carried the trade of the cities of the Hanseatic League. Edward III's preferred royal ship was the *Cog Thomas*, and cogships, mainly of foreign origin, were entering Colchester harbour in large numbers as late as 1514. The customs accounts list thirty-three alien cogships in the port in 1465–66 and forty-eight in 1513–14.[25] Under the name of *cocche*, ships of this type from Bayonne were credited by Giovanni Villani, in his *Nuova cronica*, written probably in the 1340s, with entering the Mediterranean to prey on local shipping but then exerting a great influence on the design of locally built vessels.[26] This incursion was dated by Villani to 1304, but it is probable that cogs had been seen in the Mediterranean well before this date. These ships had high sides and much straighter stem and stern posts than either hulks or longships. The precise dimensions of the Bremen cog produce a vessel 24 metres long, 8 metres in the beam and over 4 metres high.[27] This would produce an estimated capacity of 130 tuns.[28] The first four strakes laid alongside the keel do not overlap in the usual manner of clinker building but are laid with flush edges and are caulked. The remainder of the hull is clinker-built with crossbeams inserted to strengthen the vessel. There was a stern rudder fixed to the outer stern post while a single mast was stepped and would have carried a single square sail. The planks were sawn, not split, from the original logs. Vessels like this had well-designed hulls, not unduly affected by leeway. Their long dominance of the shipping trade in northern waters, in the fourteenth and early fifteenth centuries, is evidence of the success of the design. The design was also flexible and capable of considerable development. Early cogships used for war, or in waters where dangers existed from sea robbers, often had temporary platforms or castles fitted fore and aft raised above the level of the deck. These were useful fighting platforms, while missiles could also be rained down from 'top castles' fixed to the top of the mast. These platforms were gradually incorporated into the fabric of the vessel. In the after castle, where the steersman and the master could set and steer the necessary course with some protection from the weather, accommodation could be provided for noble passengers. The forecastle also provided some shelter and eventually space for guns.

In the fifteenth century this basic cog design was probably at least one source of the design of the larger two- or three-masted sailing vessels which became a familiar sight on long-distance trade routes. The shipwrights at this time were also probably inspired by the large sailing vessels from Genoa and other cities in the Mediterranean which entered northern waters both to trade and, as far as the Genoese are concerned, as war ships in the pay of the king of France, in the fourteenth century. These carracks were carvel-built (with edge to edge planking) and were built 'frame first', that is the keel was laid and the ribs of the vessel put in place before the whole was planked.

It is not at all clear when this system of building was finally adopted in the north. Henry V captured carracks from the Genoese allies of the French in 1416 but then found that repairing them was beyond the skills of his shipwrights. Carpenters skilled in this kind of work were recruited from Venice, Catalonia and Portugal.[29] Henry's own men pressed on with the building of the huge *Gracedieu* at Southampton. This ship, of 1,400 tuns capacity, had a special kind of three-skinned clinker planking, examples of which have been brought up from the wreck of the vessel in the Hamble river.[30] She was probably the largest clinker-built ship ever designed. There is no evidence that she was inherently unseaworthy, but she perhaps represented a technological cul-de-sac. It is certainly the case that, by the later years of the century, the ships built and repaired for Henry VII were all carvel-built with three or more masts, looking very like the ships to be seen in the *Beauchamp Pageant*. This is a series of drawings of the life of Richard Beauchamp, earl of Warwick, who died in 1439. The pictures were probably commissioned by his daughter Anne Neville in the 1480s. Much of the work is concerned with his pilgrimage to Jerusalem, and this provided opportunities for illustrations which include ships. These all have stern rudders and three or more masts with lateen sails on the mizzen and after masts. Cannon can be seen mounted on the deck shooting over the rail. One plate shows a sea battle, with cross-bowmen, longbow men and men hurling stones from the top castle all represented. The form of the hulls is hard to discern but may be intended to show carvel-building.[31] The household books of John Howard, Duke of Norfolk, for 1462–71 and 1481–83 also include details of naval expeditions and some information about the building of the Duke's ship *Edward*. This is often called the *carvel*, as are others like *Thomas Nokes carvel* and *John Koles carvel* in a group of ships victualled by Howard in 1470 for a sea-keeping expedition.[32]

Mariners in the north did not, however, entirely abandon the use of oared vessels in favour of sailing ships like those we have just been discussing. Vessels called galleys were built by order of King John in the early thirteenth century. Philip le Bel of France, as we have seen, created a special galley yard at the end of the same century at Rouen; galleys from Spain roamed the Channel on raiding expeditions in the early fifteenth century; and, if we look forward to the sixteenth century, Henry VIII included what were called 'roo baergys' (row barges) in his navy. There were thirteen of these, small vessels of twenty tuns capacity well armed with usually four guns apiece. They were also equipped with sails but are shown on the Anthony Roll (a contemporary manuscript with illustrations and some other details of Henry VIII's ships) as having a total of twenty-eight oars in banks of fourteen. The roll also includes an illustration of the royal ship the *Galley Subtille*; this vessel greatly resembles contemporary Italian galleys and is shown as having around forty-eight oars all told. It also had a single mast with the long lateen yard typical of Mediterranean galleys.[33]

The earlier galleys of both French and English kings are unlikely to have looked quite like this, but there is little clearly identified visual evidence for either group. It has, in fact, been suggested that to call the oared ships built by the kings of England and France in the Middle Ages 'galleys' merely serves to confuse the issue; we are here really dealing with the last manifestation of the Viking longship tradition. Perhaps closer to the 'southern' type of vessels were the balingers frequently mentioned in the records from the mid-fourteenth century onwards. The term 'balinger' has an obscure origin; the usual suggestion is that these were ships originally developed on the Basque coasts of the Bay of Biscay, particularly at Bayonne, to hunt whales ('baleiner' in Old French is a whale ship).[34] A more elaborate consideration of the linguistic origins of the word, linked to considerations of the known uses of this type of vessel, has led to the suggestion that 'balinger' is linked to the 'berlinn', the oared fighting ships and transports of the Western Isles of Scotland which were still being built in the seventeenth century.[35] The distinctive feature of these ships may have been the provision of tent-like structures for shelter on deck and a much higher freeboard than Mediterranean galleys. They, however, retained the speed and manoeuvrability of vessels which sailed well and could be rowed when necessary.[36] What is certain is that balingers were not only favoured by sea raiders, whether operating under letters of marque or as out and out pirates, but were also built by the crown for use both as warships and as scouts and rapid transports. In 1401, in the confusion caused by rebellion in Wales, Henry IV wrote to the city of Hereford saying that there was 'urgent need . . . to build barges and balingers, which, in wartime, as we are informed, are more suitable than other ships to guard the seas'.[37] During his reign, Henry V owned sixteen ships in this class ranging from the *Ane*, *George* and *Nicholas*, each of 120 tuns capacity, to the *Paul*, *Peter* and *George* (not identical with that named above) of 24 tuns each. The *Ane*, *George* (120 tuns) and the little *Roose* of 30 tuns were all two masted while the remainder had a single mast with a large square sail.[38] When parliament petitioned the king in 1442 to set up a scheme for the guarding of the seas, the MPs' hope was that the king would put together a squadron of eight great ships, each attended by a barge and a balinger (the distinction between these is not at all clear, though in this instance barges were apparently larger than balingers).[39] Balingers' reputation as fighting vessels is confirmed by the story in an Italian chronicle of how six English balingers took on a Genoese carrack in the Channel in 1416 and were only forced to break off the engagement when they had no missiles (arrows, stones and iron darts) left.[40] This was despite the fact that the carrack towered more than a spear's length over her pursuers.

The need to oppose Italian carracks in sea battles probably lay behind the development of a special class of ships in early fifteenth-century England. These were the king's (Henry V's) 'great ships', the *Trinity Royal, Holy Ghost, Jesus* and *Gracedieu.* They were intended to be the largest vessels afloat, able to overawe, lie alongside and take by boarding any vessel of the enemy; particularly at this date the carracks of the French and their Genoese allies. The oldest and smallest at 540 tuns of this group of ships was the *Trinity Royal,* a rebuild of an older vessel of the same name. The *Holyghost de la Tour* (740–760 tuns) was also a remodelled vessel. She had her origins in a captured Spanish ship, the *St Clare,* and was apparently so thoroughly rebuilt that her planking was converted from carvel to clinker. The *Jesus* (1,000 tuns) was built on the River Rother at Winchelsea, being completed in 1416. The most important of the group, however, from the point of view of her design, was the *Gracedieu.* This vessel was built at Southampton and at 1,400 tuns capacity was enormous by the standards of the day and indeed for a considerable period in the future. After the death of Henry V she was laid up in the Hamble river at first at anchor in the stream; after 1433 she was laid up on the mudflats and was then struck by lightning and burnt to the waterline in January 1439. This ensured that her remains sank into the mud and became the source of all sorts of stories about the origins of the gigantic wreck, whose timbers were just visible at low water on equinoctial spring tides. She was widely believed to be a Viking ship until the 1930s when an excavation and survey of the site confirmed her size and also allowed specimens of her woodwork to be retrieved for dating by dendrochronology. This clearly dated the timbers to the fifteenth century. These same specimens also made clear the method used for constructing the hull planking of this ship, perhaps the largest clinker-built vessel ever to sail. A kind of double or treble overlap of the strakes was used, clenched with iron nails and roves in the usual way.[41] Her planking thus always consisted of at least a double layer of timber. The accounts of her building make clear that she was at least a three-masted vessel; the other 'great ships' were two-masted with a main and mizzen mast.

Two other recent excavations, one in Brittany and the other in Wales, provide information about the construction of merchant vessels. What is known as the Aber Wrac'h I wreck was found in the mouth of the river of that name some 30 km north of Brest in 1985. The ship was wrecked when she was in ballast, so that at first all that could be seen on the river bed was a heap of stones with some frames protruding from the mass. When this ballast had been shifted, it was clear that she was a clinker-built vessel some 25 metres long with a beam of around 8 metres. Her discoverers saw some resemblances to the *Gracedieu* in her planking and she can certainly be dated to the first half of the fifteenth century.[42] The Newport ship was found in 2002 on the banks of the River Usk at Newport during the construction of a leisure centre. From preliminary results of the work on the wreck, it seems that she was much the same size as the Aber Wrac'h vessel and was laid up for repairs round about 1467, having been built some years previously.[43] No excavated ship, however, has yet been able to provide clear evidence of the beginnings of carvel-building in northern waters.

Despite the relative lack of archaeological evidence from the period after 1000, there are fewer puzzles regarding the design and construction of ships in the Mediterranean. It is generally accepted that the change from the triremes and biremes of the Ancient World to the dromons of the Byzantines occurred some time round the fifth century. A dromon had a lateen sail and an above-water 'spur', not an underwater ram at the bows. Clear written evidence on the design of a dromon exists from the time of the Emperor Leo VI in the late ninth and early tenth centuries. An anonymous treatise from about 985 makes it possible to state that most dromons of Byzantium had their oars arranged on two levels with twenty-five oarsmen per side; thus the total crew was over one hundred men, including officers. They also had a siphon or similar device on the fortified fore deck to project the Greek Fire which was their major weapon. At the prow also was the spur used to break up an opponent's oars or to make a 'bridge' for boarding parties. It is also probable that these vessels were fully decked, largely to provide some cover for the oarsmen. When Moslem forces took to the sea at the end of the seventh century, it seems that their vessels differed little from those of the Christians. In the earliest documents from Islamic sources, much of the vocabulary used is derived from Greek or is very unspecific, using terms that give no idea of the special features of a ship. From the time of the Crusades the word 'galley' is normally used to describe the ships of the Venetians, Pisans and other maritime powers of the Latin west, but it is hard to get any clear idea of their design. The suggestion has been made that chroniclers and other writers more or less never comment on the appearance of galleys because they were so standardised in character that there was no need to do this as far as contemporaries were concerned.[44] The first detailed information comes from notarial contracts and the specifications for galleys built for Charles I of Anjou in his war against the Aragonese in Sicily at the end of the thirteenth century.

These specifications are often in a contractual form between the king and the shipbuilder and do provide measurements and other technical information that is missing from the English accounts. The size of the crew and thus the number of rowing benches can be estimated as early as 1248 from a series of contracts drawn up by the notary Giraud Amalric. A typical example records the hire of a galley called *Ben Astruga* by three Tuscans for a voyage from Marseilles to Arles with 60 men, then later going to Pisa with 130 men. Internal evidence suggests strongly that this was a two-masted bireme with thirty banks of oars. The Angevin building contracts include even more technical information. Charles I ordered ten galleys in 1272 from the *justicier* of the Principat et Tour de Labour with predetermined dimensions including a length of fifty-one *goues* (40.34 metres) and a beam amidships of twelve *pans* (3.16 metres).[45] Further specifications from contracts dating from 1275 prescribe the design of a vessel called the *galea rubra de Provincia* (the red galley of Provence) as the model to be followed. These would produce a vessel slightly smaller than that from 1272, being 39.55 metres long from stem post to sternpost and 2.97 metres in the beam. These vessels were also intended to have a beak or spur (separate from the hull), 108 oars, two masts and side rudders. It seems at least possible that the oars were arranged on two levels rather than having two oarsmen per bench, but this is not entirely clear from the available evidence. Apart from the 108 oarsmen, the crew consisted of two sailing masters, four helmsmen, sixteen fighting men and two boys. If fully armed a galley like this had about thirty crossbows, quantities of darts and lances and the like, Greek Fire and the machines to project it, grapnels and rigging cutters. There would also have been silk and buckram pennons, banners and flags, a silk covering for the poop and shields displaying the coats of arms of Anjou. A ration scale was also specified for the crew, consisting largely of ships biscuits (*biscotti*) with a little salt meat (less than 1.5 kilograms a month), cheese, peas and beans, and wine (nearly 70 litres per man per month).[46] These galleys had a low freeboard; an inevitable consequence of the need to strike a compromise between a design which minimised the drag from the submerged hull and one which maximised the mechanical advantage of the oars by keeping the angle to the waterline as low as possible.[47] These galleys were in fact primarily designed to be rowed; using the sail with the oars shipped 'awing', that is raised with the blades in the air and the handles on deck, would have been extremely difficult with tacking virtually impossible. Any wind above a Force 4 (usually thought of as a pleasant sailing breeze) would have made it necessary to lower the sails.

A variant on these galleys were the ships known as *taride* or (earlier) *chelandrum*. These were not so much warships as transports, particularly horse transports, with deeper holds than the war galleys and stern ports with ramps through which the horses could be loaded or, indeed, ridden straight out to battle by mounted knights advancing up a beach. The horses were stabled in the hold, facing fore and aft, protected from the movement of the vessel at sea by being suspended by slings under their bellies. In a hot Mediterranean summer, with perhaps as many as sixty horses embarked on a vessel, holds must have rapidly become extremely hot and smelly.[48] If the weather deteriorated, many animals would have suffered injuries or even death.

Towards the very end of the thirteenth century these oared warships underwent a decisive change in design. This is mentioned by the Venetian Marino Sanudo Torsello in a text designed to encourage crusading when he says, almost as an aside, that in '1290, two oarsmen used to row on a bench on almost all galleys which sailed the sea. Later more perceptive people realised that three oarsmen could row on each of the aforesaid benches'. Regulations passed by the Venetian senate in January 1303 shed further light on this. They clearly imply that it was expected that there would be three oars (and oarsmen) per bench. This and some other evidence has been taken to mark the point when the biremes of the thirteenth century and earlier were replaced by triremes.[49] Irrespective of how the oars on biremes were arranged, it now seems clear that these triremes were so designed that three oarsmen per bench would each pull an oar. These oars were on one level but with the benches placed at an angle so that the oarsmen did not get in each other's way. The oars were also of different lengths, with that of the man sitting nearest the central gangway of the vessel being the longest. This man, the *pianero*, set the stroke for his group of three and had to be both skilled and experienced.[50] This style of rowing a galley was known as *alla zenzile*. In the early sixteenth century this was replaced by the system known as *a scaloccio* in which three or more oarsmen per bench rowed one larger oar. Much less skill was needed for this method and it has been linked with the gradual replacement of free, paid and volunteer galleymen by slaves or convicts.

The hulls of galleys were constructed on the 'frame first' system, with edge to edge or carvel planking at least by the beginning of the tenth century. Clear evidence for this is provided by the Serçe Limani wreck. Ships in the ancient world were built up on a variant of the 'shell first' system with the planking joined together by mortice and tenon joints, a method which required great skill in woodworking. A wreck from the seventh century found at Yassi Ada seems to show that by this time the idea of inserting some frames before the planking had advanced very far was gaining ground. In the Serçe Limani vessel, it has been suggested that one unit of measurement was used throughout the vessel's construction, perhaps something as basic as the measurement of the shipwright's palm.[51] Certainly by the time the surviving shipwright's notes were written, the process of hull design was governed by mathematical principles and applied geometry.[52] The first step was to determine the shape and size of the main frame. This was used as a pattern for all the other frames in the midships section of the hull. How the design of the fore and aft sections was determined is not entirely clear but it is thought to have followed similar principles.[53]

Planking (edge to edge) was fastened to the frames with nails, and caulking was forced into the seams with a special tool to prevent leaks. Before the early fourteenth century and the arrival of northern cogships in the Mediterranean, all vessels, whether the galleys or the sailing ships which also flourished in the Mediterranean, were steered by side rudders or steering oars. From this period the sternpost rudder of the north became gradually more and more common.

Despite their inherent similarities, there were some variations in the pattern of late medieval Mediterranean oared vessels. The most common were the fast lean light galleys, the *galee sottili*. These were used for warfare, for the transport of important individuals and for valuable lightweight cargoes. For more nefarious purposes, they were always the preferred craft of pirates or corsairs. They were fast under oar for short distances and could also sail well with their lateen sails, having usually one mast before about 1200 and two thereafter. Similar but smaller vessels were known as *fuste* or *galiots*. The imposing Venetian *galie grosse* or 'great galleys' were developed to meet the commercial and defence needs of the Serenissima. They were built in the state shipyard, the Arsenale at Venice, the first being launched about 1294. These vessels were rowed *alla zenzile* like their smaller counterparts, with three oarsmen to a bench, but their increased size made it necessary to have longer oars weighted on the inboard end for ease of use. At first two-masted, but later with three masts, all were equipped with large lateen sails. They sailed well and probably only used their oars to enter harbours or to hold off from a lee shore. These galleys had an average length of about 40 metres at first, but this tended to increase as time went by so that by the beginning of the sixteenth century they were some 46 metres long. The aim was to produce a vessel which had a much larger cargo carrying capacity than the light galleys but which could also defend itself from pirates and be of use in war. In many ways the design was outstandingly successful in both fields. The galleys carried valuable goods on regular trade routes. Some went from Venice via the Iberian ports to Southampton, Sandwich and Bruges; others went to Alexandria or Constantinople and on into the Black Sea. As warships their large crews (about 150 men) were a deterrent to attacks from smaller ships and by the end of the fifteenth century they also carried guns mounted on their prows. There were some problems with their seaworthiness:

these galleys under sail had a tendency to bury their prows in the waves and must have shipped a lot of water in rough weather. They also required very careful lading to ensure their stability: a decree of the Venetian Senate forbidding the stowage of cargo on the deck was probably a response to this problem.[54] By the time of the battle of Lepanto in 1571, vessels of this type had become more clearly warships, with modifications which improved their ability to serve as platforms for guns.

The Venetians were not, of course, the only people to use galleys for trade and warfare in the Mediterranean. The Florentine great galleys, which also made the journey to Flanders in the fifteenth century, were probably very similar to those of Venice. The Genoese, Sicilians and fleets from Barcelona and Valencia all relied largely on their swift and manoeuvrable light galleys for use in war and for transport and communications.

The facts that galleys were used in warfare and also carried much of the valuable trade of the Venetians and others have obscured the equally important role played by sailing vessels or round ships in the southern seas. The Serçe Limani ship already described was such a trading vessel. It was a two-masted lateen-rigged cargo ship carrying a large quantity of glassware probably from Egypt to a Byzantine port. Using the evidence of contracts to build transport vessels between Louis IX of France and others, and Genoa, Venice and Marseille, during the preparations for his crusades in 1248–54 and 1270, much can be deduced about the design of sailing ships of the day. These contracts give detailed measurements. The designs have also been tested, not by building full size replicas as in the case of some of the northern vessels but by building accurate scale models. In most cases these sailed well. Round ships between about 1000 and 1340 can be divided into one group usually known as *selandria* (about 30 metres long and about 6.5 metres in the beam) and another known as *naves* (about 34 metres long and 11 metres in the beam) which might have, by the end of the Middle Ages, two, three or even four decks. All were built on the 'frame first' system and had curved stem and stern posts, a feature which made them seem round compared with the low, sleek hulls of galleys. Most were two-masted with lateen sails, though the largest vessels might have three masts.[55] Horses, cargo and, on certain voyages, the general run of pilgrims making for

the Holy Land were carried below decks. Conditions here must have
been exceedingly cramped and smelly. There was better accommodation in the cabin at the stern, called alluringly *paradisus*. There might
also be an upper cabin known as the *vannum* or *supravannum*. These
occupied what would have been the aftercastle on a cog; these areas
would have had the considerable advantages of light and fresh air but
could become dangerous in a storm. Louis IX was forced to take
refuge in a lower cabin on his return from Egypt when it was feared
the *supravannum* might be swept overboard.[56]

The crucial factor which changed the design of these southern
round ships was the adoption of the sternpost rudder, credited to
imitation of the example of Bayonne raiders. New hybrid vessels, the
cocche, had this type of rudder and a single square sail but kept the
carvel hull of the south. One great advantage was that they required
much smaller crews to control the square rig than the huge lateen sails
of the ships of St Louis. Their superstructure maintained the familiar
raised 'castles' at the prow and the poop (but as integral parts of the
hull design) of both cogs and round ships. The best evidence of their
appearance is the little Mataro model, dated about 1450, originally
hung in a chapel as an *ex voto* offering for deliverance from some
maritime peril.[57] Its hull is carvel-built and it has a square-rigged main
sail with lateen mizzen and foresail. The Genoese in particular
developed this ship type energetically and soon used them exclusively
on the long run to Flanders and England. By the beginning of the
fifteenth century the carracks (as they were called in northern waters)
of Genoa were a familiar sight in the Channel and southern North Sea
and were by this time often rigged with a second mizzen mast carrying
a lateen sail. Their imposing size made them feared in war but was a
great advantage on trading voyages, when bulky cargoes such as alum
(a fixative for dyeing textiles, brought from the Genoese trading centre
at Chios and later also mined at Tolfa south of Florence) as well as
valuable goods such as spices could be carried. It was this ship type
that was to be the progenitor of the full-rigged sailing vessels and the
broadside-firing warships of the sixteenth and seventeenth centuries.

It is plain that most ships, particularly in the early Middle Ages,
were built not in a formally organised yard but in a suitable sheltered
spot from which vessels could be launched successfully. This might be
on the foreshore but was often on an estuary or even further up a

river, if this was wide enough and deep enough, perhaps at high tide only, to allow for a launch to take place. We know that Edward I commanded certain English towns to build ships described as galleys and barges for service to the crown in 1294–95, but there is no precise indication of where, for example, the galley built in Newcastle was actually constructed.[58] The accounts include a sum of 8s. 3½d. for wages for labourers 'clearing and making a place where the galley should be made'. A lock was bought for 'the gate of the garden in which the timber was put to be stored for the galley'. Later fir poles were procured for scaffolding and a paling was put up around the site.[59] The galley was eventually launched in May 1295 and moored for fitting out in a specially dugout dock on the edge of the Pandon Burn to the north of the town. The London galley built at the same time was constructed on a similar ad hoc site near the Tower. This was fenced round and a reed thatched hut was also put up for the stores.[60] By the mid-fourteenth century, in the reign of Edward III, when the English crown had a rudimentary administration to care for ships in royal ownership, shipbuilding and repairs for the crown were often undertaken at Ratcliff on the north bank of the Thames down river from Wapping. Henry V's shipbuilding activities took place at Southampton, but there is no more precise indication than that. The accounts as before speak of docks being dug out of the foreshore mud and fences being erected to secure the site. Some more permanent buildings were erected in 1420 when a storehouse and a forge for smiths working on the royal ships were built at Southampton out of ragstone and 'holyngstone' at the considerable cost of nearly £200,[61] but there is no clear indication of the precise location of these buildings. A building called the Long House, adjacent to the Watergate of Southampton, may have originally been built to house the spars and masts needed for royal ships, but again there is no direct evidence of this.[62]

Much later, in the reign of Henry VII when the English crown began once more to pay attention to the need for royal ships, naval accounts refer to the construction of a dock at Portsmouth. While it is true that this is the point at which Portsmouth began to establish itself as a base for the embryonic Royal Navy, this was not a true dry dock but a rather more sophisticated version of the mud docks familiar from the beginning of the fifteenth century.[63]

In France, the *Clos des galées*, set up by Philip IV in the 1290s, was at first little more than an enclosure with a basin defended by a ditch and a palisade on the left bank of the Seine at Richebourg. By the end of the fourteenth century it may have been walled; certainly there were quite substantial buildings within the enclosure. These included galley sheds, an armoury, stores, some sort of accommodation for the workmen and a house for the keeper of the galleys. This was an elaborate and even luxurious dwelling with a garden, a chapel and stained-glass windows with borders of coats of arms.[64] All this may have been a conscious imitation of the shipyards or arsenals of the Mediterranean naval powers. The word 'arsenal' itself comes from an Arabic word for 'house of work' (*dar al-sina'a*) which was used extensively for a shipyard. Its widespread adoption by Christian powers was probably because of the fame and success of the Arsenale of Venice. This probably had its origins in the early thirteenth century but at first it was only one among the many shipbuilding yards on the lagoon or in Venice itself. It became the state shipyard when it alone became responsible for building both light war galleys and trading great galleys in 1302. It soon developed into what was the largest enterprise or workplace in Europe. Shipbuilding work was centred around a basin, the *darsena arsenale vecchia*; this was later extended on two occasions by the construction of the *darsena arsenale nuovo* in about 1325 and the *darsena nuovissima* in 1470. By 1460 the whole complex, including galley sheds, armouries, gun foundries, smithies and stores, was surrounded with a wall. The main entrance from the Bacino San Marco along the Rio dell'Arsenale was provided with an imposing gateway in the latest Renaissance style. Over the archway was a relief of the Lion of St Mark while on each side crouched ancient leonine figures, loot originally from the Greek island of Delos. Even this did not include all the buildings devoted to ships and their equipment. Just outside the walls was the *tana* or ropewalk where the cordage for the galleys was made, and nearby were the *forni pubblici* where the *biscotti* (ships biscuits), the essential 'fuel' for the galleymen, were baked in huge quantities. This whole district of Venice was the home of the workers in the Arsenale, the *arsenalotti*, and is immediately obvious on contemporary maps. It must be remembered that round ships were never built in the Arsenale but in private yards all over the city and the outlying islands.

Shipbuilding was undoubtedly one of the major occupations of Venetian artisans.

The areas also known as arsenals in other Mediterranean cities never achieved a similar dedicated workforce, nor so elaborate an organisation, but they were more permanent and more prominent features of a number of ports than anything in northern Europe. They could be found, for example, at Messina, Pisa and Genoa and also in the Catalan ports, especially Barcelona. Less is known about shipbuilding on the African coast but it is clear that, when they decided to take seriously the need to wage war at sea and have a galley fleet for both offensive and defensive purposes, the Ottomans pressed the workmen and facilities of the former Byzantine yards on the Bosphorus into their service with great success.

The *arsenalotti* or workers in the Venetian Arsenale eventually became, in the sixteenth century at the peak of the operation of the shipyard, almost a separate element in the population, with special privileges. In the later Middle Ages the workers were regarded as skilled men and were normally members of the relevant guild. They worked under the supervision of a foreman shipwright or foreman caulker and were not as closely controlled by the state as the workers in the *tana*, where minimum standards of workmanship were rigorously enforced.[65] In England, by at least the mid-fourteenth century, royal accounts make clear that shipwrights were organised into trade groups or grades with different pay scales. At the top was the master shipwright or carpenter who would be in overall charge of the job. Whether he also designed the vessel being built is not clear but it seems at least very likely. The master craftsman who worked on the *Gracedieu*, John Hoggekyn, was supervised by one Robert Berde, but there is no sign that he had any responsibility for the design of the ship and he was in fact probably more in the nature of an accountant and manager than a naval architect. As well as Hoggekyn, shipwrights known as *berders*, *clenchers* and *holders* were employed. From their pay rates (varying between 8d. and 4d. per day worked) the *berders* were the most skilled, their work being to build up the shell of the vessel, the essential first step in building a clinker-built vessel. The others were involved in fixing the planks or strakes. Other trades were also involved: sawyers and fellers often worked in the woods to prepare timber; joiners built cabins for elite passengers; smiths made the large quantities of nails and other ironwork needed. We also can find in these accounts mention of occasional specialists like Davy Owen, a diver who was sent down to look for leaks in the bottom of the *Holyghost de la Tour* when she was anchored in the Hamble river in 1422.[66] In the French galley yard at Rouen there were similarly master carpenters, but there the employees were divided into the local Norman carpenters, foreign caulkers and finally labourers. From their names the caulkers were recruited from, among other places, Venice, Rhodes and Naples.[67]

The same sources also provide information about the decoration of English royal ships. Most were painted in a mixture of bright colours. When two ships, the *St Edward* and the *St George*, were repaired at Bayonne for the English crown in 1320, Thomas Driffield, the man in charge, spent considerable sums of money on colours and other materials, including varnish, eggs (to mix the pigments) and wax. The colours included white, vermilion and blue, and 'orpiment' (gold foil). The painters involved, Master John of Troia and his assistants Thomas and Marc, were well paid, receiving in sterling values about 10d. for John and between 7d. to 8d. per day for his helpers.[68] Royal ships in the fifteenth century were similarly decorated with, for example, a golden eagle on the bowsprit of Henry IV's *Gracedieu*, while his *Nicholas* was painted black with white ostrich feathers picked out in gold.[69] All vessels carried flags and banners, with those in royal ownership often carrying suitable heraldic images. The *Trinity Royal* had a 'sign' for the main sail with the royal arms and also banners and streamers with the arms of Edward the Confessor, the Virgin, the Holy Trinity and ostrich feathers.[70]

Gathering together the material needed to build a ship, in the case of England, involved bringing goods from quite considerable distances. Local timber for vessels built in Southampton came largely from the New Forest. For vessels built in London, material had to be brought from a much wider area, including woods in Essex, Kent and Surrey. Canvas for sailcloth and hemp for cordage came from Oléron in Brittany, though it was often made up into cables and hawsers at Bridport. Another source for cables, wood, spars, and the rosin and pitch needed to treat the hull, was the Baltic. These goods were brought into England by Hanseatic merchants mainly based in Danzig and imported through the port of Lynn. The iron bars to be made up into nails and the like came from northern Spain. In the Mediterranean the availability of supplies of suitable timber could cause problems. These were particularly acute in the fourteenth century for the Mamluks of Egypt, who had little alternative but turn to Christian merchants who were often willing to supply them, despite papal decrees against trading with Moslems in occupation of the Holy Land. Venice took careful steps to ensure that its shipyards had sufficient supplies both of timber and of hemp for cordage. Communal forests on the edge of the lagoon, and in Istria and in Dalmatia, had been used to supply the oak needed for the frames of galleys from the earliest times. After 1470, when the enmity of the Ottomans and the size of their fleet posed real problems for Venice, forests in Trevignano and Friuli were reserved for the needs of the state galleys. This was part of the responsibilities of the *Provveditori sopra le legne e boschi* established in 1464. In 1470 it was decreed that only the Arsenale could use oaks and other timber from the designated '*bando*' woods.[71] Later, in the sixteenth century, this care for the provision of timber extended to training trees to produce the curved timbers needed for knees to support deck timbers.

To ensure a sufficient supply of hemp, at much the same time the Venetian senate persuaded Michele di Budrio to set up hemp farms near Montagnana on the Venetian *Terra Firma* (the 'dry land' inland areas under Venetian rule). This was to prevent an interruption of the supply, which usually came from Bologna, causing trouble for the Venetian fleet. Once the raw material reached the *Tana*, its manufacture into cables and the like was carefully controlled. The hemp from Bologna was kept separate from that from Montagnana and the spinners' bobbins marked accordingly. The cables were also colour coded with labels to show their quality, the best having white labels.[72]

The scale of this organisation had no rival in late medieval Europe, but, even at the smallest port or the most remote beach, building and fitting out a ship was a complex business. It is a tribute to the persistence and perseverance of medieval shipbuilders that so many were able to complete the task, usually to the satisfaction of mariners about to take the ship to sea. By 1500 the strong regional differences between the larger sailing trading vessels had become less noticeable. Galleys were the dominant warships in the Mediterranean but were clearly less suited to the stormy waters of the Atlantic coasts and northern seas. Everywhere there were of course many small craft designed for particular purposes: fishing smacks, ferries and river boats, ceremonial barges and pleasure craft. Their design reflected both their purpose and the tradition of their home ports. The larger vessels, however, had developed considerably during the Middle Ages and the best were seaworthy ships capable, as events would prove, of completing the longest sea voyages.

The Way of a Ship

How does the master of a ship at sea know where he is and how does he determine the right path to his destination? To a modern seafarer these are easy questions to answer; even if some sudden power failure has knocked out his electronic navigation systems, help is usually at hand and a hand bearing compass, Admiralty charts and perhaps a sextant will provide some minimum back-up. Ships in our period, however, have frequently been pictured as creeping along the coast from one headland to the next fearfully avoiding passages across open waters out of sight of land. How else could a mariner find guidance across the trackless sea? Much medieval navigation was in coastal waters, of course, but this conventional picture ignores three important facts. First of all, in bad weather conditions the most dangerous place for a sailing ship to be is off a lee shore, that is when the wind is driving the vessel onshore. With adequate sea room, a well-designed vessel in good condition can ride out even a violent storm. Once, however, it is in the power of the waves and wind, smashing it onto rocks or crashing it down on a beach, the vessel is helpless. In these circumstances, mariners in northern waters at times deliberately tried to run their vessels aground through the surf in hope of saving their own lives, even if the ship and its cargo were lost.[1] The second fact is that, even within easy reach of the shore, a heavy rainstorm or fog can reduce visibility so quickly and so completely that bearings are in danger of being lost. The ship's crew literally might not know which way to turn, unless there were some other indications of their position than landmarks on shore. Third, there is ample evidence that even the earliest mariners were prepared when necessary to set out across the open sea. They and their later colleagues all needed to acquire skills in navigation which consisted of more than following a coastline.

Around AD 1000, in both northern waters and the Mediterranean, navigation skills did not depend on instruments and tables but on close observation of changes in the sea and the sky and hard-won experience. The science of astronomy and the significance of the changing patterns of the night sky, of both the stars and the moon, and in daytime of the apparent movement of the sun across the sky, had long been studied. Egyptians, Greeks and other ancient peoples had watched the skies intently, so the phases of the moon and the seasonal changes in the heavens were understood and used to measure the passing of time and in calculations of distance. Similarly the brilliant constellation of seven stars, generally known as either the Bear or the Plough, was very early realised to point to Polaris, the Pole or North Star. The Greeks used the same word, *arctos*, both for 'bear' and for 'north' while the Latin for north, *septentrio*, is said to be derived from the *septem triones* the seven 'oxen' of the Plough constellation.[2] East and west were easily located by the rising and the setting of the sun, while due south lay the sun at the meridian. In western Europe, a man standing at midday with his arms extended towards the rising and the setting of the sun and his back to the sun itself would be facing north. The winds were also given names related to the direction from which they blew. Both Greeks and Romans had named eight winds: among these, the cold blast of Boreas, the north wind, and the warm south wind, Nothus, were easily identified. Strabo in his *Geographika* (written in the first century AD) set out the whole system. This had also earlier been displayed in the sculptures of the Tower of the Winds in Athens, which dates from between 200 and 50 BC. In our period, these eight winds were familiarly used by Mediterranean sailors using these names or variants: Tramontana (N), Greco (NE), Levante (E), Sirocco (SE), Mezzodi or Ostro (S), Garbino or Africa (SW), Ponente (W) and Maestro (NW). These wind names were then used by extension to indicate direction and eventually compass points. Mariners in northern waters were equally attuned to wind direction but used the less picturesque combinations of directional terms familiar to us today. This division of the arc of the heavens into segments did not depend on any instrument but on observation and well-tried usage.

Scholars in the ancient world had also developed a sophisticated means of locating a particular place on the sphere of the earth, the system of latitude and longitude. The latitude of a place, if not the longitude, could be estimated roughly by establishing the elevation of the Pole Star or of the sun at its meridian above the observer's horizon. The Greek astronomer, Phytheas of Marseilles, had made accurate observations using a gnomon or pillar and the shadow it cast at noon on the equinox. This enabled him to calculate the latitude of Marseille to within 15'.[3] His methods were quite beyond the powers of medieval mariners, but the basic concepts behind them, the division of the heavens into named airts, the importance of close observation of heavenly bodies, the use of the elevation of the Pole Star or the sun to establish latitude (or northing and southing), were of fundamental importance to those putting out to sea even in the earliest times.

The clearest demonstration that medieval seamen did not merely creep cautiously from landmark to landmark lies in the known voyages of Scandinavian peoples. Sailing the waters of the North Sea and the Channel, and westward to Orkney, the Shetlands and Faeroes, was never easy, but it was here that the most skilled navigators of the medieval period served their apprenticeship and developed the methods which would take them first to Iceland and Greenland and, eventually, across the Atlantic to Newfoundland and the mainland of North America. The settlement of Iceland by people largely from the west coast of Norway took place in the last years of the ninth century. The *Landnamabok* includes the earliest known reference to Greenland in its record of the voyage of Gunnbjorn Olfsson.[4] He was driven west by a storm when attempting to reach Iceland and found himself eventually in sight of a group of islands off an unknown shore, before turning again to the east and homeward. This story is said to have been the inspiration for the voyages of Erik Raudi, or Eric the Red, who made the first attempts to explore the Greenland coast and eventually settled there in the 980s. The voyage from Iceland to Greenland involves about 450 miles across the open sea. When thinking of methods of navigation, perhaps the most important points which emerge from Eric's voyages and those of others who first reached unknown lands are that first Eric was able to return precisely to his starting point, Breidaford in Iceland, after three years' absence,[5] and then that the route to the new lands was also explained and taught to others and followed by the first colonists – it was not merely an accidental discovery.

These people were all experienced mariners. They were expert in the kind of sea-lore amassed by long years at sea. This depended on such things as knowledge of the cloud formations which reveal the presence of land ahead to a seaman. Experience could also give knowledge of the east-to-west progression of low pressure areas across the Atlantic, allowing the canny sailor to go west on the north of a depression and east on its south side. The presence of seabirds could also be used with care, hinting at land nearby, particularly if common gannets or puffins (which nest on cliffs and do not stray far from their broods) were present or the water was shoaling, bringing food for the birds to the surface. Sailing beneath the flight path of migrating geese would at least suggest that more distant resting places lay ahead. Elementary meteorological knowledge also came from observation and could be enshrined in collections of sayings and rhymes. The rhyme still used today, 'Red sky at night sailor's delight, red sky in the morning sailor's warning', relates to the way in which the sun, low on the horizon, is shining through dust particles. At evening this usually means that pressure is high and the weather settled. At dawn it means that a storm system is moving east and the atmosphere is full of water particles. High cirrus clouds (mares' tails) or a mackerel sky drifting east across the sky as a depression advances are good signs of a coming storm; as another rhyme has it, 'mares' tails and mackerel scales/make lofty ships carry low sails'. These and similar observations were made and well understood by Vikings.

In the same way, knowledge of the tides and their relationship to the phases of the moon was part of the basic skills of seamen in northern waters in the Middle Ages. Long before tide tables were compiled and written down, seamen needed to memorise the direction and strength of tidal streams off known coasts and headlands, and to link these to the phases of the moon. In landing places, the height of a tide was obviously important knowledge. A consideration of the facts that the tidal range at the Severn estuary is 14 metres at springs, 6 metres at neaps, a maximum of 12 metres in Mont St-Michel Bay in northern France, 5 metres at Reykjavik and 3.5 metres at Narvik makes clear that any sailor in these waters must be aware of, and be able to calculate, the state of the tide.[6] The 'Viking' sagas, the best source for details of Norse seamanship and navigation before the fourteenth century, include stories of voyages in which vessels waited for a good tide to complete a voyage. This happened to Eyvind, forced to put in at Orkney on his way from Ireland to Norway.[7] The same kind of experience could also be used to estimate likely wind patterns at different seasons of the year and thus the best time to set off.

More controversial and much debated are the methods which served for longer voyages into the North Atlantic. Did these Norse adventurers use only the kind of methods outlined above, combined with some very crude direction-finding techniques based on the observation of the Pole Star, or did they use something rather more refined? The sources which can be used to reach a decision are ambiguous. On the one hand are the details which can be gleaned from close reading of the sagas. On the other are some scraps of archaeological evidence and the results of voyages in replica vessels attempting to navigate by possible Viking methods. The starting point for both approaches is that there is no doubt, following excavations not only of known Viking sites in Greenland, but also at L'Anse aux Meadows in Newfoundland, that the Norsemen did cross the Atlantic to North America. The other pieces of material evidence concern the possibility that these voyages were made using some kind of directional dial, but one not related to the magnetic compass. The most intriguing and enigmatic artefact is a piece of an oak disc found in 1951 in the lowest levels of the excavation of the Benedictine nunnery at Siglufjord in Greenland; the disc is thought to date from *c.* 1200. It seems to have had a handle in the centre and to have been carved so that the complete circle would have been divided into thirty-two points. Also visible on the disc was a deep curved scratch which could possibly be the gnomon curve traced by the pathway of the altitude of the sun for a period around the summer solstice in the latitudes of Iceland and Greenland. The object aroused little interest at first, but was then seen at the museum in Denmark by Captain Sølver, a very experienced seaman, who was working there as a volunteer. In his view this was part of a 'bearing dial' which could be used on the open sea when either the sun or the Pole Star was visible. Once the direction of either heavenly body had been observed, a course could be set on some other bearing, with a considerable degree of accuracy. Sølver's view was vehemently attacked in the *Journal of Navigation*, in articles pointing out that the disc was far too small for this use; that no division of the heavens into thirty-two points (as on a modern compass) was known from so early a date; and that, since no tables of the height of heavenly bodies existed at this time, it could not possibly have been used in the way suggested. The object was probably a part of a butter stamp or the like, while the scratched curve was no more than the result of the tool of the workman slipping. Since then a replica of the dial has been used on the voyage, in 1991, of *Gaia*, a replica of the Gokstad Ship, and found to give positions accurate to within 3–5°, an excellent result compared with dead reckoning using wind, currents or sea state or even a visual observation of the sun alone.

A great deal of emphasis is placed both by those who accept this disc as a bearing dial and those who do not, on descriptions in the sagas of moments of danger on these voyages, when the Norsemen found themselves to be *hafvilla*, to use their own term. It is clear that this meant that they had indeed lost their bearings; they did not know where they were or what course to set. They were faced with the prospect of drifting aimlessly on grey seas under grey skies, often in thick fog, until they could once more see either the sun or the stars. At that point the ship master could once more *deila attir*, that is divide the heavens according to 'compass' points, and reset his course. Whether an instrument like the dial from Siglufjord was used, or more basic methods, it is hard to say. Perhaps the point to make is that, before the magnetic compass was in use in these waters, good estimations of bearings could be made, provided either the sun or the Pole Star was visible. It was possible in this way for Bjorni Herjúlfsson and his crew to survive their experiences when, as the *Flateyarbok* records, 'the fair wind failed and changed into northwinds and fogs and knew they not whither they went and this lasted many days'. They eventually 'got sight of the sun and could distinguish their airts' and, after approaching unknown lands, reached Bjorni's father's settlement in Herjólfsnes in Greenland.[8]

As problematic as the disc from Siglufjord is the so-called sunstone. This is mentioned in a saga relating the exploits of the eleventh-century king St Olaf. At sea in a storm, it is related that he 'looked about and saw no blue sky . . . then the king took the sunstone and held it up and then he saw where [the sun] beamed from the stone'. It has been suggested that the stone was a crystal, probably Iceland spar, and that it could polarise light.[9] It could therefore be used to indicate the direction of the sun, even if the sky was overcast. There are difficulties with this explanation: Although Iceland spar crystals will polarise light, they can only be used in this way in thin mist or light cloud. Under dark stormy skies and a blanket of thick cloud, when most needed, they would be of little help.

What then of the suggestion that the Norsemen practised latitude sailing based on the ability to estimate with considerable accuracy their 'northing' or 'southing', not using any instruments but by careful observation and experience. It is not an unduly complicated matter, for example, to observe that, as a ship sails south from Norway in the summer, the hours of daylight decrease. Similarly, the approximate point at which the sun does not dip below the horizon during the whole twenty-four hours in summer is not hard to discover if sailing in high latitudes. The suggested route from Norway to Iceland, for example, to be found in Haukr Erlendsson's version of the *Land-námabók*, reads much like a rutter (the books of sailing directions used in the fifteenth century).

From Hernum [north of Bergen] in Norway sail due west for Hvarf [Cape Farewell] in Greenland; and then will you sail north of Shetland so that you can just sight it in clear weather; but south of the Faroe islands, so that the sea appears halfway up the mountain slopes; but steer south of Iceland so that you may have birds and whales there from.

This would be a course which very nearly follows 60° North. Other routes also used by the Norsemen can similarly be interpreted as if the aim was to keep as nearly as possible to a latitude course. Another example would be that from Trondhjem to the east coast of Iceland,[10] more or less along the 64th parallel. On the other hand, it has been argued that latitude sailing is impossible without access to the necessary instruments. The directions to Iceland were merely setting out a voyage from one landfall to the next, and fortuitously this course followed approximately a parallel of latitude.[11]

Further to the south, the mariners of the British Isles, France and the other nations bordering on the Western Approaches, Channel and North Sea were as concerned as the Norsemen to observe winds, sky and sea and to build up the irreplaceable fund of sea-going experience so necessary for successful voyages. It is harder, for lack of suitable sources, to have an accurate idea of their methods before the four-teenth century but it is clear that, for example, English ships went

regularly to Bordeaux, Bayonne and the ports on the northern coasts
of Spain. Setting a course in this direction would probably involve a
period out of sight of land when crossing the Bay of Biscay, although
nothing comparable to the Norse journeys already discussed was
attempted. Often quoted is the description of the seamanship skills of
the Shipman, who was one of Chaucer's Canterbury pilgrims.

> But of his craft to rekene well his tides
> His stremes and his daungers hym besides,
> His heberwe, and his moone, his lodemenage,
> Ther was noon such from Hulle to Cartage.
> Hardy he was and wys to undertake;
> With many a tempest hadde his berd been shake.
> He knew alle the havens, as they were,
> Fro Gootlond to the cape of Fynystere,
> And every cryke in Britaigne and in Spayne.
> His barge ycleped was the Maudelayne.[12]

This speaks of the knowledge of tides and tidal streams, and of great
experience in coastal pilotage (lodemanage). He clearly had an
extensive 'mental chart' of most of the coasts likely to be visited by an
English seafarer and also had the cautious approach of the wise and
wily shipmaster. We may doubt whether any one individual could
really claim to know the entire coastline from the Baltic to Cartagena
(Cartage) on the coast of Murcia, but the general principles are clear.
Chaucer's Shipman was clearly of the old school where rule of thumb
methods and experience were what mattered. By the time Chaucer
wrote this, as he was well aware, the magnetic compass was no longer
an unfamiliar and almost magical device.[13] Although the compass
proper was probably preceded by the use of a lodestone (magnetite)
on its own, little is known about this. The first description of a
magnetic compass can be found in the treatise *De Natura Rerum* [The
Nature of Things], written by Alexander Neckham around 1187. He
speaks of how 'they touch the magnet with a needle. This then whirls
round in a circle until when its motion ceases the point looks direct to
the north.' (The needle had to be remagnetised at frequent intervals by
being stroked by a lodestone.) A reference in another of his works, *De
Utensilibus* [Necessaries], is even more revealing. While listing a ship's

stores, he included a description of a needle on a dart which turned to the north and concluded, 'and so the sailors know which way to steer when the Cynosura [Pole Star] is hidden by clouds'.[14] About twenty years later Guyot de Provins included a rather similar description in a poem, including the detail that the magnetised needle was inserted in a straw which was then floated in a bowl of water.[15] To get from this to a maritime compass as normally understood some considerable development was needed, but this had certainly happened by the later fourteenth century in northern waters and rather earlier in the Mediterranean. In 1380, in fact, Francesco da Buti's account of a *bussola nautica* differs little from that to be found on most ships by the sixteenth century. It consisted of a wooden box with a glass cover; inside was a pivoted round disc with a sixteen-point wind rose attached to a rotating magnetised needle.[16] The bittacles (now commonly known as binnacles) found in the inventory lists of royal ships in the fifteenth century were probably also very like this. The entry for 'the king's storehouse for his ships' listed two bittacles, two sailing needles, two dials and three compasses, according to the accounts for 1410–12.[17] It seems very likely that the 'sailing needles' were those of a compass, while the dials were not compass cards or wind roses but 'running glasses', small 'hour' glasses for measuring the time spent on a particular course.[18] In the 1420s, in the reigns of Henry V and Henry VI, the clerk of the king's ships noted, in the inventories taken of ships' stores, that five of the royal ships had a bittacle on board and four a dial. One, the *Petit Jesus*, had a dial and what is called a sail box.[19] By the 1430s, it was expected that any ship master setting out on a voyage which involved more than short coastal passages would have access to a compass and know how to use it. This is demonstrated by the casual mention in the *Libelle of Englyshe Polycye*, a political poem arguing forcefully for better control of the seas by the English crown, of voyages to Iceland, of how,

> Out of Bristowe, and costes many one,
> Men have practised by needle and by stone
> Thiderwardes within a litle while,
> Within twelve yere, and without peril
> Gon and come.[20]

Compass-makers are also mentioned in the records of the Hanseatic league from 1394; in 1461 Gerard of Essen was making compasses in Hamburg. The way in which the presence of a compass on board ship was normal by 1475 is shown by the listing of the gear of a vessel from Oslo in 1478. This included 'fishing gear, lead and line, compasses and all her gear', with no hint that any of this was worthy of comment.[21]

Much older than the magnetic compass was the simple device, listed above, which could help the experienced ship master establish his position and whether he was standing into danger. This was the sounding lead, a heavy lead weight attached to a fine rope or line marked out at regular intervals (standardised as six feet) by a series of knots or other markers. These were the basis of the measurement of the depth of water in fathoms. This simple piece of equipment could establish the depth of water under the vessel's hull and also, when 'armed', with tallow being forced into a hollow on the bottom of the weight, could bring up samples of the sea bottom for inspection. The great practicality of this device is made abundantly clear from the text of the 'rutters' or books of sailing directions which survive for the Channel coasts and adjacent waters from the fifteenth century, and which probably record information previously held in the memory of a ship master. These books thus record the painfully acquired knowledge of generations of seamen and show how even in this field 'book learning' was taking its place alongside oral and experiential teaching by this date.

The oldest surviving manuscripts (in English, and in Low German) of sailing directions for these waters are all 'library copes'. That is, they were copied for interested gentlemen as part of their book collections; we can only presume that the battered salt-stained copies used on board ship were discarded when they fell apart. The English rutter survives in two copies of the same text, known as the Hastings and the Lansdowne Manuscripts. The latter belonged originally to Sir John Paston II, who was certainly not a seafarer, and was copied by John Ebesham, his usual scribe. The German text, now known as *Das Seebuch*, survives in two different versions which are now bound up together. All date from the second half of the fifteenth century but very probably include earlier material.

Looking closely at the Hastings Manuscript, its contents can be divided into seven sections. These cover different geographical areas

and also differ in their content and format. A recent analysis has not
only considered these aspects in detail, suggesting different origins for
the material, but has also tried to work out if the proposed courses are
good or whether they would lead a mariner and his ship to disaster. In
this analysis twenty-five of the thirty-two courses from England to
France included are identifiable; 23 per cent are good, that is would
certainly bring a vessel safely to the intended destination;
40 per cent are 'acceptable' and 28 per cent seem dangerous. Before
condemning medieval seamanship, this may be because of copying
errors or confusion over some of the place names. The correct adjust-
ment to make for the state of the tide is also not included, except in
two cases. Courses between England, Ireland and the Isle of Man do
rather better proportionately, with 82 per cent rated as 'safe'. All the
courses include bearings and often some material on tidal streams,
though not enough for an inexperienced pilot; soundings are
mentioned more rarely, although the final leaf of the work is a picture
of a vessel taking soundings off a rocky shore. Bottom samples are
mentioned only in the Bay of Biscay. There is little help on the best
way to enter any particular harbour, with virtually no mention of
useful landmarks. The manuscript may be more of an *aide-mémoire*
for a captain who was already familiar with the area from Berwick to
Spain than a full-blown pilot book. We will look closely at the last
section which sets out two routes, possibly for the masters of ships
with pilgrims from Compostela, returning to England from Coruña.

Part of the text (with modernised spelling and wording) reads as
follows:

Here are the grounds of England Brittany and Scilly.

And you come out of Spain and you are at Cape Finisterre go
your course north north east; and when you estimate you are two
parts over the sea and are bound in to the River Severn you must
go north and by east till you come into soundings; and if you
have 100 fathoms deep or else 90 then you shall north until you
sound again in 72 fathoms in fair grey sand and that is the shoal
that lies between Cape Clear and Scilly; then go north till you
come into sounding with oozy mud and then go your course east
north east or else east and by north and you shall not fail by

much [to see] *stepilhord*, this rises all around a hill like a high-crowned hat.[22]

This description is said to be 'complete and usable'. The complete work was probably put together from various different sources, but even so it marks a clear movement towards a more literate approach to navigation and the setting of courses than the simplicity of the directions in the Viking course to Greenland. It is also, along with material like the tide tables for Brittany which were produced at much the same date, a testament to the sophistication of the thinking of medieval seamen. To use sailing directions like these, whether written or held in the memory, a mariner had to have developed a complex 'cognitive map'. This allowed him to use the wind rose of the compass (or the direction of the winds) to reconcile solar time and lunar time to predict tides and to estimate direction and distance. Men of culture and education, like Chaucer, expected their readers to have such knowledge. In the Franklin's Tale, the lover wishes for perpetual spring tides

> then shall she [the sun] be ever at full always
> And spring flood last both night and day.

Mariners needed not only understanding of the way tides were connected to the cycles of both sun and moon but also hard-won practical information. Once acquainted with the 'establishment of the port' (high tide at a particular location in relation to lunar time), they could predict the state of the tide on any day at any time with reasonable accuracy.[23] They could make sense of such directions as 'All havens be full at WSW moon between the Start and the Lizard'.[24] Equally they could estimate the strength and direction of tidal streams, very necessary information off headlands and in narrow channels, in much the same way. The Hastings Manuscript rutter when giving courses for the east coast of England includes these directions for entering the Thames.

> And going out of Orwell to the Naze you must go south west. From the Naze to the marks of the Spits [a sandbank], your course is west south west. And it [the tide] flows south and by

east bring your marks together so that the parish steeple be a little to the east of St Osyth's Abbey than go your course over the Spits south till you come to 10 or 12 fathoms then go your course with the Horseshoe [sandbank off Shoeburyness] south south west. And if it be on flood come not in 8 fathoms and that shall bring you to 11 or 12 fathoms then go your course in to Thames with the green bank [possibly the isle of Grain on the Kentish shore] west south west and at the Horseshoe it flows south and north.[25]

To make full sense of this, the seaman needed also to have the details of the 'establishment' of the ports ashore firmly in his memory to be able to calculate the state of the tide at any particular moment. *Das Seebuch*, the Low German collection, is usually considered a better all-round pilot book with fewer gaps in its information.

Further south, however, mariners from Genoa, Venice, the Balearic Islands and other major Mediterranean sea powers would not have been impressed by sailing directions like these and had little use for tidal calculations while sailing in the Mediterranean.[26] Written sailing directions for voyages in the Mediterranean had been known and used in ancient times. The *Periplus of Scylax of Caryanda* dates from the fourth century BC and gives details of ports and landmarks in the Mediterranean and the adjacent coasts of the Atlantic. A little later a similar book, the *Stadiasmus of the Great Sea*, was produced which gives directions from Alexandria westwards. Distances in both works were given in units of a 'day's sail' while direction was described in terms of the wind needed to reach the desired destination. The wording of these and similar later works has been held to imply that Greek and Roman sailors were familiar with coastal maps or charts, even though none has survived from this period.[27]

By about AD 60, when the *Periplus of the Erythraean Sea* was compiled probably by a Hellenised Egyptian, the genre had developed further. It was no longer just a list of distances and wind directions but a combination of this kind of information, with useful tips for a merchant trading in distant lands; in this case the Red Sea and the Arabian Gulf. The book at times reads almost like a modern pilot book; this, for example, is the description of Musera (Moosa) in Oman: 'the anchorage is safe and good upon a sandy bottom where the anchors have good holding'.[28] This entry also seems to imply the very early use of a sounding lead or a similar instrument.

The continued use of these and similar books into the Middle Ages is, of course, very doubtful, but it is clear that later versions of very similar collections of sailing directions were familiar to shipmasters in the Mediterranean from the thirteenth century and possibly before that. These were often intended to be consulted in conjunction with 'portolan' maps or charts. The earliest surviving example of this kind of writing is the *Compasso da Navigare*. The slightly older *Liber de Existencia Riviarum et Forma Maris Nostri Mediterranei*, which exists in a manuscript in the Cotton collection in the British Library, is more a listing of distances and coastal features than sailing directions aimed at mariners. It dates from about 1200; this dating is confirmed by the omission of places, for example Aigues Mortes, not founded until later in the thirteenth century. It was probably written in Pisa and is of interest here because it clearly relates to an early map of the Mediterranean which does not survive. It is written in Latin and notes for example of Tortosa, 'this city is on the east side of the river. From here begins the sea of Spain . . . the mouth of the River Tortose is 1100 from Valencia.'[29]

Much more clearly intended for use at sea is *Lo Compasso da Navigare*. This describes a whole circuit of the Mediterranean by sea, beginning at Cape St Vincent going eastwards along the north coast, and then westwards along the southern coast, eventually ending at Safi in Morocco, to the south of Casablanca, thus including the area of the Atlantic to the immediate west of the Straits of Gibraltar. It is written in Italian, with the oldest surviving version dating from around 1250. It gives courses with distances (in units now called 'the little sea mile') and bearings (using the wind names for directions) for longer voyages in sections called *Peleio*. More detailed pilotage information is also included for major ports. Thus the *Peleio* for courses from Malta includes 'from Malta to Cape Pasaro 80 miles by *maestro* [north west]' and 'from the castle of Malta to La Licata 105 miles by *maestro* [north west] *ver la tramontana poco* [and a little to the north, that is, nor nor west]'.[30] Describing the entry to Seville up the Guadalquiver river, the *Compasso* reads from the said mouth as far as the city of Seville is 60 miles by the river . . . 5 miles to the south west is a rock called Peccato which shows above the water . . . Beware of the bank called Zizar to the west and likewise of another bank to the east called Cantara . . . In entering the said river by ship you must first take soundings and note the buoys and when the water comes in and the tide rises go by the course marked by the buoys.[31]

This description makes plain not only the everyday use of the sounding lead in southern waters but also the existence of sophisticated buoyage systems for marking a channel. The Guadalquivir was notoriously prone to silting and shifting sandbanks, a factor which led to the growth of San Lucar and Cadiz as ports on the coast at the end of the Middle Ages. In the Netherlands the estuary of the Scheldt was similarly dangerous for sailing craft, and buoys are marked on a chart from the sixteenth century. It was more usual in the north to use prominent features on shore (the steeples of churches and the like, for example St Osyth's Abbey mentioned above) as leading marks to guide a vessel safely into harbour, or to build towers, like that at Stralsund on the Hiddensee which dates from 1306.[32] The directions in the *Compasso* are also clearly intended to be used with a chart, quite likely an earlier version of the Carta Pisana of 1274, the oldest surviving marine chart. The existence of such an invaluable aid to navigation had been definitely recorded some five years earlier when Louis IX of France, *en route* for Tunis in 1270, was shown his position on a chart by the sailing master of his ship when stormbound in Cagliari Bay. The Carta Pisana, and later similar examples, was drawn on a sheepskin parchment. The coastal outlines are easily recognisable and drawn to scale, but the most prominent feature of the map is the network of courses on rhumb lines. Two touching circles are drawn on the map and, within each, lines are drawn connecting the sixteen points of the wind rose, familiar to all Mediterranean sailors, marked on the circumference of each circle. Using this chart and the sailing directions, and, most importantly, a magnetic compass, a sailing master could now lay his desired course with a degree of certainty. A ship master in these waters, from at least the mid-thirteenth century, needed basic mathematical skills and a degree of literacy to profit from these innovations.

There is, however, a need for some caution in adopting this view. Did, in fact, mariners in the Mediterranean at this date have access to a compass which could be used on board ship? Or were they still using the crude magnetised needle, stuck through a straw, floated in a bowl of water, a device which could indicate north but was hardly suitable for laying off precise courses, or for use at sea in anything but a flat calm. There is a degree of uncertainty about the date at which a useful ship's compass was developed with the needle attached to a pivoted wind rose card enclosed in a small box. Ramon Lull writing in 1286 gives the impression that such a device already existed. Francesco da Barberino, a Tuscan lawyer and notary, writing in the early fourteenth century, however, included in a long and ponderous treatise on how to live a good life a section on how to cope with shipboard life. This first of all mentioned direction finding on board ship with the possibly obsolete 'bowl and needle' method. He then went on to suggest that, if his reader had the misfortune to be shipwrecked, he should make sure to have with him a small round box with a compass needle under glass, something which sounds more like a pocket compass. This would allow him to discover the north even under water and thus make his way to the nearest shore. Perhaps both references owe more to the literary imagination than sea-going reality.

This controversy aside, there is other good evidence of a more 'paper-based' attitude to navigation in southern waters than in the north. One of the problems facing a mariner related to his course 'made good'. That is, while his ship might have travelled a certain distance through the water, because of the influence of ocean currents, the effect of the wind on the hull of his vessel (leeway) and the need to change course according to the wind direction, he might not have travelled the same distance to his desired destination, that is the distance or course 'made good'. An attempt was made to deal with this problem by means of a set of mathematical tables. The earliest copy to survive was made in 1428 in Venice, although they were certainly in existence earlier than this, perhaps as early as 1286 when another reference in Ramon Lull's *Arbor Scientiae* seems to describe something similar. The rules or tables were known as the *Toleta de Marteloio*; the rules were based on the construction of right-angled triangles and some elementary trigonometry, but the ship master was not expected to do this at sea. As set out in the surviving copies, the first table in the rules has three columns each with eight entries. In the first is the name of a 'quarter wind' (south, south west, west etc.), in the second is the course made good, and in the third is the distance off course a ship may be depending how many 'quarters' lie between the vessel and its desired objective. A second table then indicates the course (quarter wind) which should be adopted to get back on track.[33] Even if the master using these rules had to be able to divide and multiply, he still also needed the same almost indefinable skills shown by northern mariners to be reasonably sure of the distance his vessel had travelled through the water. Experience was enhanced but not superseded by the *Toleta*, the compass and the marine chart.

The scholars and mathematicians who had devised the *Toleta* tables were also involved in the adoption by mariners in the Mediterranean of a method of establishing their position at sea by taking the altitude of heavenly bodies. We know a great deal more about this development in this area than the inferences and speculation on which we largely rely when discussing this approach in northern waters. The work of classical scholars, who had first developed this idea and who had also put forward the system of latitude and longitude to define a position on the globe, was better known in this area. The greater degree of state involvement in sea travel and eventually exploration may also have supplied the stimulus for the wider diffusion of these techniques and the parallel development of schools of careful and precise cartographers. We should not forget that the first well-authenticated voyage of Europeans to the Canaries took place before 1336, when Lancelotto Malocello visited the islands (Lanzarote is named after him). The islands can be clearly identified on a map of 1339 made in Majorca by Angelino Dulcert or, to give the Italian version of his name, Dalorto.[34]

The connection with Majorca is not surprising, since this was also the home of Abraham Cresques, the supreme map maker of the age, who produced the so-called Catalan Atlas for presentation to the French king Charles V in 1375. This was more than a marine chart since it incorporated maps based on the most up-to-date knowledge of the Orient and Africa, including on one a picture of the fabulously wealthy king of Mali, Mansa Musa; but its outlines of the coasts of the Mediterranean, the Black Sea and western Europe followed that now familiar to contemporaries from portolans.[35] The way in which these charts were now seen as part of the normal equipment of a well-found vessel is demonstrated by the decree of Peter IV, king of Aragon, that every royal galley should carry at least two charts. By 1399 chart-making was a recognised occupation in Barcelona. In the summer of that year a Florentine merchant ordered four world maps as gifts to present to rulers he hoped to influence in his favour on a business trip to Aragon, Bordeaux, England and Ireland. The contracts drawn up with the cartographers describe them as Master Jacome Ribes of Mallorca and Master Francesco Becaria of Genoa, both resident in the city. More details of the progress of the contract are recorded in letters in the Datini Archive in Prato; in these Ribes is called 'cristiano novella, maestro di charte da navichare' and Becaria 'di Genova, dipintore di charte da navichare'.[36] Ribes was in fact the son of Abraham Cresques and had assumed a new name on his conversion to Christianity. He is usually also identified with the cartographer called Mestre Jacome de Mallorca who was working for Henry the Navigator in Portugal between 1420 and 1427.

By the end of the fourteenth century, Mediterranean navigators were using compass, chart, sailing directions and *Toleta* tables as a matter of course. These combined to form a well-tried and serviceable system in the hands of an experienced ship master. The account of a voyage by a galley from the Habibas Islands near Oran to the Spanish coast in 1404 shows how it worked in practice. The sea was very heavy 'and the wind blew from the west very fresh. The sailors at once made ready. They set up their magnetic compasses, they opened their charts and began to prick and measure with the dividers, for the course was long and the weather adverse. They observed the hour glass and entrusted it to a watchful man. They hoisted the storm try-sails, fixed the auxiliary rudders and shipped the oars.' After a rough crossing to the Spanish coast and a day stormbound at San Pedro de Arraez, they reached Cartagena in safety.[37]

There is, however, no mention of the observation of heavenly bodies, particularly of the use of 'altitudes' to establish a position. On land, at this date, there is no doubt that this was something frequently undertaken by scholars and others, with the necessary calculations and instruments commonly in use. The Cresques family of map-makers, for example, also produced astrolabes and other similar devices. We have already discussed the possible way in which mariners in northern waters used heavenly bodies to establish direction and estimate their 'northing and southing'. We can also note here the use of extended fingers to give rough estimations of angles. These methods, which did not need elaborate instruments or calculations, were probably familiar to southerners as well, particularly if they had voyaged to England or the Netherlands. The innovation in the fifteenth century, first developed by the Portuguese, was to adapt the systems used on land for use at sea. An astrolabe, as used by a scholar astronomer, was a costly, elaborate and complex instrument. The mariner's astrolabe derived from it was relatively simple; it consisted only of the main circular plate of an astrolabe hung from a swivel ring; in the centre of the circle was fixed a pointer or alidade with sights at each end. This could be turned so that the height of the sun or star could be observed through the sights. The angle of altitude could then be read off from the scale engraved on the rim of the circle. To perform this operation on the heaving deck of a ship at sea must always have been problematic. It is likely, though there is no direct evidence of this, that 'sights' were taken ashore. There is also a reference to a lance being used to measure the height of the sun. Slightly easier to use was the quadrant, also simplified for nautical use. A metal quarter segment of a circle, it had a pinhole sight on one edge and a plumb line attached to the centre point. If the heavenly body was sighted through the pinholes the plumb line would fall on the scale marked on the rim of the quadrant at its correct altitude; but again it is hard to imagine how the line could have been prevented from swinging on a ship at sea, making an accurate reading virtually impossible. Probably on both the lance and the quadrants predetermined 'heights' were marked with an indication of the place referred to.[38]

It has been suggested, however, that the further south Portuguese mariners penetrated along the African coast, a process underway after about 1415 and their capture of Ceuta, the greater the need became for some reasonably accurate method of determining a ship's position. It is certainly the case that the 'direction and distance' method of navigation the Portuguese were used to was subject to increasing errors on longer voyages. The rediscovery of the works of Ptolemy, the Hellenistic geographer, by the west, and their translation into Latin in 1409, may also have increased interest in the use of latitude and longitude for this purpose. Certainly, by the 1480s navigation as practised by Portuguese long-distance sailors had become a much more scientific and mathematical process, with much less reliance on the almost instinctive methods based on the accumulated experience of generations of seamen.

The initial impulse was associated with the court of Prince Henry the Navigator at Sagres. He is credited with summoning there the best astronomers and cartographers of the day, including Mestre Jacome of Mallorca. Henry's traditional role as the inspirer of Portuguese voyages to Africa has been questioned, but there is little doubt that there was a concerted effort on the part of mariners from this small and impoverished kingdom to establish a sea route to the fabled river of gold in the south, in the territories of Musa Mansa, and also to settle the Atlantic islands. At some point on these voyages the first observation of the Pole Star by means of an instrument by mariners was undertaken. This may have necessitated going on shore, but the first certain record of this being done dating from 1456–57 is ambiguous on this point. A young Portuguese gentleman noted in his account of his travels that 'I had a quadrant when I went to those parts. And I marked on the scale of the quadrant the altitude (*altura*) of the Atlantic Pole. And I found it better than the chart'. His reference to marking the altitude on the scale confirms that this was probably the usual practice of mariners. The known altitudes of the Pole Star at various prominent locations on the coast could be marked off on the scale by a scratched letter or other sign until something approaching a list of coastal 'latitudes' had been compiled.[39]

This method worked well enough; it made possible the system of 'latitude sailing' which we have already discussed in relation to some of the Viking voyages. It could also be adapted to observations of the altitude of the sun at noon when mariners reached far enough south to find that the Pole Star was no longer visible or was so low in the sky as to be unusable. To take sun sights with reasonable accuracy, however, the mariner needed further help from mathematicians and astronomers. The apparent movement of the sun as the seasons changed had to be understood and allowed for. Were the mariner and his ship to the north or the south of the equator? Was the sun overhead at noon to the north or the south of the equator? How could the position of the vessel in degrees of latitude be calculated from the position of the adilade on the scale of the astrolabe when the sight was taken? The answers to these and other questions were provided by new sets of tables and rules which came to replace the old *Toleta*. By lucky chance much older material was incorporated and thus preserved for later historians in the earliest printed copy of the *Regimento do Astrolabio e do Quadrante*. This dates from 1509 but includes tables dating from 1480–81 when the Portuguese established the fort of San Jorge at Mina in the Gulf of Guinea. It includes three 'Rules', the Regiment of the North, the Rule for Raising the Pole and the Rule for the Sun, a list of *Alturas* from the equator northwards, and a calendar beginning on 1 March setting out the sun's declination day by day and its position in the Heavens relative to the Signs of the Zodiac, the usual method of astronomers at this date. The first rule set out how to observe the Pole Star; the second established a new method of getting back on a desired course now that the Marteloio was no longer used (largely a matter of learning certain figures by rote); while the third set out how to use the sun to calculate a latitude. This was not entirely straightforward and involved calculations made on the spot. Perhaps one example will give a flavour of the method. A letter to the king of Portugal in 1500 informed him how the pilots on an expedition to Brazil had gone on shore to take a sun sight. They found '56° and the shadow was [from] the north'. By this, according to the *Regiment of the Astrolabe*, 'we judged we were 17° distant from the equinoctial and therefore had the height of the Antarctic Pole in 17°'. The calculation was 90° − 56° = 34° (zenith distance of the sun); 34° − 17°(declination) = Lat. 17° South.[40] None of these calculations or instruments helped with the problem of establishing longitude. For this sailors had perforce to rely on meticulous dead-reckoning and a very cautious approach to the estimation of the distance sailed. Even so, large errors could easily creep in, leading to uncertain landfalls and, at times, the horrors of shipwreck.

By the end of the fifteenth century, therefore, the art of navigation had also in some sense become a science, at least in the hands of the most skilled mariners of Spain. Portugal and Genoa. Bartolomeu Dias and Vasco da Gama used the methods of the *Regimento* on their long and difficult voyages to the Cape of Good Hope and to India. Da Gama had been sufficiently impressed by its utility to bring back to Portugal an example of the *kamal*, a simple Arab device for taking the

altitudes of heavenly bodies which was easier to use on board ship
than an astrolabe. In northern waters, the use of instruments other
than the compass and the sounding lead was apparently still
unknown. We can speculate that, for example, the shipmasters from
Bristol, who by the end of the fifteenth century went regularly to
Seville, must have encountered on the quayside or in the tavern
shipmen experienced in the new ways. There is, however, no evidence
of the use of astrolabes, quadrants or cross-staffs by English seamen
until the second half of the sixteenth century. Similarly, northern
seamen clearly valued rutters or books of sailing directions, and small
printed or manuscript tide tables, but did not use the tables of dec-
linations and latitudes, or the calendars used in conjunction with
astrolabes and the like. There is also little evidence of the existence of
charts, or of their being part of the normal equipment of a northern
ship master, until the sixteenth century. The attitude of at least some
of their number is well expressed by the remarks of an 'old salt'
recorded by William Bourne, a fervent supporter of mathematical
navigation, in 1571:

> I have known within this twenty years that them that were
> auncient masters of shippes hathe derided and mocked them that
> have occupied their cardes and plattes and also the observation
> of the Altitude of the Pole saying: that they care not for their
> sheepskinne for he could keepe a better account upon a boord.
> And also when they dyd take the altitude they would call them
> starr shooters and would aske if they had striken it.[41]

When John Cabot set off, in 1497 and 1498, from Bristol on his
voyages across the Atlantic, which resulted in the discovery of Newfoundland, it is possible that these were the first ships to leave an
English port equipped with the instruments of 'southern' navigators.
His son Sebastian probably went on these voyages as a boy and later
became the head of the Spanish pilots' school, charged with teaching
these methods. He then returned to England to assist Henry VIII in
making plans for more ambitious English voyages. As late as 1540,
however, English ships were said to rely on Italian and French navigators.[42] Before we decry the conservatism of northern mariners, we
should remember that the 'southern' system had not solved all the

problems faced by navigators at sea by their use of instruments and tables. There was still a great need for the kind of experience and close observation of changes in the sea and sky, and of the way of the ship, which had served the Vikings so well in earlier centuries. The words of an Arabic manual written as early as AD 434, describing the qualities of an ideal pilot, still held good:

> He knows the course of the stars and can always orientate himself; he knows the course of signs both regular, accidental and abnormal, of good and bad weather; he distinguishes the regions of the ocean by the fish, the colour of the water, the nature of the bottom, the birds, the mountains, and other indications.[43]

The problem of how to establish longitude accurately would not be solved until the eighteenth century. The varying difference between 'magnetic' north, as shown by the compass, and 'true' north was not fully appreciated until the later sixteenth century. Chartmakers equally did not grapple with the problem of how to represent the curvature of the earth on a flat parchment or paper map until much the same date.

The spread of charts, tables, sailing directions and the like in the maritime community did, however, have other results. One was undoubtedly to raise the status of the profession of navigator. He was now more likely to be an educated man of some scientific and mathematical ability than a rough and ready practical seaman like Chaucer's Shipman. These innovations also opened the way to the increasing knowledge of the furthest reaches of the world which so excited Europeans in the sixteenth century. The routine use of the compass also had economic effects which contributed to the growing success of the seaborne trade of western Europe in our period. There seems to have been more navigation in the winter months in the Mediterranean and thus a greater frequency of longer trading voyages in the fourteenth century and later. After around 1300, Norse sagas no longer include accounts of ships completely losing their bearings at sea, in the state known as *hafvilla*. The course followed on the voyage from southern England to the Gironde for wine, or to northern Spain for iron, after about 1400, recorded in books of sailing directions, was set on compass bearings from the coast of Brittany across the Bay of

Biscay.[44] This also contributed to the commercial success of this traffic and greater safety for both ships and mariners

At no time in the past had mariners always hugged the coast, creeping fearfully from one cape to another, but by 1500 they had the possibility of using a wider range of methods to set their courses and establish their position, many of which could be used in unfamiliar as well as home waters.

4

Making a Living

In about 1006, at the beginning of his career as writer and teacher, Aelfric, a monk at Cerne Abbas in Dorset,[1] wrote a set of dialogues in Latin as 'class texts' to help his pupils in the monastic school gain confidence with the ecclesiastical and intellectual language of the age. He used the familiar types of Anglo-Saxon society as his characters. Among them was the merchant, who was represented as saying,

> I go aboard my ship with my goods and I go over seas and sell my things and buy precious things which are not produced in this country and bring them hither to you . . . brocade and silk, precious gems and gold, various raiment, and dyestuffs, wine and oil, ivory, and mastling [brass-stone], copper and tin, sulphur and glass and the like and I wish to sell them dearer here than I buy there, that I may get some profit wherewith I may feed myself and my wife and my sons.[2]

For a sea-girt nation this was the dominant image of both the merchant and foreign trade; it involved exotic goods from distant lands with a sea journey as the essential prelude. The status of those who ventured overseas was even more strikingly recognised by the writer of a document setting out the ranks of society in England in the first quarter of the eleventh century, who included among those worthy of the title of thane (the level just below that of an earl) the trader who prospered, 'that he crossed thrice the open sea at his own expense'.[3]

Certainly the use of the sea as a highway of trade was a prime reason for undertaking regular voyages and making this a way of life and a source of livelihood. Not all trade by sea was either as profitable or as prestigious as these early commentators suggested and, of course, a different view would have been prevalent in lands where maritime concerns did not loom large or which were landlocked. In this chapter, the focus will be on the ways in which the sea and maritime trade dominated the economy and the way of life for many: in northern waters, we will consider England, and the cities of the Hanseatic League; and in the Mediterranean, the maritime republics of Venice and Genoa, and Egypt and the Maghreb, the coastal area of North Africa. There will also be some discussion of the pleasures and terrors of sea travel in the Middle Ages.

As has been seen, ship design changed, particularly at the end of the thirteenth and the beginning of the fourteenth centuries, producing more seaworthy vessels, and as navigation became less experiential and more scientific, maritime trade routes expanded and were followed more frequently. Around AD 1000 very few Mediterranean mariners ventured into the Atlantic and to the North, while voyages to the South were equally rare for northern sailors. By 1500 the nations of Europe were linked by sea by a web of well-used trade routes, and some intrepid mariners had penetrated into much more distant seas. Map (4) shows these routes and the most frequently visited ports.

Englishmen were not, however, either very adventurous or very innovative traders for much of the Middle Ages. The main item of English overseas export trade until the fifteenth century was raw wool supplemented by tin, and small quantities of hides, pewter dishes and the like. The wool went mainly to the markets and textile weaving centres in Flanders and the Netherlands and to Italy. English merchants and vessels were virtually confined to the cross-Channel traffic which involved only a short sea voyage. From the time of Edward I, English kings also saw the wool trade as an invaluable source of tax revenue and, as a consequence, as an irreplaceable form of security for loans. The establishment of a staple system, whereby a named town or towns was the only permitted market for trade in a particular commodity, increased the ease with which royal taxes could be levied and provided a quid pro quo for English merchants in the form of a quasi-monopoly and the partial exclusion of alien merchants from the trade. A compulsory staple for trade in wool was first established in 1313 at St Omer. Over the succeeding years it moved to Antwerp (1315), Bruges (1325) and eventually returned to a group of English towns in 1327. These moves were caused not by commercial necessity but the complex and fluctuating politics of the relations between France and England and the rulers of the Nether-lands. The outbreak of war with France in 1337 caused even more confusion, but support for the existence of a staple both from the community of wool merchants and from the crown tended to increase. The crown itself lost both honour and money in a disastrous attempt to deal directly in wool itself in 1340–41. After the fall of Calais to the English, this seemed the natural location for a wool staple. A first attempt to set it up on a firm basis in 1363 came to an end in 1369, but by the beginning of the fifteenth century the Company of the Staple, a corporation of wool merchants, firmly controlled the traffic in wool, the bulk of which had by law to go through Calais. This ensured that the shortest sea route continued to be by far the busiest for medieval English mariners. Most wool left from the port of London, with minor flows going through the east coast ports and Southampton, and went straight across the Channel.

Also in the fifteenth century the export trade in English cloth began to grow rapidly. By the mid-1440s exports of cloth exceeded in value those of raw wool; although the calculation of comparative values for the two commodities is not easy, because of the nature of the evidence, it seems that in the decade 1441–51 the average annual value of exported broadcloths reached £89,660 while that of raw wool was only £51,080. Twenty years earlier the average annual value of wool exports had been £77,780. From the point of view of mariners this important change at first made little difference; much of the cloth was in a 'white' undyed and semi-finished state and was bound for the textile towns of Flanders as before. Some, however, was bound for the Mediterranean in the galleys and carracks of Venetians and Genoese, who also had a dispensation to export raw wool directly via the 'Straits of Morocco' (Gibraltar), as the legislation had it. The cloth trade in general was not subject to such close official supervision as that in wool and did, as time went by, become very involved in the process by which English traders and mariners began to venture further afield.[4] The need to find new markets for a valuable commodity like this drove mariners and merchants to travel north to Iceland (and, eventually, in the sixteenth century, Muscovy) and south to the Mediterranean.

A better idea of the operation of the staple system, however, and in particular its maritime aspects, can be gained from looking at the business correspondence of a family of London staplers, the Celys, as well as the customs accounts. The Cely family's papers, a large collection of letters, accounts and other documents, survive by happy accident. At the end of the fifteenth century, Richard Cely, the survivor of the two brothers who had run their family partnership since around 1476, sued his widowed sister-in-law for the repayment of debts. The family papers were needed as evidence but were never returned by the courts after the case was over; they remained as part of the records of the court of Chancery kept first of all in the Tower of London and then in the Public Record Office.[5] The organisation by the Company of the Staple of the export of wool from England to Calais at this date (and very probably at earlier periods) was complex. The staplers used middlemen (in the Celys' case their main agent was William Midwinter of Northleach) to collect raw wool for them in the producing areas. The raw wool and also wool fells (fleeces) were brought to the ports (by the mid-fifteenth century almost invariably London) overland in carts, packed in standard bales (sarplers) and sorted by quality.[6] Once in the city, the carts had to make their way through the crowded streets to the weigh beam where the number of fells and the weight of each sarpler was officially recorded and the customs paid. The bales were repacked in canvas covers then numbered and painted with the shipper's personal mark. The customs seal or cocket was also attached to each bale. If a wool fleet was about to leave, the bales would go directly to the wool quay to be loaded on the waiting vessels. The shippers, the members of the staple or their apprentices, would carefully record the numbers of each bale and where it was loaded in the ship. It was the usual practice to divide the shipment among a number of vessels, to minimise the risk of a total loss, so this was a vital part of the process. The Celys' factor in London, William Cely, wrote anxiously to George Cely in Calais in November 1481:

> You shall receive off the *Thomas of New Hythe*, Robard Ewen, master, 1 pack half a hundred 14 fells and a little fardel [bundle] of fells that is allowed for 3 fells with the Customer and the said fells lie next aft the mast lowest under the fells of Thomas Betson and the little fardel lies just to the mast upperest of my master's fells.[7]

The Company of the Staple, at this date, seems to have organised three main wool fleets per year, one in the spring (March or April), one in the summer (May to early August) and one in the autumn (September or October). The size of the fleets varied considerably: forty-one ships left London in July 1478 with 1,160³/₄ sacks of wool and 268,227 fells, but only fourteen the following May.[8] The danger from pirates even on the short Channel crossing was apparently so great that it was usual for the wool fleet to be convoyed by an armed escort. The Celys' own vessel, the *Margaret Cely*, was used in this way in July 1486. She was victualled for the voyage in London with no less than 56s. 8d. being spent on twenty-eight barrels of beer. There were, it is true, forty-five people on board, twenty-eight soldiers of the escort and seventeen crew, but even so this seems a very generous provision.[9] Earlier, in March 1475, when war with France was imminent, the cost of the convoying vessels (three from London and one from Ipswich), including the victuals of the men aboard, reached the large sum of £171 5s. 0d.[10] If no fleet was scheduled, the sarplers would be stored in a wool house to await the next sailing, although, on occasion, sales of wool were made in London, despite this being forbidden by the staple regulations.

Even though the voyage to Calais was short, the merchants, waiting in London for news of the shipments, fretted anxiously about the weather or news of delays. In December 1483, a ship called the *Battle* was delayed and William Cely wrote to his master, 'the Boston fleet is come to Calais all in safety thanked be God, save the *Battle* which is yet behind and she hath in a hundred sarplers, wool and fells and they hear nothing of her here yet. I pray God send her well hither.'[11] Once the wool fleet arrived in Calais, the vessels were unloaded and the sarplers registered in their owner's name by the Staple collectors. A fee was payable and also the wool was inspected to see that it was of the quality described or 'awarded'. Often this was done by selecting one sarpler from a batch to be examined; something which gave an opportunity for sharp practice. In 1487 the bale selected from a Cely cargo (no. 24) was found to be 'very gruff wool' by the packer but the wool from another bale was repacked in no. 24's canvas covering before this could be recorded. William Cely reported happily to his masters that this was 'fair wool enough'.[12] The Flemish merchants who bought English wools came to Calais to inspect what was on the market and then transported their purchases overland to the textile towns. The financial side of the trade was extremely complex, so much so that, despite the survival of the Cely papers, including some accounts, and the existence of the rather similar Johnson papers from the sixteenth century,[13] it is not easy to be sure how profitable it was for an individual merchant. Apart from the system of royal customs duties and subsidies on the export of wool, a fifteenth-century merchant of the Staple had to deal not only with different systems of wool weights existing in Calais and England (using modern weights, the 'standard' wool sack weighed 364 lbs in England but only 315 lbs in Calais) but also with a ferocious tangle of accounting difficulties. Moneys of account (the system of pounds, shillings and pence, or the rival system of marks valued at two-thirds of a pound (13s. 4d.)) were not related to the actual coins in use. In England the silver coins minted were the groat worth 4d., a half groat, penny, half penny and farthing. There were in addition three gold coins: the 'old' noble, first struck after the English victory at Sluys in 1340 (which had on the reverse an image of the king on a ship), the *rial* or rose noble and the *angel* noble (with St Michael on the reverse). In 1465 these gold coins were worth 8s. 4d., 10s. and 6s. 8d. respectively, provided they were 'good' coins, that is to say, of the correct weight. There were, however, relatively few of these English coins in circulation in Calais after the closure of the Calais mint in 1442. Much more common was a mish-mash of the coins, both gold and silver, struck in the duchy of Burgundy, France, the Rhineland or other European mints. The company of the Staple displayed in the lower hall of their headquarters in Calais, the Place, a table of current coinage values, and thus the exchange rate, but this might differ from that in other places, particularly Bruges or London, creating a possible trap for the unwary merchant and an opportunity for the authorities to manipulate the exchange rate. The complications caused by the circulation of many different coins is well illustrated by one transaction of George Cely in 1480. He sold some wool fells to a merchant who paid half the total in cash at the rate of 25s. 4d. Flemish to a pound sterling. He gave George 93 Andrews (Burgundian gold coins) valued at 4s. 6d. Flemish each, 18$\frac{1}{2}$ crowns (French) at 5s. 4d. each, 6 Venetian ducats and 2 salutes, at 5s. 6d., 1 Rhenish gulden, at 4s. 4d., 5 Utrecht gulden, at 4s., and £8 0s. 2d. in double briquets (Burgundian silver coins). The total according to Cely came to £37 5s. 8d. Flemish and he then gave his customer change in 12 Guilhelmus (silver shillings of William IV count of Holland) valued at 4s. 4d. each and a further 14d. in small coins.[14] Only a proportion of the price was paid in cash. The purchaser was contracted to pay the remainder due on the transaction by a bill of exchange usually payable at the next mart, for example the Antwerp Bammis mart in the autumn.

Much more demanding of the skills of seamanship was the wine trade. This was centred on the wines of Bordeaux and the surrounding areas and involved the voyage from English south and west coast ports, from London to Bristol, to La Rochelle or the Gironde and Bordeaux itself. From the early twelfth century until 1453 the duchy of Aquitaine, of which Bordeaux was the prime city and port, was a possession of the English crown, so it is not surprising that most wines drunk in England at this time came from this region. In the later part of the fifteenth century, after the loss of Aquitaine to the French, more wine came from Spain and Portugal, and a limited amount of the highly desired sweet malmsey from the Venetian island of Crete. The Hastings Manuscript rutter includes a section, with soundings only, for the passage from the Gironde to Beachy Head; this would, of course, need to be expanded to include bearings, distances and tidal information to be usable by a navigator unfamiliar with these waters. The existing notes were, however, useful as reminders for seamen who made the voyage on a regular basis. As it stands, this section is hard to interpret and may, in fact, be a translated copy of a Portuguese or Spanish set of sailing direc-tions which included *alturas* or the altitudes of heavenly bodies used to calculate latitudes. A recent attempt to plot the course suggested by this supposition on a chart produced a 'good' course from Ushant to the Gironde, clear of all dangers and taking the best line. An earlier part of the same manuscript describing courses in 'spayne and bretayne' seems to imply a course following the coast much more closely, with waypoints suggested on headlands and islands including Penmarch, Belle-Ile and Oléron. On reaching the Gironde the ship master is warned about the sandbanks on the south shore. This section may date originally from earlier than the first course mentioned. Other evidence also suggests that St Mathieu (near Brest) was often used by English vessels as a 'half-way house' on the way to Bordeaux; this might be to take on fresh victuals or to wait for favourable winds.[15]

It is clear that this trade, often grain outward to Bordeaux and wine
inward to various English ports, was generally seen as profitable.
Even royal ships, when not needed for sea-keeping duties, might be
involved. William Catton, the clerk of the king's ships in the early
years of the reign of Henry V, hired out royal ships to merchants for
the voyage to La Rochelle or Bordeaux for wine, raising sizeable sums
for the expenses of his office in the process. The freight charge varied
between 10s. and 22s. 6d. per wine tun so that a voyage by one of the
larger ships could raise a considerable sum. For example, a voyage to
Bordeaux in early 1413 by the *Cog John* raised £207 10s. 0d., with a
cargo of 207 tuns, 1 pipe of wine, at the rate of 20s. per tun. Even at
the much lower rate of 8s. 6d. per tun, the *Redcog de la Tour* brought
in £52 9s. 9d. with a cargo of 123 tuns 1 pipe from Bordeaux in May
1416.[16] Wine was being sold wholesale in London in these years for
between 133s. 4d. and 93s. 4d. per tun. Later in the same century,
after the English had lost control of Aquitaine, the port books or local
customs books of Southampton give us a picture of the way the distribution of wines was organised from Southampton. Relatively few
vessels brought large cargoes of wine into the port from Bordeaux or
Spain. Sometimes two or more ships would travel in company to
reduce the risk from pirates, particularly off the Breton coast. Once
the wine was landed, it was bought in small lots by local men and then
very often sent on by sea to consumers up and down the south coast
and the Isle of Wight. A mariner named John Shepard, who was particularly active in 1469–70, had something like a regular carrier's
business bringing kerseys into Southampton from the island and
taking back, along with one or two tuns of wine, goods such as
feather beds, tallow, olive oil and salt fish. As another example, in
October 1494 a boat from Rye delivered wine to Arundel for the earl
and to Chichester for the bishop, a small part of a large shipment
probably from Spain.[17]

In Bristol, the wine trade was of great importance, with ships both
from Bayonne, the shipping centre of Aquitaine, and from Bristol and
other west country ports bringing in large quantities. Before the
English loss of the duchy in 1453 and their virtual ejection from the
wine trade from Bordeaux for the next twenty years (see chart of wine
imports through Bristol for the fifteenth century, p. xii),[18] Bristol was
the most important wine port after London, with Hull as its nearest

rival. In the later part of the century, only London and Bristol were substantially involved in the trade, with much of the wine coming into London being carried in Italian ships. Like Southampton, Bristol was also the centre of vigorous coastal and river traffic, distributing wine and other luxury imports to Irish and west country ports such as Tenby, Newport, Barnstaple, Cork, Limerick and Galway and up the Severn to Gloucester and Tewkesbury. At Worcester, wine was loaded onto carts for journeys overland as far as Warwick and Coventry.[19] A development in the fifteenth century which does not seem to be mirrored in other ports was the rise in Bristol of great family fortunes based not on trading but on shipowning. One of the most prominent merchants in Bristol in the late fourteenth century was William Canynges the older. The basis of his prosperity was the cloth trade to Spain and Bayonne, though he owned one ship, the *Rodcog*, at his death. His son John continued as a merchant, building up a property empire of no fewer than twenty-eight shops and other buildings and empty sites in the town. His grandson, William the younger, built an even more impressive fortune largely as a ship-owner. William of Worcester, a contemporary who wrote a description of Bristol in his *Itineraries*, claimed that Canynges employed no fewer than 800 men on his ships, controlling perhaps as much as a quarter of all the shipping in the port. Worcester claimed that the *Mary Canynges* and the *Mary Redcliffe* were of 400 tuns and 500 tuns capacity respectively, while the *Mary and John* was an enormous vessel for the day at 900 tuns. If the total capacity of all Canynges's ships was close to 3,000 tuns, and if each ship made two trips a year to the Gironde for wine, he could, in theory, have received over £10,000 in freight charges at current prices. These are large assumptions and take no account of all the uncertainties which were the lot of the shipowner – storms, adverse winds, damage, pirates, unreliable or even fraudulent clients – but that such a large sum can be plausibly suggested gives some idea of the potential of the trade.[20]

A detailed illustration of the complex nature of the financing of shipowning can be found in the Cely Papers. These include accounts for the operation of the *Margaret Cely*. This was originally a Breton vessel called the *Margaret of Penmarcke* which the Cely brothers bought in 1486 and operated in partnership with William Maryon. She cost £28 to buy and was then re-equipped, with £4 spent on armaments including guns and 40s. on such necessary items as kettles, a compass and a glass (timer); new rigging and sails were also fitted. After two short voyages to Zeeland and Calais, it was decided to go to Bordeaux for wines, the real purpose of acquiring the ship. This entailed laying in victuals for the crew of fourteen including enormous quantities of beef (three oxen are mentioned), biscuit and firewood for the galley. All told, including buying the ship, £91 18s. 0½d. had been spent by the time she set out for Bordeaux. This did not include the crew's wages nor further provisions and items such as new anchor stocks and water barrels bought in France. Her return cargo was 55¾ tuns of wine, with the total freight charges coming after various discounts and deductions to £49 19s. 6d. George Cely finally accounted for small dividends of just over a pound to his partners, but the return was nowhere like those suggested for Canynges. The *Margaret Cely*'s voyage to Bordeaux in 1488 is another good example of the uncertainties of this kind of venture. After victualling in London, again largely with beef and biscuit, the vessel left Gravesend on 14 September and by the beginning of October was at Plymouth, where she stayed for five weeks. She then crept along the coast to Fowey where she stayed for a further two weeks, leaving on around 13 November. Fair winds then brought her to Bordeaux in a few days. She left for home in early January, making a fast passage and entering the Pool of London about 16 January. Even so the voyage had lasted four months, during which the crew's living expenses had all been met by the owners. When George Cely made up accounts in May 1489, which covered all voyages made by the *Margaret Cely* in 1487 and 1488, the partners were out of pocket to the tune of about £23 for his brother Richard, £41 for George and £14 10s. for William Maryon. The only profit came from goods shipped in their own names. Canynges had much larger ships and thus could profit from economy of scale, but he also employed much larger crews and would have been equally subject to delays due to bad weather and adverse winds.[21]

Whatever doubts there may be over the profitability of shipowning, it is, however, clear that Bristol men and mariners were more ready to take chances and to seek out new markets by sailing new routes than those from the south coast ports. Southampton ships routinely sailed across the Bay of Biscay to Bilbao, mainly for cargoes of iron. Bristol men followed this route but also sailed south to Seville, not being daunted by the tortuous and difficult passage up the Guadalquivir. In 1473 the *Mary* Redclyffe unloaded a cargo from Seville of 134 tuns of oil, and 146 tuns of wine as well as soap and sugar. The total value of the cargo was £572 10s.[22] William of Worcester also recorded the story of Robert Sturmy of Bristol in his *Itineraries*. Sturmy attempted to open the Mediterranean to direct trade in English goods, instead of via Italian intermediaries, as early as 1446. He loaded his ship the *Cog Anne* with wool, cloth and tin, as well as 160 pilgrims for the Holy Land, and saw it set sail from Bristol in the autumn. The vessel seems to have reached Jaffa, the port for Jerusalem, in safety and there disembarked its passengers. On her return voyage, however, off the coast of the Peloponnese, near the Venetian trading post and colony of Modon, the ship was wrecked and her master and the crew drowned. Eleven years later Sturmy, now one of the leading citizens of Bristol, sent a much larger venture into the same waters. He set out on board the *Katherine*, with two other ships laden with large quantities of wool, cloth and tin, for the Levant via Gibraltar in mid-1457. The aim was to sell the cargo directly to Turkish or Egyptian traders, buying spices and other luxuries for the return leg. This would cut out the middlemen, particularly the Genoese. Sturmy's ship was in fact attacked by the Genoese near Malta, taken and spoiled. It is possible that Sturmy himself was killed in the attack; certainly his widow proved his will on 12 December 1457. The taking of his ships and the loss of the cargo caused a violent reaction from the English authorities, who arrested all the Genoese in London in retaliation and confiscated their goods. The situation was only resolved by the payment of around £6,000 by the Genoese. This was divided up among those who had invested in Sturmy's venture.

Another trade, which involved a lengthy and sometimes dangerous sea passage, was the Iceland voyage. The *Libelle of Englyshe Polyce*, a robust piece of propaganda for a more determined commercial policy on the part of the crown in verse form, written about 1436, put Bristol in the forefront of the trade.

> Of Iceland to write is little need
> Save of stockfish; yet forsooth indeed
> Out of Bristol and coasts many one

Men have practiced be needle and by stone
Thitherwards within a little while,
Within 12 years, and withouten peril,
Gone and comen, as men were wont of old
Of Scarborough, unto the coast(e)s cold.

This ignored the involvement both in trade and in the fisheries, particularly off the Westman Islands on the south west coast of Iceland, of boats
from Lynn, Hull and other east coast ports (including Scarborough).
This had begun in about 1412, according to the Icelandic annals.[23] It
was, however, accurate in seeing stockfish, air-dried cod, as the main
inward item of trade. This was popular 'fast day' and Lenten fare not
only in England but also in most of western Europe. Icelanders were
happy to trade stockfish for all manner of cloth, ironwork and
hardware, timber, and personal and household items hard to come by in
their bleak and cold island. The voyage there, as the *Libelle* hints, was
not without its dangers; nearly eight hundred miles across the stormy
North Atlantic was a formidable undertaking. Bristol ships would have
sailed for Iceland from ports like Galway on the west coast of Ireland.
The course would then have been a little west of north, easily made good
with a south-west wind by fifteenth-century ships. Landfall would also
have been made on this course at the settlements on the west coast. The
course from Lynn or Hull would lie more to the north west and might
well involve pauses at the Orkneys, Shetlands or Faeroes. Mariners from
all ports, however, would undoubtedly have felt more secure if able to
follow a compass course as the *Libelle* implies.[24]

Trading with Iceland was not just a matter of employing seaworthy
vessels with experienced masters and establishing what goods were
acceptable to both parties. It also involved the relations between the
rulers of England and first Norway, ruling Iceland from 1262, and
then Denmark, overlords of Norway as well as southern Sweden
following the Union of Kalmar in 1397. Denmark's interests were
primarily financial. The Danish king tried to insist that all trade with
Iceland went via the staple at Bergen, as this entailed the payment of
high tolls to himself. English direct trade with Iceland threatened this
useful source of income, no matter how welcome it was to the Icelanders. English fishermen and merchants were faced with royal
efforts to ban the trade in both England and Denmark, then with the

possibility of obtaining licences to avoid the ban. All this created opportunities for the independent-minded to sail to the North, ignoring all attempts at control, while others like John Forster of Bristol with nine licences between 1466 and 1478, and the forty-three merchants shipping Icelandic goods to Hull on three ships in 1471, played the system to their own advantage.[25]

Another factor in the situation, however, was rivalry with the traders of the Hanseatic League. This confederation of trading cities, mostly in the lands of the Holy Roman Empire, extending from Cologne on the Rhine in the west, to Riga and Reval on the Baltic in the east, emerged as an informal cooperative grouping in the early thirteenth century. By the mid-fourteenth century, their organisation had become much stronger, with the development of the *Hansetag*, sometimes also called the diet or assembly, which, under the leadership of Lübeck, promulgated decrees and took decisions for the League as a whole. The importance of Lübeck and the way in which the trade and organisation of the League developed is well illustrated by the career of Johannes Wittenborg, whose account book for the years 1346–59 survives. Wittenborg came from an old-established Lübeck family with extensive landed property and involvement in League politics. He traded with Flanders, England, Scania, Prussia, Livonia and Russia. From the west he imported cloth, principally from Valenciennes and Louvain. From the east he imported furs and wax to sell in Bruges and he also traded in bulk goods, barley, malt and beer. He sailed to England himself in 1348 and was also in Bruges in 1356. His success in business led to his becoming a member of the council of Lübeck in 1350 and he attended the important Hanseatic diets at Rostock in 1358 and Griefswald in 1361, when he was *burgermeister* of Lübeck. His career, however, did not end happily. He had supported the decision of the League to go to war with Denmark and was commander of the league's naval forces in the Sound in 1362. His life as a merchant was, however, no preparation for command at sea and he was held responsible for the defeat of the Hanse by the king of Denmark, arrested on his return to Lübeck, tried by the council and eventually beheaded in the market place. Even wealth and strong family connections could not save him from the wrath of his fellow citizens when they felt their interests had been fatally harmed.[26]

The ships of the League dominated trade in the Baltic and became increasingly important in the North Sea and in ports on the east coast of England and in the Netherlands during the fourteenth century. It has sometimes been suggested that before the fourteenth century most bulk goods coming from Prussian ports or Gotland were unloaded in Lübeck where the goods were placed on carts for transport to Hamburg; there they would be again loaded onto ships for the voyage to Flanders or across the North Sea. It is clear, however, that ships were making what was called the *ummelandfart* (the voyage round Jutland via the Sound) much earlier than this. The ship type, the cog, characteristic of the League towns, was well fitted to this journey, which was a natural extension of the voyages to Skania for herrings which had been the root of the Wendish ports' prosperity.[27] The total number of towns and cities in the confederation varied from time to time, with around seventy being considered as full members, the most important being Cologne, Bremen, Hamburg, Lübeck, Rostock, Stralsund, Visby (Gotland) and Danzig. All these conducted a major part of their trade, the lifeblood of each city and the League as a whole, by sea or via a navigable river. The League also controlled *Kontors* or major trading centres in Novgorod, Bruges, London and Bergen. Their centre in London, the Steelyard, had originally been set up by merchants from Cologne, but by the thirteenth century it was occupied by merchants from all the Hanseatic cities. It extended down to the banks of the River Thames where there was a wharf; stretching back from this were various buildings, including living quarters, a hall, warehouses and stores. Those living there were expected to obey strict rules regarding their clothing (no ostentatious garments) and behaviour. Picking the fruit in the garden and bringing loose women into the enclave were both strictly forbidden. A somewhat similar regime existed in Bergen and Novgorod, although the latter had a system of winter and summer merchants alternating at the Peterhof, as this Kontor was called. In Bruges, by far the most important centre, there was a hall from the mid-fifteenth century but no living quarters. In 1457 there were over 600 Hanseatic merchants and their assistants and apprentices living in the town, exerting very considerable economic power. The cogs which came to the wharves in London and Bruges were laden with a very wide range of goods. Some were high value including wax and the furs – fox, squirrel and sable – brought from Novgorod and eastern Europe, and weapons and armour from Cologne; others were essential bulk goods – timber and its byproducts like pitch, salt herring, grain, osmund or Swedish iron and hemp for ropes. Their return cargoes consisted largely of cloth with small quantities of wine. In the late 1450s over ten thousand cloths a year were exported from England by the Hanse. As well as the kontors, there were also smaller trading centres spread throughout the northern regions. In England, King's Lynn was the base for one group of merchants, whose warehouse still exists though now easily overlooked as it is hidden behind a Georgian frontage. In the Shetland Islands, where the herring fishery flourished in the fifteenth century, there are small stores built by Hansards, which may date from this period, in Busta Voe on the main island and Symbister on the island of Whalsay.[28]

The Hanse *kontor* at Bergen more or less controlled all the seaborne exports of Norway by the fifteenth century, with Hanseatic vessels dominating the seaways through the Sound to the Baltic or across the North Sea to King's Lynn and other east coast English ports. By this time the seafaring tradition of the Norwegians, bound up with stories of the epic voyages of the Vikings, seems to have almost completely decayed. One reason for the welcome given to the first English traders in Iceland was that the Norwegians seemed unable to send the six annual ships with supplies to Iceland which had been specified in the treaty of 1262. In fact in the same year in which the Iceland annals noted sadly that there was 'no news from Norway to Iceland', it was also recorded that a strange ship had been seen off Dyrholm Island. When men rowed out to it, they discovered 'fishermen out from England'.[29] The Hanse merchants at Bergen were not prepared, however, to tolerate English competition for Icelandic stockfish, and pressure from Lübeck and other leading cities lay behind Danish attempts to ban English voyages to northern waters. The value that merchants at King's Lynn placed on their Hanseatic connections perhaps lay behind their willingness to accept this restriction, unlike other English ports including Hull.

The quasi-monopoly which the Hanseatic cities were able to establish in the most important northern trades has been put down to the superiority of their ships, as well as the harmony in maritime and business practice between the members of the League. Their characteristic vessel, the cog, was larger and handled better than vessels of other designs, an advantage particularly noticeable from the mid-fourteenth to the mid-fifteenth centuries. Their fleets were also larger and better coordinated than those of possible rivals. League members could command around one thousand ships at the end of the fifteenth century; these would have been able to transport a very large amount of cargo. Perhaps one-third normally traded via the Sound between Denmark and Sweden, *en route* to England and Flanders for cloth, and to Gascony for wine and for the salt produced in the Bay of Biscay at Bourgneuf; one-third were employed in trade within the Baltic; and the remainder would sail to Iceland or within the North Sea.[30] In 1403 the diet laid down rules which kept most ships in port between 11 November and 22 February, and from 1426 ships could not be sold to foreigners. Convoys were also organised on longer routes with armed escorts; for example, a minimum of ten vessels was needed for the passage through the Sound. Maritime law for the merchants and shipmasters of the Hanse was at first based on the customs of Hamburg. This was later heavily influenced, as were the laws of virtually all northern maritime nations, by the Laws of Oléron. The Hanseatic version was printed in 1505 in Copenhagen as the *Götlandisches Wasserrecht*, a title which acknowledged the importance of one of the oldest members of the League, Visby on the island of Gotland. Trading partners, particularly England and the cities of Flanders, found the Hanse's grasp on trade in northern waters highly restrictive. English cloth merchants chafed angrily at the customs privileges the Hanse had extracted from the English crown in the early fourteenth century which meant that Hanseatic merchants paid duties which were not only lower than those paid by all other aliens but also lower than those paid by denizens. All attempts to receive reciprocal favourable treatment in the ports of Danzig, Lübeck, Hamburg or other League members were unsuccessful, leading eventually to open conflict in the early 1470s.

Despite the hold of the Hanseatic League over seaborne and land-based trade in the Baltic, and on the coasts adjacent to the North Sea, it seems that the total amount of trade passing through the port of Lübeck, by far the richest and most important of the member cities, was dwarfed by the seaborne trade of the leading Mediterranean cities, particularly Genoa and Venice. It is not easy to make direct comparisons of the total traffic of these ports in the later Middle Ages because of the lack of suitable quantitative evidence. Although there are figures from customs or other tolls charged on goods passing through the ports, there was no uniform way to levy such tolls; and there were frequently all sorts of exemptions for various privileged groups. The survival of records of this kind is also very erratic, especially in Lübeck. It is possible, however, to compare the trade of Lübeck with that of Venice and Genoa for a short period in the fourteenth century. This shows that the total value of trade through the port of Lübeck between 1379 and 1384 was 350,000 golden *gulden*, units whose value was comparable with that of Genoa's golden *genovini*. The total trade of Genoa, even in this depressed period in the aftermath of the arrival of the Black Death, was 1,700,000 *genovini*. In 1492, nearly a century later, the trade through the harbour at Lübeck was valued at the equivalent of 330,000 Venetian ducats; the 1497 figures for Venetian trade with Alexandria and Beirut alone (a relatively small proportion of total Venetian trade) show a total value of 590,000 ducats, including imports worth 475,000 ducats.[31] No northern port could produce such impressive totals until the sixteenth century and the shift of seaborne trade away from the Mediterranean towards the Atlantic.

Our first look at seaborne trade in the Mediterranean, however, will be concerned not with the great Italian trading cities but with the merchants of the North African coast. This is because, for the eleventh and twelfth centuries, when Italian sources are still somewhat scanty and uninformative, there is a source from Egypt which supplies much of the kind of personal information about ships and traders which was almost entirely lacking in northern Europe. This is the great collection of commercial documents, letters and many other kinds of writings which was found in the Geniza of the old synagogue in Cairo at the end of the nineteenth century. A Geniza was a repository for all sorts of written material thought to be of no further practical use. Jewish tradition rejected the throwing away as rubbish of any document which might have some religious significance, and from this grew the habit of consigning obsolete or damaged writings to a special place. In the case of Cairo this was the boarded up section of the attic over the women's gallery of the Ezra synagogue, which had been founded in the ninth century. The Geniza had no doors or windows and could only be reached by a ladder going up to the hole through which additions were originally pushed. When the Geniza's contents were finally examined it became clear that much of the material related to the business life of the community and the economy of the region before the thirteenth century. A general survey of the contents of the letters, contracts and other documents makes clear that, for both Jewish and non-Jewish merchants based in Egypt and adjacent areas, trade with the *Rum* or the Christian nations on the northern shores of the Mediterranean and Byzantium to the east was vital. It was the arrival of traders from these areas that opened the market and set the prices. If their arrival was delayed or prevented, letter writers bewailed their fate; 'This year [1133] business is at a standstill for noone has come from the west', wrote one correspondent. Earlier, in about 1085, an Alexandrian wrote to a colleague in Cairo, 'the alum has not yet arrived; here are *Rum*; we shall offer it to them and we hope they will buy it'. The letter writers did not in fact have a very high opinion of the commercial acumen of their western customers. Around 1060 one wrote in amazement of how the latter had happily paid exorbitant prices for dyestuffs (indigo and brazilwood), being unwilling or unable to distinguish between first-quality and inferior goods. 'For every quality they pay the same price. Likewise, the flax – they buy the poor quality for the same price as the excellent and are not prepared to pay more for the latter.'[32]

Westerners travelled to the markets of Egypt, Tunisia and the Maghreb much more frequently than the eastern merchants ventured to the north. The Geniza documents are concerned almost entirely with the activities of Jewish merchants, but this generalisation seems to hold good for Moslems as well. Jewish scholars from France or Germany travelled to Egypt to consult religious authorities but virtually none made the journey in the reverse direction. Nor were there commercial contacts between these communities. The Jewish merchants traded almost exclusively with Christians from Italy and Byzantium who came to them in Egypt and the Maghreb to purchase all manner of exotic merchandise.[33] The goods exchanged in the markets of Alexandria and the other cities on the coast were extremely varied. Some of the commodities bought or sold by Isaac Nisaburi, a Persian Jew living in Alexandria around 1100, are good examples. He traded in dyes, including saffron and brazilwood, medicinal plants, glass, silk, brocade robes and silk scarves, corals from Christian Europe, perfumes, wax, millstones and a variety of more mundane things.[34] Other merchants also traded in metals, oil, precious stones, spices such as pepper, cinnamon and cloves, and books, including both Jewish and Moslem religious and legal texts. Bulk goods, which were seldom handled by the Geniza merchants, included foodstuffs, notably wheat, rice, and barley, and timber, which were imported in large quantities. Even though much of the Geniza evidence dates from the period of the Crusades, notwithstanding the conflict in Syria and Palestine, both merchants from *Rum* and their Jewish and Moslem counterparts were not in the least willing to interrupt this traffic.

It is clear that, wherever possible, transport of goods by water was much preferred to sending them overland. In Egypt, the Nile was used extensively for this purpose, with boats sometimes going on to Cairo after crossing from Sicily. The river was not easy to navigate, with its shifting sandbanks, fierce currents and sudden squalls. One man, the servant of an Egyptian aristocrat at the end of the eleventh century, wrote feelingly of a river journey, 'we went down the Nile and stayed several days on the river, enduring great horrors on it'.[35] Another traveller complained that he was 'several times on the brink of being drowned' on a river journey from Cairo. River boats were also vulnerable to attacks when moored, sometimes from robbers, sometimes from predatory government officials. Sea routes to the west extended along the coast of North Africa to Morocco and to southern Spain. Eastwards there was some contact with Byzantium, but more usually the sailings ended at El Ladhiqiya, where goods from Damascus could be loaded. The usual pattern of trade was for Arabic and Jewish merchants to travel from one market to the next selling their goods as the opportunity arose and buying in the same manner. Silk from Andalusia might be sold in Tunis and the proceeds invested in spices which had come from the East Indies via Syrian or Egyptian traders. If trade was bad in one town, merchants packed their goods and moved on to the next.

Despite the fact that sea traffic only operated in the summer months, usually from around March to November, the letters make clear how vital sea traffic was to traders; both goods and potential customers came in this way and a continual theme is anxiety about the whereabouts or the hoped-for arrival of ships. There was even a system of watch points to track the progress of ships sailing near the shore between Alexandria and Tunis. The prices in the market were in fact determined by the flow of shipping. This applied particularly to trade in silk which was almost treated as a kind of investment. A trader from Alexandria in 1100 wrote:

> There are only twenty-three days left until the Feast of the Cross [September 28–29, the last date for the convoys to sail back to the West], but not a single ship has arrived from the West [Tunisia] and no news about ships has come through; in addition the winds are unfavourable, they are neither east nor west winds. This very day people have offered 23 dinars for [10lbs] of coarse silk but noone wants to sell. Everyone is refraining from selling until the situation clears up.[36]

When the decision was taken to send goods by sea, we get a much more detailed idea of what this entailed from this evidence than from that available for northern ports. Space had to be booked in a vessel well in advance, as ships often travelled in convoy, sometimes with an escort of armed vessels. The merchant (or his agent) came on board the day before the ship was due to leave and spent the night, either in prayer or in writing last-minute letters (including, of course, some of those which survived in the Geniza). He may or may not have been expected to sleep on the cargo bales in the hold but was certainly expected to provide bedding, utensils and food for himself. Voyages could be delayed because of the weather or wind direction but, once under way, the ships did not always creep from one port to the next but could take a more direct route. With favourable winds it was considered that it should take eight days to sail from Tripoli to Seville, mostly out of sight of land. Stories of storms and shipwrecks, however, lost nothing in the telling. On his way to Jaffa from Tyre, one merchant ran into a storm:

> We were without sails and oars and the rudder was broken. Likewise the sail yards were broken and the waves burst into the barge. Realising that our ship was a mere river boat, small as a ferry, we cried 'Allah, Allah'. We threw part of the cargo overboard and I gave up all hope of life and for all that I carried

1. A Battle at Sea. This image comes from an illuminated edition *c.* 1270 of Vegetius' *De Re Militari*, a classical treatise on the art of war which has a short section on war at sea. The picture is of a medieval action with the crews of the two opposing ships locked in close combat. Both longbows and crossbows are being used, as well as spears and other weapons. *(Fitzwilliam Museum, Cambridge)*

2. The Seal of John Holand. John Holand was Admiral of England 1435–42 and this is his admiralty seal. It shows a stylized representation of a single-masted ship of a rather earlier date with fore- and after castles and a top castle. In the top can be seen a stock of spears. The long streamer flying from the masthead was the accepted sign of a vessel ready for war; on the sail are the royal leopards of England. The ridges and knobs on the hull are probably a stylized version of clinker planking and clench nails. *(National Maritime Museum)*

3. The Battle of Sluys Froissart's Chronicle. This is a conventional picture from a fifteenth-century MS of the battle in 1340 between the fleets of France and England but it shows clearly the appearance of ships of the cog type. *(Bibliothèque Nationale, Paris)*

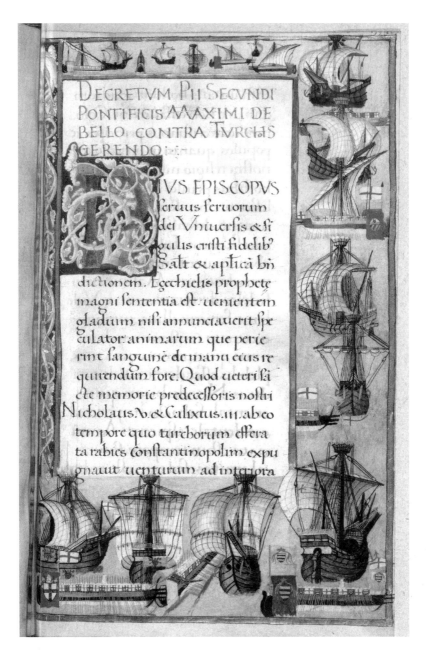

4. A decorated decretal of Pope Pius II, 1464. The decretal related to a proposed crusade against the Turks. The decoration around the opening page consists of pictures of Mediterranean vessels of this date. Both galleys and round (sailing) ships are represented flying the crusader cross. *(Bibliothèque Nationale, Paris)*

5. The Master of WA Kraek *c.*1470. This well-known engraving has often been described as the best representation of a carrack, a ship type introduced by the Genoese and later copied by the English. It gives a detailed and convincing picture of the ship's rigging and also other fittings like the rudder and grapple at the bow. There also seem to be a cannon in the aftercastle and a smaller gun in the top castle. Recently the possibility was raised that this was not a picture of a real ship but a plan for a float in the elaborate processions popular in fifteenth-century Burgundy. A possible copy of this picture appears in a contemporary tapestry in Paris. *(Asmolean Museum, Oxford)*

NAVE·DEL·ARMER·

6. The Battle of Zonchio. This woodcut was produced very shortly after the battle which took place in 1499 between the Venetians and the Turks off the coast of the Morea. Two large Venetian sailing vessels engaged a Turkish one but a fire on this ship spread rapidly to the others and all were burnt to the waterline. The oared vessels present then withdrew with little further action. *(The Trustees of the British Museum)*

7. Beauchamp pageant ships, Cotton Julius. This Beauchamp pageant was a celebration of the pilgrimage to Jerusalem of Richard Beauchamp Earl of Warwick in 1408–9 probably commissioned by his daughter c. 1485. It shows vessels of this later date engaged in close combat. *(The British Library)*

with me . . . Finally, through God's grace we reached Caesarea;
however, both my clothes and goods were completely soaked.[37]

He then took refuge in the local synagogue. Another merchant was
wrecked on an island somewhere near Sicily and was marooned there
for twenty days with nothing to eat except nettles. He did eventually
reach Sicily, but he and his companions 'were so exhausted from our
sufferings on the sea that we were unable to eat bread or to understand what was said to us for a full month'.[38] Some travellers were not
above using amulets or other magic formulae to prevent such
disasters; amulets have been found in the Geniza which included 'holy
names'. These would be placed in a jar and thrown into the sea and
this would (or so it was claimed) calm the storm. Despite these
dangers, the Geniza material gives the impression of a lively and
generally prosperous trading community, well able to afford the cost
of packing goods for transport by sea, meeting the freight charges and
making a profit.[39]

If we turn to their customers from the land of the *Rum*, principally
merchants from the Italian cities, we are not so dependent on one
source, even if it is one of exceptional richness, particularly for the
later medieval period. The major ports on the Mediterranean all had
some system of customs duties or tolls, leaving records of varying
completeness. There were usually other official records as well, legal
records and, particularly in the fourteenth and fifteenth centuries, the
papers of individual merchants. The accounts both of individuals and
of the governing body of the city can be very helpful as can the papers
of notaries whose expertise in civil law led to their being closely
involved in the drafting of contracts. The most voluminous collection
of private papers is probably that of Francesco di Marco Datini of
Prato. These papers survive largely because of the terms of his will
which, in the absence of any heirs, established a charity for the benefit
of the town in his magnificent house. Here his executors preserved his
account books, letters and other documents, which were largely
undisturbed until the nineteenth century.[40] As a trader, Datini had connections and business partnerships the length and breadth of Europe,
from England to the Levant and Crimea. His letters reveal the
influence of the political situation in Italy at any one time on his
choice of route and on his decision whether to ship goods by land or

by sea. At first he primarily used the port of Pisa, establishing an office in the city in 1384. This prospered under the care of resident factors but by 1390 the turmoil in Tuscany caused by the supporters of Gian Galeazzo Visconti, the duke of Milan, and the enmity between Pisans and Florentines made trade increasingly precarious. The letters have stories of piracy and of attacks, including that on a vessel trying to get up the Arno to Pisa. It escaped two armed vessels at the mouth of the river but then just short of the city was attacked from the banks by bowmen and bombards and forced to flee back to sea.[41] In 1392 Datini transferred his base to Genoa, where he conducted trade with Spain and the Balearics, forwarding goods to the east while bringing back return cargoes from the Balkans and Black Sea. Much of the trade was in goods related to textiles, raw wool, dyestuffs, mordants and silk, but it also included exotic spices and furs and occasionally slaves from Romania. The bill of lading of a ship arriving in Genoa from Romania on 21 May 1396 included 'thirty-seven bales of pilgrim's robes [made of the coarse *schiavina* wool], 191 pieces of lead and eighty slaves'. Spices, including pepper, were also included on the final leg of the journey from the Far East, either overland to the Black Sea ports or up the Red Sea or Persian Gulf and then by caravan to the Mediterranean coast. We have already mentioned the maps ordered in Barcelona which by some unknown process ended up 'secretly and well wrapped so that no man can see them' in Datini's Barcelona *fondaco*.[42] Perhaps information of possible commercial value was not lightly shared with others.

A wider view of seaborne trade and the way it was organised, however, can be gained by looking at the affairs of two of the leading maritime powers, Genoa and Venice. Both these port cities were republics that lived by trade but, apart from this basic similarity, their citizens and merchants had very different ideas on the way in which trade and shipping should be organised. The very nature of Venice, on its lagoon with all travel in the city being either by foot along alleyways and over bridges or by boat on the canals, created a society in which seafaring and trade were the norm. In Genoa as well, hemmed in by the mountains of the Ligure, and confined to a narrow coastal strip, the sea seemed the way to riches and adventure. The merchant oligarchy of Venice, however, devised a system for the control of ships and trade which placed almost all the power in the hands of the ruling bodies of the Most Serene Republic or Serenissima. In the earliest days of the republic most trade had been with near neighbours on the Adriatic coasts. In 1082 the city was, however, granted trading privileges in Byzantium in return for helping the Byzantines withstand the attacks of the Normans from Sicily on imperial lands in the Balkans. Before the end of the century, the First Crusade, and its unexpected success in taking not only the Holy City of Jerusalem but also ports on the coast of the Levant, created even more opportunities for lucrative trade in both exotic and expensive goods and more prosaic bulk cargoes. These openings were taken up and largely controlled by the Serenissima itself, issuing decrees. These were drawn up at first by the Rogati, the executive committee of the Senate, and can be found among the general collection of decrees. From 1440 the orders relating to all manner of matters concerning ships and the sea were separated into a collection called the Senato Mar. They were implemented by various groups of state servants, some at the Dogana or Customs, some at the Arsenale, some specially elected from the Senate like the *Savii ai Ordini* whose responsibility it was in the 1320s to have ready, by the beginning of December, directions for the way in which galleys were to be armed for voyages starting in the spring.[43] It is not surprising that most of the evidence relating to maritime affairs in Venice comes from official sources.

Although the great Venetian merchant galleys, the *galee da mercato* or *galee grosse*, were the best known of their vessels, and much has been written about their voyages and the way in which they were organised, they were only one highly specialized group in the Republic's merchant fleet. There were at least five ways in which a Venetian voyage overseas might be set up, controlled and financed by the beginning of the fourteenth century. Some privately owned vessels, usually round or sailing ships, might be operated freely with little or no state control. In other cases, privately owned ships might find aspects of their operations regulated by the Senate, while other similar ships would need licences for their undertakings. Finally, galleys (the *galee da mercato*) owned by the Serenissima might be put up in an auction (the *incanto*) giving the right to a private individual to operate the vessel. Other galleys, also communally owned, were completely controlled and operated by the state.[44] All shipmasters and merchant shippers found that aspects of their business needed to be in accord with maritime law. For Venice, this had been set out in a code by the Doge Ranier Zeno in 1255, with later amendments by Andrea Dandolo in 1347.

Most small sailing ships plying up and down the coast of the Adriatic, or to Venetian towns in Istria, were not interfered with by the Senate but the same could also apply to longer voyages which had not yet been deemed sufficiently profitable or important to the prosperity of the whole community to attract the attention of the authorities. This applied to the very first voyages beyond the Straits of Gibraltar to Seville, Lisbon and Bruges. If, however, traders were dealing in exotic, luxury or high value goods, such as spices, silks or expensive cloth, or were exporting bullion on the usual routes, these goods had to be shipped in a galley. The authorities also laid down conditions for round ships, usually carrying bulk goods, if the voyage was thought to be dangerous. The most important of these was that the loading of such cargoes in Venice had to take place within a certain period (confusingly known as the *muda*, a term which was also applied to convoys of merchant ships). In April 1351 any large cog or ship wishing to go to Cyprus was required to notify the Council and to embark fifty good crossbowmen, in addition to the usual crew, at the cost of the merchants who had goods on board. Four at least of the crossbows should be *a turno*, the most effective kind.[45] If conditions on one of the trade routes concerned with this type of traffic became very insecure, with threats from corsairs or the enemies of Venice, the Senate might determine the number of ships which could make the voyage in a particular season. Shipmasters and shippers would be expected to honour any commitment to take part. The fleet would have a *capitano* and be expected to follow a prescribed route and timetable. The most tightly controlled voyages were those of the state galleys, the *galee da mercato*, whether the *patronus* had bought the right to operate the vessel in an auction or whether he was a state employee. He would have to swear an oath which set out his obligations not only in the management of the galley and the crew but also in relation to the commercial aspects of the voyage. These fleets were first sent in 1332 to Romania (that is to Constantinople, then through the Dardenelles to the Black Sea with the terminus at Tana on the Sea of Azov) or to the Levant (Cyprus and Beirut). In 1346 Alexandria was added as an additional destination, while in 1374 the first state galleys made the long voyage through the Mediterranean, up the Atlantic coast of Portugal and finally to Bruges and Southampton (usually visited on the return leg of the journey). In the fifteenth century galleys also went to Aigues-Mortes (1402) and to Barbary (the ports of the Maghreb, from 1436).[46] These 'state' voyages could be disrupted by political events and conflicts between, for example, Genoa and Venice, but there is no doubt of their importance to the prosperity of the city. In the deliberations of the Rogati, in 1470, a period of tension in the eastern Mediterranean with the Ottomans besieging Negroponte, we can see the nervousness of those in Venice as they waited for news of the galley fleet, sending streams of instructions to the *capitano*. On 15 March galleys were ordered to make the maximum speed possible, not even stopping for water, because of the need to keep our affairs safe 'against the known machinations of the Turk'. In April the same year the galleys for Aigues-Mortes were instructed to increase their armaments to have two bombards on board. Other instructions regarding the provision of biscuit for galleys or the need for more armaments were issued nearly every day.[47]

We can get some idea of the goods carried on these galleys, particularly those which made the long voyage through the Mediterranean to England and the Low Countries, from the records of the cargo unloaded at Southampton in April 1440 from the galley of Francesco Dandolo. More than forty shippers are listed. Some were prominent merchants, others were clearly members of the crew like the assistant scribe or purser (*subter scryvano*) who imported six barrels of wine and one barrel of black soap. The goods as a whole varied enormously; there was a fair amount of wine and cloth or items connected with the wool trade in general but also things like spurs, knives, mirrors, ginger and candy peel, and tapestry cushions for benches.[48] The cargo loaded at Southampton for the return voyage to Venice consisted entirely of broadcloth and kerseys.

The mention of trading on their own account by crew members highlights an accepted feature of the terms on which seamen enrolled in the crews of both galleys and cogs or round ships. All crew members had the right to load a small quantity of goods to employ in trade as seemed best to them. In other respects the employment of the crews of galleys was tightly controlled. Once a patron had succeeded in obtaining the right to a vessel in the 'auction', he would set up his table outside St Mark's in the Piazza, usually with a banner of his coat of arms flying above his scribe. The scribe would carefully record the name of those galleymen who came to 'sign on' for the voyage. The advertised destination and the reputation of the patron made a considerable difference to the ease with which a crew could be put together. These galleymen or oarsmen, who would form the bulk of the crew, were not slaves or convicts. They came from all over the Mediterranean, but many were from Dalmatia or Greece. Some had got into debt, others were in fact destitute but, hard though their life was, they had some protection from the state and were paid.[49] Their diet, something which could not be neglected when their physical strength was essential to the operation of the galley, was laid down. About 1310 each should have received a little less than 4,000 calories a day. Most of these came from the *biscotti*, hard, specially baked biscuits which did not rapidly become mouldy at sea. They also received wine, cheese, salt pork and beans. The pork and beans were made into a kind of stew or thick soup (*minestra*) with the pieces of meat distributed so that each man received some on alternate days. Wage rates reflected the hierarchy on board. Leaving aside the officers, skilled oarsmen or seamen, including those who tended the sails, received higher pay than the ordinary *galeotto*.[50]

In the galleys travelling in convoy, the ultimate authority was held by the *capitano* chosen and employed by the senate. Neither he nor his suite of secretaries, chaplain and servants was involved in the trading aspects of the voyage. Each galley had its own patron, generally with one or two counsellors; there would also be a sailing master or *nauclerus*, pilots, helmsmen, artillerymen, a caulker, ship's carpenter, cooks and victuallers, a barber surgeon, a chaplain and trumpeters. One very important post was that of the scribe (*scribanus*) or purser, whose job entailed keeping precise accounts not only of the crew but also of all the merchandise loaded or unloaded, bought and sold, during the course of the voyage. Although all crew members were expected to have personal weapons, the senate also insisted that there should be between thirty and fifty crossbowmen on board. There would also be a small group of young men from the leading families of Venice (known as the *nobili da pope*); these dined with the patron but they were also paid and had the usual right to embark a small package of their own trade goods. In effect they were being trained for the demanding role of organising and controlling similar voyages in the future. All told, a merchant galley of 120 oars would have a total crew of 300 men if manned to the optimum level. The patron could expect to have some of his expenses reimbursed but the ultimate success or failure of the commercial aspects of the voyage was his responsibility.[51]

A more detailed understanding of the regulations surrounding these galleys can be gained by looking closely at the terms of the auction of a galley destined for Aigues-Mortes in December 1422. The galley would be chosen from the best in the Arsenale and would operate in many ways in a similar form to those going to Flanders. Spice would not be charged freight to Aigues-Mortes but all other goods would pay at the same rate as the Flanders galleys. Sicilian sugar would pay 2½ ducats for each *cantar* (*c.* 50 kg). Loading would begin on 13 January next, the ship having been delivered from the Arsenale three days earlier. If cotton was to be loaded it had to be ready six days before the end of the period for loading spices and cloth. Silks and similar goods could be loaded up to the very day of departure; no silk of any kind could be loaded other than at Venice, nor could spices, no matter who was the owner. There were also regulations about choosing another destination if Aigues-Mortes was unsafe for any reason and the amount each officer could load for his personal trade. The successful bidder, Ser Arsenio Duodo, paid 128 Venetian pounds 1 sol. to become patron of this galley on what was probably a reasonably profitable venture.[52] Clearly the purpose of many of the regulations was to protect the profits of the Venetian state and its leading families. Spices could be carried with no freight payment because the profits from their sale would be high enough to cover the expenses of transport. Restricting the loading of cargoes ensured that the convoy would leave on time and that the goods would reach the market at the expected time. Forbidding the loading of possibly cheaper or inferior goods elsewhere kept up prices and protected the Venetian reputation for quality.

The orders issued in April 1485 to the captain of galleys bound for Sluys and London are even more detailed. The captain had to send a courier from Sluys to Venice as soon as he had docked there and a second one a fortnight later. He was also to buy four pieces of ordnance for each galley as a first call on his freight receipts which would be given to the Arsenale on his return. He was obliged to fund the necessary presents for the king of England and the duke of Burgundy himself. One preoccupation of the orders was to make sure that the galleys and their cargoes were divided between the London market and the market in the Netherlands in the most profitable fashion and to control stops at intermediate ports.[53] The aim, as before, was to ensure the greatest possible profit for the state and the safety of these large and valuable vessels and their cargoes. By 1485, however, the system which had depended on the acceptance of tight discipline by both merchants and galley patrons was facing problems. Too often galley departures were delayed, upsetting the regularity of the voyages and causing goods to miss the market. By the end of the century, there was also a growing tendency for individuals to abandon the convoys and put together individual voyages operating outside the rules imposed by the senate.[54]

The round ships or cogs, with no oarsmen, had much smaller crews and were normally only obliged to obey the general rules included in the codes of Zeno or Dandolo. Only on voyages when the situation at sea was very insecure, and the cogs sailed under the protection of *galie sottile*, were their masters burdened with anything like the detailed instructions given to galley patrons. Round ships of from 450 to 750 tons burden had crews of between thirty and fifty men, sometimes increased by order of the Senate when piracy was rife or encounters with enemy vessels were feared. Not surprisingly, freight charges were much lower on these ships than on the galleys, but these ships were confined, by senate decrees, to bulk trades, being laden with cargoes which included grain, salt, cotton, sugar, oil and wine. High value goods, including silks, spices and the best woollen cloth, were only permitted to these vessels in extraordinary circumstances; for example, in 1495, when a storm sank two out of three of the Flanders galleys, round ships were allowed to transport English wool and Flemish cloth to Venice in that year. Venetian reluctance to entrust valuable cargoes to these ships may have had justification, as they were more likely to be wrecked or taken by pirates. Cargoes on sailing vessels were normally insured (athough the rates were not high), but some Venetian merchants thought it unnecessary to insure goods on a galley, so good was their record for punctual and safe arrival at their destination.[55]

In Genoa, a rather different attitude was taken to the operation of vessels engaged in long distance trade. The Genoese did not have early close ties with Byzantium, but, perhaps because their neighbours, the French, were instrumental in the First Crusade (one of the most prominent leaders was Raymond, count of Toulouse), and because they had been involved with the Pisans in attacks on Moslem cities on the North African coast, they sent the first European fleet to the Holy Land. Genoese vessels brought supplies to the Crusaders during the siege of Antioch in 1097. This was turned to commercial advantage, as the leaders of the expedition obtained from Bohemond of Taranto, the future prince of Antioch, the grant of a church, a well, a *fondaco* (trading centre) and thirty houses in the city. This constituted the core of a trading colony in the Levant. Other fleets from Genoa provided valuable help to the Crusaders. One group of Genoese ships is said to have been dismantled at Jaffa so that the timbers could be used to build siege engines for the attack on Jerusalem. Certainly by 1104 Baldwin, the king of Jerusalem, had granted the Genoese a charter giving them valuable tax exemptions and property and privileges in coastal cities, including Jaffa and Acre.[56] At much the same time other Genoese were establishing contacts with the Balearic Islands, the coast of Spain and North Africa. They were also rivals to Aragonese and Pisan merchants for influence in Sardinia and Corsica. Although the more warlike expeditions did have backing from the authorities of the republic, for example when assistance was given to Alfonso VII of Castile for his assault on Almeria in 1146, much of this development in trade and shipping routes depended on individuals. Perhaps, as a result, the most important sources for gaining an understanding of Genoese commercial and maritime activities are not the official records of the state but the papers of notaries which survive in cartularies in the state archives. The earliest are those of a certain John the Scribe which cover the years 1155–64. A second collection covers 1179–1200 and there are increasing numbers throughout the thirteenth, fourteenth and fifteenth centuries.[57]

These papers reveal a stable and sophisticated system for dealing with the legal and practical aspects of organising overseas maritime trade on what would now be called a 'private enterprise' basis. In the earliest documents most vessels have one owner who is also the shipmaster. The first galley to sail from Genoa to Bruges of which there is a record was owned by Nicolo Spinola. It left Genoa on 17 April 1277. The next year three vessels made the voyage, the *St John*, the *St Anthony* and the *Alegrancia*. These were to call at an English port as well as Bruges. The contract, dated 12 May 1278, bound the galley patrons to supply to the contracting merchants, all from leading Genoese families, their three galleys all ready prepared for the voyage with a sufficient crew armed with crossbows and other weapons. The outward cargo was alum, a mineral fixative essential for dying woollen cloth, and a fundamental commodity in Genoese trade with north-western Europe.[58] It later became more and more usual for the ships to be owned (and built) in shares known as *loca*.[59] These were eventually regarded as a form of investment and could be bought and sold freely in various fractions related to the size of the vessel. Before a voyage the merchants involved often formed informal groups to decide on their respective share of the cargo. They would then go before a notary to conclude the agreement with the shipowners (who might or might not also be among the merchants concerned). The agreement set out the *naulum* (freight rate and any special provisions), the obligation of the shipowners to provide the vessel and to under-take the voyage, and that of the merchants to load sufficient cargo, pay the freight and load by a set date. Both sides then provided pledges or guarantees to ensure the due performance of the contract. There were variations in the contracts for voyages to different areas. On voyages to southern Spain, Ceuta and Bougie in North Africa, for example, no charge would be made for the transport of some goods outward if the return voyage was also guaranteed. Generally no charge was made for the passage of travelling merchants and their servants, particularly if the agreement was also for the return journey.[60] The assumption was that the profits on the inward cargo would ensure that the enterprise was successful.

A contract for the hire of a ship between a noted Genoese entre-preneur, seaman and pirate, Benedetto Zaccaria, and a partnership of shipowners registered in January 1382 goes into great detail. It includes the fact that the ship was to be fully rigged with good new cotton sails; it would also have a crew of fifty-five all told. Once it had left Genoa the course and choice of ports would be decided by the pilot employed by Zaccaria. No other merchants' goods were to be loaded except with Zaccaria's express permission, apart from the goods allowed to the crew for their private trade according to Genoese custom. For this Zaccaria would be charged 160 Genoese pounds per month, with various extensions possible.[61]

By the fifteenth century a radical change had taken place in Genoese shipping. Galleys were no longer used on commercial voyages, except for the special case of those making the long voyage to Caffa in the Crimea and Tana on the Sea of Azov. They were by now seen almost exclusively as warships. Unlike both Venice and Florence, trade with the western Mediterranean and with Flanders and England was conducted in carracks. These large sailing vessels were very well suited for the bulk commodities which had become the staple of Genoese trade with the West. The most important of these was alum. The Genoese, at this period, had control of the best-quality source of this mineral, through their monopoly of the production of the mines at Phocaea in Anatolia. This had originally come into Genoese hands following their support for Michael Paleologus in the 1260s and his successful attempt to oust the Latin emperor from Constantinople. Zaccaria was personally granted both the mines and the island of Chios and exploited both energetically, the island becoming the linchpin of Genoese maritime trade with the Levant. It was not, however, a colony or possession of the republic of Genoa in the same way as Venetian towns in the Peloponnese like Modon or Coron. At first the personal possession of Zaccaria, from 1346 Chios was governed by the *Maona*, a cooperative association of shipowners and merchants much of whose business was based in the island or adjacent territories. Alum was also mined from the second half of the fifteenth century in papal territory at Tolfa in central Italy. This was also accessible to Genoese traders though not under their direct control.

The variety of the cargoes of these carracks, and their importance both to Genoa and to merchants and artisans at their destination, is well illustrated by the goods brought into Southampton by four carracks in April 1436. Large quantities of oil, wax, Syrian and Turkish cotton and sugar were landed, but the major commodity was no fewer than 2,970 bales of alum. This did not, however, prevent both leading shippers, from families like the Spinola and the Lomellini, long prominent in Genoa, and also other dealers in a small way of business, probably crew members, bringing in all manner of goods including ginger, raisins, figs and silk, and, on this occasion, 'dent d'olifant' (worth £7 6s. 8d.) and an ouche of gold with '1 grant perle par le myluy environee de ii saffiers et vi rubyes'.[62]

Although the Genoese state stood aside from the organisation of overseas trade and the ownership of shipping, there were regulations drawn up and enforced by the authorities of the republic. These concerned, in particular, trading ventures into the eastern Mediterranean and beyond. We have already described how Genoese ships were deeply involved in the Crusades and trade with 'Oltremare'; this had led to voyages to Byzantium where the Genoese faced bitter competition from the Venetians. The events of the Fourth Crusade and the establishment of the Latin empire largely by the activities of Venice had left the Genoese with few friends in the area. By supporting Michael Paleologus in 1261, when he recovered the throne of his forebears, however, the Genoese were able to strengthen their position in the east and their hold on its trade. In 1267 they established their own base across the Bosphorus from the imperial city at Pera, with the emperor's help. Before the end of the century, individual Genoese adventurers controlled islands in the Aegean, and the Republic also had colonies at Caffa in the Crimea and Tana on the Sea of Azov. There were other groups of Genoese merchants at ports on the Danube and in modern Romania and Bulgaria. This entire zone the Genoese called Romania. An anonymous poet of the period wrote:

> And so many are the Genoese
> And so spread out throughout the world
> That wherever one goes and stays
> He makes another Genoa there.[63]

To bring some order into this explosive activity a new office was set up in Genoa in 1313, the office of the Gazzaria (the Crimea). Its regulations were intended to control voyages, exclusively by galleys, to this region (and from 1340 also those to Flanders and England). It set out, in much the same way as in a Venetian galley captain's orders, the number and deposition of the crew. For example, twelve crossbowmen must be carried, although eight can at any one time be used as oarsmen. The galley must be properly provided with arms and armour for the crew; it must be fully equipped with oars, lanterns and the like, and also be adequately victualled with *biscotti* and sweet water. The design of the galleys was also laid down, with careful requirements to make sure that merchandise did not encroach on the space needed for arms. From 1330 it was laid down that no galley should be loaded so heavily that the three markers on the hull were submerged. These laws were enforced by officials charged with inspecting the vessels while still in the shipyards. Galleys intended for voyages to Flanders and England across the stormy waters of the Bay of Biscay were expected to have a higher freeboard than those used only in the Mediterranean but, as we have seen, this route was rapidly taken over by the sailing carracks with their very roomy and high-sided hulls.[64]

The two city states of Venice and Genoa, therefore, by determination, the intelligent seizing of opportunities and intimidation of outsiders, came to dominate maritime trade in the Mediterranean in the fourteenth and fifteenth centuries. They faced, as they had always done, rivalry from other Italian cities, and from the Catalans and Aragonese, but their galleys and sailing ships were the ones most frequently seen on the long-distance trade routes. Their domination was, however, more fragile than it seemed. In the east the advance of the Ottoman Turks was stripping away trading bases both in the Black Sea and in the Aegean from European control. In northern waters the experience and the boldness of local shipmasters was increasing, making them more ready to undertake long voyages to the south. Any sign of weakness by the traders or seamen of either state would allow other maritime communities to seize the opportunity for their vessels to dominate these routes.

As well as these long voyages with an element of adventure and even glamour surrounding their cargoes of luxuries and the more mundane salt, wine and oil, there were many much smaller vessels of many different origins going from port to port in search of cargoes. These acted as a vital means of communication in coastal areas with few roads, and distributed, at village level, goods of all kinds and, incidentally, news and gossip from the wider world. It is hard to find much information about shipping of this kind since the mariners involved seldom needed the services of notaries or came to the attention of the authorities. There are, however, some details available of the activities of a *burchio* (a small flat-bottomed craft with a single lateen sail) which belonged to the estates of the Malatesta family and appeared in their factor's accounts. In 1409–10 the *burchio* was based

at Fano on the Adriatic and generally sailed between Pesaro and
Ancona, although it made one voyage further north to Cesenatico.
Between July 1409 and June 1410 it completed forty trips, despite
being held up at Ancona for a whole month in January 1410 and
being wrecked and badly damaged on the beach at Senigallia in
February. In this period no fewer than six masters commanded the
vessel while fourteen crewmen in all were employed; four were needed
to operate the *burchio* at any one time. Two of the masters and the
great majority of the crew were Slavs from Dalmatia or Ragusa. The
most usual cargoes were firewood and other timber, though occasionally horses, barley, wine, cartwheels and other things were carried.
Although the work was hard (the crew had to load and unload the
cargo and drag the boat over the beach to launch it), the pay was
reasonable and vessels like this were clearly essential to transport
heavy and bulky goods, especially when the coast roads were poor.
The crew of this vessel, if on a somewhat larger scale, were performing much the same function as John Shepard and his colleagues along
the coasts of Sussex and Hampshire.

Travelling merchants and seamen can be regarded as having a professional interest in maritime affairs. The sea was part of the fabric of
their lives, and its terrors, and also its moments of beauty, were
accepted as such. What, however, of passengers whose journeys made
a sea passage inescapable but who had little, if any, previous experience of life at sea? There is not a great deal of evidence which casts
light on matters like this but what there is relates in the main to two
groups of travellers, first of all royal or aristocratic persons and
secondly pilgrims going either to the shrine of St James at Compostela
or to the Holy Land. The letters of Jacques de Vitry, who had been
appointed Bishop of Acre in 1216, provide early evidence of how he
personally approached a sea voyage. He travelled by round ship and
saw to it that he and his servants should have no fewer than four areas
for their exclusive use. These were a sleeping space, a space to store
their own food, a kitchen area and a space for the horses which
accompanied the party. They took with them food for three months –
a pessimistic estimate of the length of the voyage which, on this
occasion, lasted forty days, including fifteen days in ports *en route*.
The victuals taken were basic provisions, including wine, biscuit, salt
meat and some condiments. This was in addition to the ship's own

stores, which included beans and some fresh and dried fruits. Vitry also provided an illuminating sidelight on shipboard life in a sermon in which he mentioned that mariners hid harlots in the hold and also stole the food stored there and siphoned wine out of the barrels kept in the same place.[65] The evidence for journeys by royalty consists largely of accounts which give us an idea of how such voyages were organised. In 1386 Jeanne de Navarre married John IV, duke of Brittany. Detailed accounts exist of the preparation of the three ships which went from Nantes to northern Spain to fetch the bride and bring her back to her new home. On the outward voyage the vessels were victualled with bread, flour, beef, salt pork and dried fish; all to be washed down with large quantities of wine. The quality of the food was dubious at best, as nearly half the beef was rotten and had to be thrown overboard. There were also small amounts of spices (ginger and pepper), butter, cheese and fresh fish. The wedding party reached San Sebastian after an uneventful voyage. There was then some delay until they sailed to Bayonne to embark the princess and her train. A special apartment for her was built on the largest ship, probably on the aftercastle. Although the main part of the construction was wooden, it may only have had a tent-like roof made of waxed and greased cloth, inadequate protection for a voyage across the Bay of Biscay in September. Pewter dishes were bought, as well as wooden and earthenware bowls, cloth for towels, lanterns, candles and coal for the kitchen fire. Some special provisions were also loaded: onions and garlic, some finer bread and cakes, and wine decanted into bottles rather than drawn straight from the barrels. Nevertheless the voyage must have been something of an ordeal for Jeanne, since the vessel was extremely crowded and horses were also being carried in the hold. She left Bayonne on 4 September and reached Le Croisic at the mouth of the Loire about three days later.[66] Very similar alterations were made to the English ship carrying Philippa, the daughter of Henry IV, to Denmark for her marriage to Eric X, king of Denmark, in the early fifteenth century.[67]

Henry, earl of Derby (the future Henry IV of England), made several Channel crossings from Dover to Calais in the 1390s when *en route* to Prussia to join a crusading expedition with the Teutonic Knights against the pagan Lithuanians. The detailed accounts of these voyages highlight the high prices charged by the owners of horse transports. Getting eleven horses across the Channel cost 22s. 4d. on one occasion, with sums up to £4 10s. 1d. for an unknown number of animals at a later date. Some of the party went straight from Boston to Danzig and five pilots were hired for the voyage at a total cost of £11. The ship concerned also had to be towed, initially, down river from Boston to 'Chopchire', presumably at the mouth of the Witham on the Wash. This again was expensive, costing 46s. 8d. The ship which carried the earl himself was specially adapted in much the same way at those for the princesses already described; chambers (or cabins) called the hall, chamber and chapel were built by carpenters from Lynn with canvas hangings and some sort of a 'port-hole' with a covering of Flemish cloth. Cabins were also made for a cook and other officials.[68] No royal personage would, apparently, embark on a sea voyage unless strenuous efforts were made to increase the comfort of sea travel.

A little later, in 1422, Felice di Michele Brancacci was sent by the Florentine Republic as ambassador to the sultan of Egypt in Cairo. He kept a diary of his mission which allows a close look at his voyage across the Mediterranean. He left the port of Pisa on 12 July and crept slowly along the coast southward, stopping for water and supplies on the way. He reached Messina on 25 July. By the 30th he was at Corfu, despite heavy seas on the crossing from Sicily. He then went by Crete (5 August), and Rhodes (9 August). Here he was delayed for a week because of a conflict in the port between a Catalan ship and two from Genoa. He finally reached Alexandria on 19 August. The journey time of just over a month would have been about average for this route at this time of the year. His journey home began on 15 November when his galley sailed from the same port. Brancacci himself was still suffering from the effects of a severe bout of fever and had to be carried on board. The voyage began well but, after leaving Rhodes, the galleys faced contrary winds and storms off Modon. They were forced north to Corfu and did not reach Messina until Christmas Day, after the current in the straits forced the galley to run aground. They set off again on New Year's Day in a flat calm, being only able to make progress under oars, but on the night of 4 January a violent storm drove them to take shelter in a haven on the uninhabited island of Volcano. It was not until 21 January that they were able to leave, having endured snow, rain and high winds for over two weeks. Their route homeward then lay by Palermo and Gaeta and they eventually reached Pisa on 11 February. It is not surprising that Brancacci then thanked God for His grace which had brought them safely home at last. Some thanks, perhaps, were also due to the skills and experience of the galleymen and the patron and the pilots who had brought the vessel through all these difficulties without disaster.[69]

Pilgrims, unless they were of high rank and able to afford special arrangements,[70] often faced similarly difficult voyages but in conditions of greater discomfort. Many pilgrims from England made the journey to Compostela in Galicia, to the great shrine of St James, by sea. William Wey, a fellow of the newly founded Eton College, made this journey in 1456, leaving from Plymouth on 17 May. On the same day, he tells us, ships left with other pilgrim parties from Portsmouth, Bristol, Weymouth, and Lymington. On this occasion the voyage lasted four days. On the way back, there were no fewer than thirty-two English ships in the harbour at Coruña waiting for returning pilgrims. This time they met contrary winds and were forced back into the port on the first attempt at leaving but, again, when the wind changed, they were at sea for four days, 5–9 June.[71] Earlier in the century, Margery Kemp set out from Bristol. Before embarking, she prayed fervently that God should preserve her and the ship 'from vengeance, tempests and perils in the sea that they might go and come in safety'. Her outward voyage in fact took seven days and the inward five days.[72] Some verses from much the same date also paint a vivid picture of the voyage. The pilgrims go on board but soon 'their hearts begin to fail'. The master shouts at the crew to get the sails up and for the passengers to get out of the way.

> With 'how! hissa!' then they cry
> 'What ho mate thou standest too nigh
> The fellow may not haul the bye'.

The ships boys lie out on the sailyard as the sail is set and then the boatswain instructs the crew ominously to make the boat ready for the pilgrims because

> Some are like to cough and groan
> Or it be full midnight.

Once the ship is under way, after more shouting of incomprehensible orders, the pilgrims are warned that a storm is approaching.

> This mean while the pilgrims lie
> And have their bowls fast them by
> And cry after hot malmsey
> Thou help for to restore.

Some try and eat a little dry toast but can manage nothing else.

> Some laid their books on their knees
> And read so long they might not see
> 'Alas my head will cleve in three'
> Sayeth another certainly.

The shipmaster ordered the carpenter to make cabins but night brings little peace.

> A sack of straw were there right good,
> For some must lie then in their hood,
> I had as lefe be in the wood
> Without meat or drink
> For when that we shall go to bed
> The pump was nigh our bed's head
> A man were as good to be dead
> As smell thereof the stink.[73]

The journey to the Holy Land and the major Christian shrines in Jerusalem was, by the early fourteenth century, organised on a regular basis. The Venetians arranged transport to Jaffa either in one of the galleys on the route to Beirut or in a sailing ship. The master of the ship then dealt with the necessary formalities with the Mamluk authorities on arrival at the port, making arrangements for the journey from Jaffa to Jerusalem. It was even possible to set up an extension to the standard pilgrimage, as it were, by going into the desert to St Catherine's monastery at the foot of Mount Sinai. The pilgrimage was undertaken by sizeable numbers of people but accounts of the journey by participants which include details of the voyage and descriptions of its pleasures and horrors only become relatively frequent in the fifteenth century. One voyage in the spring of 1458 produced no fewer than six different accounts of their adventures by pilgrims. The most important are those of Roberto da Sanseverino, a nobleman from Milan, Gabriele Capodilista from Padua, and William Wey from Eton. Also on board on this occasion was John Tiptoft, earl of Worcester, a pioneer of Renaissance scholarship in England, but no separate account of his experiences survives. The most detailed and informative narrative, a little later in date (1480–83), is that of Felix Fabri, a Dominican friar from their convent at Ulm, covering two journeys to Jerusalem and a trip to Sinai.[74] He, perhaps, is the nearest to a 'travel writer', producing his two-volume *Evagatorium Fratris Felicis Fabri* (the Wanderings of Brother Felix Fabri), originally for his brother friars, as something to be read 'with pleasure and amusement in the intervals of more fruitful studies or on holidays thereby eschewing idleness and obtaining recreation. Therefore I have dared among great things and true, grave things and holy, to mingle things silly, improbable and comical.'[75] These words from his introduction perhaps convey a warning to be very careful in the interpretation of all these 'Jerusalem stories'. Are they intended to be sober factual reports or are they to a greater or lesser degree embroidered or even fictionalised accounts? *The Travels of John Mandeville*, perhaps the nearest thing that the late fourteenth century had to a best-seller, mingles a reasonably accurate description of, for example, the church of the Holy Sepulchre in Jerusalem and of the village of Nazareth with increasingly fantastic stories like that of the one-footed men of Ethiopia or the gravelly sea in the country of Prester John.[76] Even if pilgrims with literary ambitions did not go quite this far, it is noticeable that more or less all of them seem to have survived fearsome storms at sea, whether on the outward or the homeward journey. The storms are also described in a somewhat schematic way and the sea itself is often seen as a fearsome thing divorced from 'everyday life'.

Taken together, however, these narratives provide a more detailed and livelier picture of life at sea than can be put together from the official records. The pilgrims would travel in a group and would, on arrival at Venice, book their places on one of the galleys or ships sailing to the Holy Land. This process was closely controlled by the Senate, with officials, the *Cattaveri*, making sure that all the regulations were complied with. There were also *tholomarii* or Piazza guides who helped the pilgrims equip themselves for the voyage. The pilgrims had to provide their own bedding and a certain amount of extra food and drink beyond the basic provisions provided by the galley master. The groups were not always harmonious. Margery Kemp's companions tried hard to get away from her without success, while she complained bitterly that when it was time for the pilgrims to make up their beds on the galley her sheets were stolen by a priest.[77] The pilgrims were very cramped, lying head to tail in the hold, with a bed space marked out that was about eighteen inches wide. Fabri describes a 'kind of hall' reached by four hatches and ladders from the rowers' deck.[78] Wey recommended pilgrims to try and sleep on the poop, for beneath the hatches it was 'right evil and smouldering hot and stinking'. In this confined space (if following Wey's advice) had to be stored extra food and things like 'a little cauldron, and frying pan, dishes, platters, wooden saucers, cups of glass, a grater for bread and such necessaries' usually kept in chests.[79]

Life on board the galley followed a regular pattern. A *Missa Secca* would be said daily and sometimes the crew sang together a long chant which included the Pater Noster, Ave Maria and prayers to a long list of saints thought to favour seafarers including St Mark, St Cecilia, St Andrew, St Barbara and St Nicholas.[80] Fabri noted that the galleymen had hard lives and were drawn from many nations, including Slavs, Greeks, Macedonians and Turks. He was aware of the way they traded on their own account, and admired the skills of the helmsmen and pilots. Apart from mealtimes announced by trumpet, the pilgrims often found time hanging heavily on their hands. It was hard for them to find any place to read or even talk without being in the way of the crew. Fabri found the noise and general confusion extremely difficult, complaining about other pilgrims who got drunk or who gambled incessantly. Theft of personal possessions was rife, 'for example while you are writing if you lay down your pen and turn your face away your pen will be lost even though you be among men whom you know'. There was also the need to spend some time each day 'hunting and catching lice and vermin'.[81] Meals were a welcome diversion but, once any private supplies were exhausted, as Capodilista said, travellers on a galley 'must accustom themselves to biscuit that is black, meat that is hard, and wine that is thoroughly unpleasant'.[82]

Some pilgrims, however, did find pleasure in being at sea in good weather. Robert de Clari, leaving Venice at the start of the Fourth Crusade, found the spectacle of the galleys putting to sea most exciting. 'It was the most beautiful sight since the creation of the world; because there was a hundred pairs of silver or bronze trumpets which all sounded our departure and so many drums and other instruments it was marvellous.'[83] He felt that the sight of all the ships with sails raised and banners flying expressed the joy he and all the crusaders felt at setting out on this expedition. Later, in the early fourteenth century, Ludolph de Sudheim was amazed to see flying fish.

There are some marvellous [fish] which lift themselves out of the water and fly for quite a long time like butterflies, but I don't know how long they can stay in the air. I asked experienced sailors about this, wanting to know where the fish came from. They replied that in England and Ireland very beautiful trees grow on the shore bearing fruit like apples. In these apples, worms are born, and when the apples are ripe and fall they break open and the worms fly away because they have wings like bees. If they touch first on land they become airborne and fly with other birds. If they touch first at sea they become sea creatures and swim like fish but from time to time they also use their natural ability to fly.

Perhaps wisely, Ludolph remarked that he wasn't sure if trees like this really existed but he recorded what he had been told.[84]

Storms at sea were terrifying in the extreme. The darkness of the sky alarmed the passengers long before the storm broke. The screaming of the wind in the rigging and the violence of the waves all served to convince them that their last hour had come. Some of these features perhaps became stereotyped in these narratives but even so we do gain some understanding of the horror and, at times, the excitement of being at sea in these conditions. The crew was usually far too occupied in ensuring the survival of the vessel to take any notice of their cargo of exhausted, seasick and frightened pilgrims. On his return voyage from Jaffa in 1480, Fabri's ship ran into a storm just north of Corfu. Very soon everything on board, including all the pilgrims' clothing and their food stores, were soaked in sea water and the galley fire was out. Fabri wondered 'how it can be that water being as it is a thin, soft and weak body can strike such hard blows . . . for it makes a noise when it runs against the ship as though millstones were being flung against her'. Despite this, however, he was prepared to stay on the upper deck and watch 'the marvellous succession of gusts of wind and the frightful rush of the waters'.[85] On the spring voyage in 1458 the galleys ran into rough weather shortly after leaving Ragusa on the outward journey. The head wind made it impossible for the galleys to make progress and the mainsail was lowered and the mizzen reefed right down. The patron, Antonio Loredan, then adopted an old sailor's expedient to try and alleviate their situation. He wrote all the saints' names he could remember on slips of paper and put them in a hat. As each one was drawn out by a pilgrim, he vowed a mass to that saint if they reached the shore in safety. Then all the slips were thrown into the sea. Jewish merchants in the twelfth century had seen the crew do something very similar in the same circumstances. Much the same was done on the return journey in another storm off the coast of Syria.[86]

Although it did not make for such stirring reading, the most trying aspect of these voyages, and often also of those by both the merchant galleys and the round ships, was their slowness. Neither galleys nor round ships could sail close to the wind and therefore they could spend days in port or drifting at sea waiting for a favourable wind. Stops on the way could make a journey more enjoyable for the passengers (Ludolph de Sudheim suggested this was one reason for choosing a galley which took a more direct course rather than a round ship), but being unable to make progress at sea could be both tedious and alarming. Fabri noted how the water became foul, at first 'lukewarm, whitish and discoloured' and then 'putrid and stinking'. The usual route taken by the galleys went down the Adriatic with stops at Ragusa, Durazzo, Corfu, Candia in Crete, Rhodes, Cyprus (Limassol) and Jaffa. The *Loredan* galley left Venice on the evening of 17 May 1458 and reached Jaffa on 19 June. This was in fact a speedy voyage; on the return journey, sailing from Acre with another patron, Sanseverino left on 10 October in the same year and did not reach Ancona until Christmas Day. He was finally at home in Milan by mid-January

1459. Fabri's first pilgrimage in 1480 reached Jaffa after six weeks at sea. He returned to Venice on 21 October after a much delayed voyage home of well over two months. His second journey began on 2 June; by 15 June they were at Modon and on 1 July, having sighted Mount Carmel, all the passengers began to sing the *Te Deum*. He returned from Alexandria having made the journey to St Catherine's at Sinai. The galleys sailed on 14 November and reached Venice in mid-January, being storm bound for days off the Peloponnese and unable to double Cape Melos. He disembarked from his vessel 'glad of our enlargement from that uneasy prison, yet, because of the companionship which had grown up between us and the rowers and others, sadness mingled with our joy'.

By the end of the medieval period the fierce joy with which Norse poets had written of the sea was no longer commonly felt by those who could be called mariners or whose living was bound up with the world of ships. Overseas trade within the confines of the Mediterranean or the routes to the North as far as Iceland was no longer an unusual or very adventurous endeavour. The economic health of much of western Europe, particularly the maritime states, depended on these sea routes and the goods exchanged, whether luxuries which came predominantly originally from the East, or essential bulk goods, timber, salt, wool, tin, salt fish, which made up so many cargoes. A seaman's life was hard and would continue to be so for many centuries. Even if navigation techniques and instruments improved, and ships became more seaworthy in their design, the perils of the sea remained and could only be endured. We should not, however, lay too much emphasis on fear of the sea and sea travel. Certainly it existed but most trading voyages ended successfully and most travellers reached their destinations. The discomforts on ship board were probably not much worse than those in roadside inns while the sense of companionship to which Fabri refers could greatly enhance a journey no matter how tedious.

War at Sea

The image of war at sea in the popular imagination is that of ships of the line in the Napoleonic era, with epic fleet actions like those associated with the names of St Vincent and Nelson. In these, large three-decked, full-rigged sailing vessels manoeuvred in order to smash the enemy with a well-aimed broadside. On board, gallant officers attempted to maintain control as cannonballs smashed through the rigging, and the roar of the guns, the smell and smoke of gunpowder and the screams of the dying combined to create a vision of chaos. Linked with this image are the theories of control of the seas, the deployment of fleets and the uses of sea power associated with the American nineteenth-century historian and commentator Admiral Mahan.[1] Do the images of a fleet action, or notions of rulers consciously striving for naval superiority, have any relevance for our period? Were 'control of the seas' and the use of blockade against trade and fleets a realistic possibility at this time? Can we say that by the beginning of the sixteenth century the conduct of war at sea was beginning to edge towards the model so familiar from the later period? One problem to take into account is that, while war is conventionally seen as an activity initiated by states and rulers usually for political ends, not all violence at sea in our period can be so easily categorised. Attacks or even campaigns by individuals cannot be written off in the Middle Ages as just piracy and thus a 'law and order' matter. Piracy in this period has been called 'a cross-cultural phenomenon, an unceasing form of guerrilla warfare, . . . a kind of kidnapping or mugging and a routine investment'. So ubiquitous an activity should not be left to linger 'at the periphery of the historian's vision'.[2] It was in many ways a kind of unofficial warfare. In this chapter we will look at both the public actions of rulers and this kind of activity, sometimes called 'the war on commerce', or the *guerre de course* in the convenient French phrase, and attempt to assess their importance.

The divide between the Mediterranean and off northern shores, noted already in ship design and in the organisation of seaborne trade, is again of importance when considering all kinds of warfare at sea. We will therefore begin by looking at developments in the North Sea, Channel and Western Approaches. Precise details of fleet operations and sea fights in these areas are hard to come by, especially in the earliest periods; what information there is comes from saga literature, often written down long after the events, or from chronicles, usually kept by monks with little knowledge of or interest in naval matters. We should also remember that the difference between a warship and a merchant vessel, so obvious in modern times, was hardly noticeable in our period. More or less any vessel might find itself involved in a sea fight and needed some basic form of armament, even if this was no more than the swords and daggers of the crew. Kings of England and other rulers had a well-established right to requisition any vessel in port in their realm (with little regard to the origins of the ship or its master) to take part in a naval expedition, when the need arose. The number of ships in royal ownership, what might be thought of as the core of a royal navy, was usually no more than a handful. These royal ships, by the fourteenth century, had 'castles' or raised platforms at both stem and stern and a fighting platform at the head of the mast (the top castle), but by the early fifteenth century these were probably a normal feature of all, except the smallest, of the sailing ships of the north. It was the need to accommodate cannon on board ship, in a manner which allowed them to be used to greatest effect, which led to the emergence of sailing ships specifically designed for war at the beginning of the sixteenth century.

In northern waters, the Vikings, from around the eighth century, used their maritime prowess to extend their power. The *Heimskringla* or *Lives of the Norse Kings*, collected and written down by Snorre Sturlason in the twelfth century,[3] makes clear how essential ships were in the feuds and wars of his forebears in all the lands reached by the Vikings. Snorre also presents a picture of how the sea, as highway, and as the setting for both casual violence and heroic conflict, was an inescapable part of the lives of the men of the north. Rulers are routinely called 'ruler of ships' or 'sea king'. When, in 872, battle was joined in Hafursford (near Stavanger) between King Harald Hairfair

of Norway and the forces led by Eric of Hordaland, the bard
described how

> Ships came from east-way,
> All eager for battle,
> With grim gaping heads
> And rich carved prows.[4]

The battle was not, however, in the open sea but in the relatively
sheltered waters of the fjord, near enough to the shore for the van-
quished to flee by 'leaping up on land and thence by the upper ways
south through Jaederen' (the flat land between Stavanger and
Egersund). Later, at the end of the tenth century, in the *History* of
Olav Trygvason accounts of battles on, or near, water are even more
prominent. The Jomsvikings had fleets of as many as sixty ships; at the
end of one battle we learn how many were slain and the ships 'drifted
about, full of warm bodies'.[5] King Magnus the Good's struggle against
Earl Swein Ulfson in 1044 gives an even clearer picture of the type of
amphibious warfare which was the principal mode of fighting among
these people. Battle was at first joined by Magnus's men rowing
forward against Swein's forces; Swein adopted the tactic of roping his
ships together, creating in effect a kind of fighting platform. A tremen-
dous tussle ensued which began with the firing of many arrows. Then
came hand-to-hand fighting with men leaping from one ship to
another until Swein's ships were cleared of warriors. The bard
describes the scene:

> The billows, stirred by the storm,
> Beat their legs and their skulls
> To the edge of the sea:
> The ocean howls about the corpses.

Some who managed to escape the carnage made their way home to
Zealand where Tjodolv the Scald described their resistance to
Magnus's pursuit. His words leave no doubt that this kind of warfare
involved the use of ships as transports and as means of attack but
virtually always in shallow waters near the shore:

We brought down a shore raid;
In the midst of the land the ship
Is moored. With words alone
Swein will not ward the land.[6]

The attacks of the northmen on the British Isles seem to have been conducted in much the same way, even if they were preceded by a much lengthier sea passage. The Anglo-Saxon Chronicle, however, does not describe the raids with the same poetic verve and knowledge of this kind of warfare shown by Snorre Sturlason. The events are mentioned in a brief and laconic fashion. Thus in 837 the annal reads:

Ealdorman Wulfheard fought at Southampton against thirty-three ships' companies and made great slaughter there and won the victory.[7]

Only in the description of an Anglo-Saxon victory at Brunanburgh in 937 is there an echo of the saga accounts. The Norse king, forced by the attackers to the prow of his ship with a handful of companions, then flees 'over the waters grey' to save his life.[8]

Alfred has been dubbed the founder of the Royal Navy. This may overstate the importance of his leadership but the passage from the Anglo-Saxon Chronicle which is the source of this belief demonstrates very well what this meant at this time. In 897 'predatory bands' of Danes from East Anglia and Northumbria were harrying the south coast of Wessex. Alfred's response was to order the building of new ships to meet those of the marauders. They would be, we are told, twice as long as the Danish ones with at least sixty oars; swifter, steadier and with more freeboard than those of the enemy, and designed to be unlike either Danish or Frisian ships. When a party of Danes appeared near the Isle of Wight, the new ships trapped them in an estuary and blocked the way to the open sea. Some of the Danish ships were drawn up on the beach with no crews on board. The English took two Danish ships at the river mouth but one escaped. The English could not mount a pursuit because some of their own ships had also grounded at low tide; the two sides then fought each other on the foreshore but, as the tide came in, the beached Danish ships were afloat first and were able to put to sea, only to be driven onshore in a storm and wrecked on the Sussex coast.[9]

This is the same kind of raiding and fighting on the coast, half on board ship, half on dry land, that the *Heimskringla* describes. Given the design of ships at the time and the fact that commanders had few means of discovering an enemy's whereabouts or his intentions, this was probably all that was possible. The events of the summer of 1066 confirm this impression. At various times four fleets were at sea in the Channel and North Sea. The fleet of Harold Godwinson, king of England, raised to protect the land from invasion, spent the summer months cruising fruitlessly off the south coast or in harbour, searching for the enemy. Tostig, Harold's estranged brother, raided up the east coast until he was able to join Harold Hardrada's fleet of Norway off the Yorkshire coast. Once ashore their joint forces were annihilated at Stamford Bridge, outside York. William of Normandy's fleet spent most of the summer blocked by contrary winds, first in harbour at Dives, later at St Valéry; only a fortunate wind shift at the end of September allowed him to cross the Channel. There was no naval engagement and no opposed landing for the invaders. The decisive engagement was on land outside Hastings, 'at the grey apple tree' in the words of the Chronicle.[10]

After the Norman Conquest, the most noticeable development at first was the change not in tactics in sea warfare, nor in the technology employed, but in the political conditions which might lead to war. Until the beginning of the twelfth century the Danes were still powerful and a force to be reckoned with, particularly in coastal regions. In the eleventh century it was possible to think in terms of a North Sea empire encompassing the British Isles, Scandinavia and the Baltic coasts. By the twelfth century, however, England and indeed Scotland were looking south, mainly to France and Flanders. The Conquest had established strong ties between the English realm and the rulers, counts, dukes, kings and emperor of continental Europe. The Channel ceased to be a frontier. It became an awkward barrier within the possessions of one ruling family. By the reign of Henry II, the territories held by the king of England in France, under various titles, were more extensive than those on the English side of the Channel. After the loss of Normandy, following the battle of Bouvines in 1214, France and England faced each other once more across the

Channel. The pattern of hostility between the two realms was to continue with fluctuating intensity for the remainder of the Middle Ages. Flanders, linked to England by trade and to France by the feudal loyalties of the counts, was inevitably drawn into these quarrels from time to time. Other nations with a seaboard in these northern waters were minor players, intervening when and if it seemed that some advantage might result, whether to an individual trying his hand as a corsair, or to a state making or breaking an alliance.

For reasons of political geography alone, the sea and ships loomed larger in the minds of Englishmen than in those of the French. Until Philip Augustus defeated John of England and took control of Normandy, the French crown had had no direct access to the Channel coast. Both the duke of Brittany and the count of Flanders were vassals of the king of France, but the king continued to have little real power in either territory. Much of the Atlantic coast of France was part of the duchy of Aquitaine, whose immediate ruler was the king of England. On the Mediterranean the area around Perpignan and Roussillon was Aragonese territory, while further west lay Provence, which was under Angevin control until 1486. Only a small area around Aigues-Mortes, at the mouth of the Rhône, was in French royal hands at this time. England's long coastline influenced the attitudes of its rulers, even if John Fortescue's reference in the 1470s, in his book *The Governance of England*, to 'this realm of England, which is an island', tacitly ignores the separate existence of Scotland.[11] The remark, however, expressed the fact that for most Englishmen to travel abroad meant to travel overseas, and that it was feared that any major invasion would come from the sea.

Most warlike activity in the waters of the Channel and North Sea reflected some aspect of the rivalry between England and France. This was a power struggle between rival royal dynasties, motivated by desires for land and influence, with, by the time of the Hundred Years' War, the beginnings of a nationalist element. Economic or commercial considerations only came into play when freelance or semi-official 'pirates' attempted to capture a valuable cargo or prevent 'interloping' in a valuable trade. The definition of both 'pirate' and 'interloper' was often vague in the extreme. Our first concern will be with royal action.

King John has, perhaps, a stronger claim than Alfred to be considered the founder of the royal navy. Faced with a hostile France across the Channel, he established a fleet of galleys and also a rudimentary system of logistical and administrative support for them. His 'galleys' were at least partly powered by oars but were modifications of the kind of ships shown in the Bayeux Tapestry, not vessels like those used in the Mediterranean. A base for the royal ships was established at Portsmouth and, in the reign of Henry III, there was a building for seven galleys at Rye with auxiliary stores.[12] Later kings tended to base the small squadron of royal ships in the Pool of London near the Tower, the centre of the royal ordnance, until the reign of Henry V when the greatly expanded administration of the clerk of the king's ships was moved to Southampton, with ships (by this time all primarily sailing vessels) based either off the town or in the more defensible Hamble estuary.[13] Across the Channel, the French king Philip IV established a base for royal galleys, probably with advice from the Genoese, on the left bank of the Seine at Richebourg just outside Rouen in 1295. This *Clos des galées* was capable of building oared fighting vessels for the French crown, as well as repairing them, but by the end of the fourteenth century it housed little more than decaying hulks.[14] Its final destruction by fire by the English when they took Rouen in 1418 had little real significance for the effectiveness of French royal activity at sea. This depended much more on the actions of Castilian and Genoese seamen and their ships, hired by the French crown, than on the resources of France itself.

What might be called 'official' Anglo-French warfare at sea was, of course, dictated by the political situation between these two realms and the existence of a state of war between them. The battle of Damme (1213) and the battle of Dover (1217) illustrate this well; it is also the case that the first of these was a sea battle in the old Nordic style, while the latter perhaps pointed to a future in which the side with better shiphandling skills and more seaworthy vessels was victorious. At Damme in Flanders (now some considerable distance from the sea) the French fleet sent there by Philip to prevent the Flemings from siding with the English lay in a shallow anchorage. The English fleet had sailed for the Zwyn waterway with no very clear idea of what their tactics should be; they probably had no idea they would find the French fleet in the port. They were also surprised to discover that most of the French ships were unmanned and unguarded, with their crews on shore foraging and sacking the town. The English took the vessels which were not beached, with their cargoes, and burnt the rest before much resistance could be organised. At the battle of Dover (1217), the situation was different. The French under the dauphin already had an army ashore in England, profiting from the confusion of the last years of John's reign. William Marshal, earl of Pembroke, guardian of the infant Henry III, was well aware that it was vital to prevent this army being supplied and reinforced. The chronicler Matthew Paris, although a monk at St Albans, often had access to letters and other documents and, on this occasion, apparently interviewed a reliable eyewitness, Hubert de Burgh, for the details of his account. He explains how the French relief fleet was commanded by Eustace the Monk, a semi-legendary figure as a sea-rover,[15] but by all accounts a competent seaman. He and his ships arrived off Dover after a swift passage before a strong southerly wind. The English, under de Burgh's command, put to sea to meet him, but instead of making straight for the enemy they set a course across the Channel towards Calais, perhaps a deliberate ruse to confuse the enemy. The French feared that their aim was to attack the undefended town, but a fortunate shift in the wind allowed the English to go about and come up on the rear of the French forces and then grapple with them. In the ensuing mêlée, Eustace's ship was taken by the English; he himself was found hiding in the bilges, dragged out and beheaded without more ado. On this occasion, although in the Straits and with the action clearly visible from the cliffs, the battle was fought on the open seas, with skill in reading the wind patterns and in handling a group of ships playing a vital role in the victory.[16]

This intermingling of actions either in harbour or very near the shore with those on the open sea continued into the fourteenth century. One engagement of which there is a detailed account by a near contemporary is that between the forces of Philip IV of France and Guy de Namur, the count of Flanders, at Zierikzee in Zealand in 1304. Philip was attempting to assert his authority over Flanders, in theory a vassal state, but which had been in rebellion since 1302. The battle and its outcome were of minor significance in the quarrel as a whole, but the forces engaged and the tactics used throw light on the way sea battle could develop at this period. Our source is a verse history by a Guillaume Guiart (which was extensively discussed from the naval point of view in a paper given to a gathering of French intellectuals in the summer of 1798 in the midst of the French Revolution).

It paints a picture of great interest. Zierikzee itself was in the hands of French allies but was besieged by Guy and his forces. The aim of the French fleet was to bring up reinforcements and lift the siege. The ships approached in two squadrons; the first made up of *grands nefs*, large sailing vessels of the cog type. These were a mixture of hired Spanish ships and ships arrested in the Channel ports for the king's use. The second squadron was composed entirely of galleys hired from Genoa, under the command of Renier Grimaldi. All these ships and some others from Flemish allies had to get up the Scheldt to the town; this they could not do at first, as the wind and tide were against them. It took them eight days to reach Zierikzee. There the leading sailing ships went immediately into the attack, using crossbows against the defending ships. In his haste, however, the French commander misjudged the tide; as it ebbed all the French ships grounded and became sitting targets for the missiles of the defenders. The defenders also tried to use fireships against the enemy but at this juncture the wind shifted, making them drift back towards the Flemish vessels. The tide turned again in the midst of this confusion. Soon the French floated off the shallows and renewed the attack with vigour, using springals and crossbows and then boarding the Flemish ships. Grimaldi's galleys, which had hung back and played no part in the fighting, now also attacked under oars with great success. The leading Flemish ship, in an attempt to turn the battle, steered for Grimaldi's galley under full sail and succeeded in breaking up one bank of oars in a collision. It could not get grapples aboard, however, and it was soon clear that the French forces had prevailed. The siege was lifted.[17]

As far as we know, no royal ships were used in this engagement; not even the galleys from Rouen, with Genoese hirelings being preferred. The fight began with showers of missiles of all kinds but in the closing stages became a boarding action. There is no record of any vessel being sunk. The action was in shallow waters off the town and within easy reach of the shore, but even so the forces of the winds and the tide had a crucial part to play in the shaping of events. The action of the Flemish commander in deliberately closing with Grimaldi's galley and disabling it, in the midst of the battle, was a considerable feat of seamanship even if ultimately of no avail. By this time it is possible to see war at sea becoming more specialised in some respects. The tactics, showers of missiles followed by boarding and hand to hand fighting,

were no different from earlier encounters, but without some understanding of wind and tide and seamanship victory was hard to
achieve. Later actions in the course of the Hundred Years' War seem
to confirm these impressions. At Sluys in 1340, the English fleet,
although outnumbered, seems to have managed to trap the French in
the estuary hemmed in by sandbanks on a falling tide. They pressed
forward with the usual showers of missiles and then boarded the
French ships, successfully taking a large number. As Edward III
reported in a letter to his son written on board the royal ship *Cog
Thomas*, three days after the battle, French casualties were very high:
they 'lie dead all along the coast of Flanders'. There was a ghoulish
joke going the rounds in England that summer that the fish were
speaking French because of the number of bodies in the sea.

   Much more a matter of seamanship, shiphandling and sturdy
vessels seems to have been the engagement known rather enigmatic-
ally as Les Espagnols sur Mer.[18] Some ten years after Sluys, the English
fleet, mostly consisting of impressed ships but with at least nine royal
ships present, with access to better intelligence than usual, waited off
Winchelsea for the Spanish fleet in the pay of the French to make its
way home down Channel from Flanders. Froissart's account of the
ensuing battle is lively and circumstantial and may be based on information from Robert of Namur, a participant. Leaving aside details
like the king, dressed in a black velvet jerkin and a black beaver skin
cap, ordering his minstrels to play dance tunes as he waited for the
look-out to sight the approaching enemy, we get a graphic picture of
the engagement. The Spanish came on sailing very fast, a north-east
wind behind them. The king ordered his ship to steer straight for the
nearest vessel, with which it collided 'with a crash like thunder'. One
of the top castles on the Spanish ship was dislodged by the impact and
all the men in the top were drowned as it fell into the sea. The seams
of the king's ship were also sprung and it was leaking badly, but after
a fierce hand-to-hand fight on the decks of the two ships grappled
together, the English managed to overpower the enemy as their own
vessel sank. Froissart continues with other incidents, including the
sinking of the ship carrying the Prince of Wales, and his rescue by the
duke of Lancaster and the near loss of Robert of Namur's ship to the
Spanish. He lays emphasis on the advantage that the Spanish had, as
their ships were larger and heavier than the English, but even so they

lost fourteen out of a fleet of forty, many loaded with valuable cargoes of Flemish cloth and linens. Some details may be those expected in chivalric histories but the importance of the engagement is confirmed by the details of the careful preparation of the royal ships before the battle, listed in the dockyard accounts. The sinking of at least two ships is significant, as is the awareness shown of the importance of wind direction and speed.[19]

Dramatic actions like these were rare events. Although the victory at Sluys was widely lauded, and celebrated in the permanent and valuable form of the striking of a gold coin with the triumphant Edward III on his *Cog Thomas* on the obverse, it had little influence on the course of the war as a whole. No medieval navy could 'control the seas' in any real sense of the term. The mounting of a blockade or even of regular naval patrols was beyond the financial and logistical capacity of a medieval monarchy. The only area where a form of blockade was successfully carried out was in the confined waters off southern Sweden. Denmark and the Hanseatic League isolated the southern ports of Norway in 1284, preventing the arrival of vital grain fleets.[20] In many ways a more effective tactic was that most often used by the French and their Castilian allies. Raids, usually by galleys, on coastal towns, causing widespread destruction of property and some loss of life, engendered a climate of fear and unease among the inhabitants. Southampton Water, the Solent and the Isle of Wight were particularly vulnerable to this kind of attack, with at least eight serious raids in the period 1336–77, but there were also raids on west country ports, ports in Sussex and Kent including a very serious one on Winchelsea in 1360, and up the east coast. There was, of course, nothing innovative about this tactic. It mirrors that used by those who raided coastal villas in the Roman period or the activities of the Norsemen of the ninth and tenth centuries. The traces of the raids are still clear in excavations within the walled area of medieval Southampton where, for example, in the High Street there are 'widespread layers, approx. 10cm thick of burnt material including roofing slates'.[21] Froissart describes the raid in 1338 as being by a mixture of Normans and Genoese, who raped and pillaged through the town and then set sail again for Dieppe loaded with plunder.[22] In many ways the disruption to economic and social life in the raided areas, the distraction from preparations for more formal warfare and the impression created in England of being defenceless against attacks from the sea all worked to the advantage of the French and could be said to be a more worthwhile method of using ships and crews than the maintenance of an expensive fleet. The tone of petitions presented in the House of Commons amply testifies to the unease caused by these raids. On the one hand, the Commons were very reluctant to contribute to the provision of ships or to pay for watchers on the coast; on the other hand, towns like Scarborough in 1383 pleaded for help:

> The said town stands open to the sea and from one day to the next is attacked by barges and various other ships from Scotland and from France and by Flemings and other enemies of our lord the king so that many mariners of the said town and coasts there have lost ships which had been lately captured by the said enemies to the value of £2,000 so that the said town and the coasts surrounding it are on the point of being ruined and destroyed unless swift remedy is found.[23]

In the fifteenth century, however, particularly in the early decades, there were significant changes in the ways ships were used in warfare. These were closely related to political events and to advances in ship design. At first, until the succession of Henry V of England in 1413 and the reactivation of the Hundred Years' War with the Agincourt campaign in 1415, activity at sea, involving French, Flemish and English vessels and their allies, was a matter of small-scale coastal raids and semi-official attacks on merchant ships. From the time of the English invasion of 1415 until 1420, when Henry V was recognised as heir to the king of France by the treaty of Troyes, the Channel was the scene of naval activity inspired by the crown, with fleets, largely led by royal ships, on a scale not seen before. Even the accounts of raids in the opening decade of the century show a greater appreciation of seamanship than before. The activities of one small group of Castilian galleys, led by a Castilian noble with considerable experience of Mediterranean warfare, were recorded in a biography written by his standard-bearer. In this, an encounter between the Castilian galleys and some English balingers in the Channel is fully described. The galleys were sailing west past Calais but were deterred from trying to enter the anchorage by bombards (artillery fire) from the town. The next day, now joined by some French balingers on course for England, they came up with an English squadron, a mixture of great ships and balingers, hove to in mid-Channel for lack of wind. The Castilian captain ordered the attack. Both sides used crossbows and missiles, including on the Castilian side flaming arrows and a fire ship. The wind now got up and the great ships of the English bore down on the Castilian commander, preparing to board him. His vessel was only saved by what the writer calls 'a splendid feat'. The Spanish account is not entirely clear, but it seems that a French balinger turned into the wind and then went about in such a way that she was able to ram amidships one of the vessels threatening the Castilian galley, disabling her by shearing off the bowsprit and cutting the forestay. The galley was then able to make good her escape.[24] Here, in an action between a mixed force of sailing and oared vessels on the one hand and only sailing ships on the other hand, a sailing vessel had come to the rescue of a galley.

Henry V set in motion what might be called a naval policy within six months of his accession. The more or less moribund office of the clerk of the king's ships was reinvigorated and more vessels joined the royal ranks, some newly built or refitted, some as gifts or forfeitures. The most interesting group were clearly what were known as the king's 'great ships'. These, the *Trinity Royal*, the *Holyghost*, the *Jesus* and the *Gracedieu*, were all much larger than average English sailing ships. The smallest, the *Trinity Royal* (540 tuns), was a refitted version of an earlier ship of the same name; the others were all substantially newly built. Their design was heavily influenced by that of the Genoese carracks which frequently visited English harbours, particularly Southampton, and which had proved themselves very effective as fighting ships in the Mediterranean. Their sail plan (at least two masts with the mizzen carrying a lateen sail) made them easier to handle than single-masted cogs. Their high-sided hulls, with a pronounced tumblehome, made them hard to board, while the height of the deck above the water level and the height of their masts, equipped with topcastles, made them good platforms for the projection of missiles, now including some rudimentary shipboard guns.

As Henry V was undoubtedly aware, the Genoese were allied with the French, and their carracks would be the main opposition to English ships in the Channel. Certainly it was actions between the

English and the Genoese which provided the most important of the engagements in the Channel. In August 1415 the *Trinity Royal* led over 1,500 vessels out from Southampton Water towards France, rejoicing in the good omen of swans mingling with the fleet.[25] The expedition made landfall at Harfleur, a town soon taken and garrisoned by the English. By the summer of 1416 this garrison was suffering badly from lack of supplies, and French attacks. A relief force led by the duke of Bedford, on board the *Holyghost*, was opposed by eight Genoese carracks; the French had also hired galleys under the command of Gioanni de' Grimaldi, but these had withdrawn after the death of their commander in a skirmish. A group of Spanish and Basque ships were also said to have fled, without taking any part in the action, when they saw the power of the English fleet. The result was the successful raising of the siege and the capture by the English of four Genoese vessels, immediately absorbed into the squadron of royal ships when these prizes reached Southampton. We have no details as to how this was achieved; just the bald statement that the battle was very cruel.[26] The tactical decision which a commander had to take in these circumstances was how to divide his forces between the small, quick, manoeuvrable balingers and large, high-sided, lumbering carracks. The difficulty faced by a force of balingers when trying to take a carrack was well illustrated by a fight in the Channel some six weeks after the success off Harfleur. Six balingers put out from Calais to chase a carrack sighted making her way up Channel, probably to Sluys. The balingers easily caught up with her, but, despite a desperate fight which went on until their missiles were exhausted, they could not board her and she eventually made good her escape, having suffered heavy casualties.[27]

The need for a vessel which could not be overawed by any carrack probably lay behind the decision to build the 1,400-tun *Gracedieu* at Southampton in 1416. This vessel was something of a wonder to contemporaries, managing even to impress the captain of a Florentine galley fleet which put into Southampton in 1430. Luca di Maso degli Albizzi called it the largest and most beautiful ship he had ever seen, when he was taken to see her and the other great ships at anchor in the Hamble river.[28] She was, however, ready for action too late to serve any real purpose. The English had mounted regular patrols in the Channel with well-armed squadrons of ships every summer since

1417; the *Gracedieu* joined the patrol in 1420, but by that time the Genoese carracks were no longer in the Channel, both coasts of which were in the hands of the English or their allies. She never went to sea again, although efforts were made to keep her in reasonable repair till about 1430.[29]

It was, in fact, enormously expensive for the crown to keep even a small group of ships in good repair. Wooden hulls, upper works and hemp rigging needed constant attention, whether the vessel was at sea or at anchor. The fact that Normandy was in English hands, and Brittany and Burgundy (controlling the Flemish coast) were England's allies, meant that expenditure on naval affairs was not a priority after 1420. The death of Henry V in August 1422 introduced a further complication. Royal ships were the personal property of the monarch and the king's will directed that all his ships, with the exception only of the great ships, should be sold to pay his debts. This was done by 1427, after which only the great ships and one or two others in poor repair remained. By 1452, despite the complete reversal of the situation in France and along the southern coasts of the Channel with the resurgence of French power, the office of clerk of the king's ships ceased to exist. It had done little more for years than sell off old stores. The crown of England then possessed no vessels of its own for the next twenty years.[30] The office of clerk was not resuscitated until late in the reign of Edward IV, while Henry VII was responsible for ordering the recreation of a small group of royal ships equipped with the latest form of shipboard guns.[31]

This gradual decay of English maritime strength did not pass unnoticed, nor was it welcomed by merchants and others whose interests were threatened. In 1436, in a document known as the *Libelle of Englyshe Polycye*, the author bewailed the fact that the importance of controlling the Straits of Dover was ignored by the crown. He looked back to Henry V's great ships, 'the great dromons/which passed other great ships of all the commons' and asks:

> What hope it was the king's great intent
> Of those ships and what in mind he meant?

> It was not else but that he wanted to be
> Lord round about environ of the sea.[32]

For him the sea was the 'wall of England' which ensured peace in the land and also good relations with neighbours. Some time later the Commons petitioned the king, in the 1442 parliament, to re-establish the system of patrols to 'keep the seas'. Even the most optimistic of the MPs from London and other trading cities must have privately acknowledged that there was very little chance of the implementation of their scheme for eight great ships, each with an attendant barge and an attendant balinger, to be at sea from Candlemas to Martinmas for this purpose.[33] The cost in wages and victuals alone was estimated at £4,568 6s. 8d. at a time when the crown was gravely in debt, with expenditure exceeding revenue by nearly £50,000 per year, not counting the expenses incurred in France.[34] By this time if ships were needed for the transport of troops and their equipment, for the general support of land armies or for the suppression of disorder on the high seas, recourse had usually to be made to the arrest of privately owned merchant ships. In 1450, for example, no fewer than eighty-three ships were arrested to transport troops to Aquitaine, including twenty-four large vessels of over 200 tuns. These came from most south and west coast ports, including Southampton, Dartmouth, Plymouth and Fowey.[35] Seakeeping expeditions were set up by a system of indentures, in effect contracts with a named individual, who was charged with setting up an expedition for a declared purpose with promised payment from public funds, usually the customs revenue. This was what might now be called 'privatised' defence.

As England descended into the confusion and chaos of the Wars of the Roses, some of the most important noble families also became shipowners. In the case of the Howard family this may have been mainly for commercial reasons, but Richard Neville, earl of Warwick, the most notorious of the power-brokers embroiled in the quarrels of York and Lancaster, maintained a squadron of vessels and was able to use it effectively in the support of the house of York from 1457 to 1460. At first he was involved in seakeeping by indenture on behalf of the government of Henry VI. By 1458, however, his activities at sea were for his own benefit or that of the Yorkists. For the first time, Calais (he had been captain of Calais since 1456) was used not as a jumping off point for a land army or as a centre of trade but as a 'naval base'. From its harbour either his own ships, or those paid for by him and under his command, set out into the Channel. Some of their activities were regarded by his enemies as piratical; others as intended to raise his own prestige among the English maritime community. In the Paston Letters, there is a vigorous account of a battle between the Spanish and Warwick's fleet which involved, or so we are told, twenty-eight Spanish ships, including sixteen large ones, and five large vessels, three caravels and four pinnaces from Calais. The English on this occasion were forced to retreat and the Pastons' correspondent reported that Warwick had sent for more ships.[36] The next summer, in June 1459, his fleet chased two Genoese carracks and some Spanish ships and, having taken at least one of the carracks, seized her valuable cargo.

As the political situation deteriorated in England, Warwick's ships had a strategic role to play. Those loyal to Henry VI were clearly determined to try and eliminate this squadron. It made only too clear the inability of the royal government to provide adequate defence either for English shipping or for port towns and was a useful instrument in drawing the allegiance of southern coastal counties away from the king and towards the Yorkists. For a time, in the autumn of 1459, Warwick's ships were laid up in Sandwich harbour under the control of the king's commissioners, but in the new year John Dinham, one of Warwick's captains, with a new force of ships, mounted an early morning raid on the town and got away with all the captured ones. These forces were then instrumental later in the year in ensuring the successful invasion of England by Warwick and the future Edward IV, the young earl of March. The duke of Exeter, commissioned to lead a fleet against Warwick, had in the end recoiled from any encounter, leaving Warwick's ships free to scour the Channel at will and eventually to land the Yorkist forces in Kent in June 1460, the start of the campaign which ended with the enthronement of Edward IV.[37]

It was clear to at least one thoughtful observer of events at sea in the waters around England in the fifteenth century that a well-financed group of royal ships was a necessity for a sea-girt nation. It is not fanciful to interpret the views expressed by John Fortescue in The Governance of England as having their origins in events since the accession of Henry IV. Henry V had created and maintained a force of ships which could 'keep the seas', with the help of merchant vessels, which was a valuable weapon of war. Since his death a series of ad hoc arrangements had led to a lack of security for merchants and other seafarers and the unavailability of suitable large ships in times of war. Fortescue thus wrote:

> And though we have not always war upon the sea yet it shall be necessary that the King have always some fleet upon the sea, for repressing of rovers, saving of our merchandise, our fishers, and the dwellers upon our coasts; and that the King keep always some great and mighty vessels, for the breaking of an army when any shall be against him upon the sea. For then it shall be too late to make such vessels. And yet without them all the king's navy shall not suffice to board with carracks and other great vessels, nor yet to break a mighty fleet gathered of purpose.[38]

Fortescue gives pride of place in seakeeping to the repression of rovers or pirates, and to many contemporaries this probably loomed much larger than the relatively infrequent sea battles or skirmishes between national forces. Rovers and raiders of coastal towns could easily bring ruin to an individual or community. How common and how destructive was piracy in northern waters in our period? This is not an easy question to answer largely because the definition of piracy was so loose and vague at this time. All nations with a seaboard on these waters accepted that in times of war all the vessels of a belligerent, of whatever kind, were fair game to the enemy: but what about the goods of belligerents in 'neutral' vessels or the situation in times of truce? What about the status of what would now be called privateers, those with some sort of royal sanction for their behaviour, perhaps engaged in licensed reprisals for some earlier outrage? These were problems that were not easily resolved in a period when communications were slow and shipmasters often illiterate. There was also, of course, a strong economic motive for seizing valuable cargoes and valuable ships and taking them into the nearest friendly port. Remedies did exist for those who suffered from the loss of their possessions by robbery at sea. An English statute of 1353 allowed restitution on proof of ownership by the claimant without the full rigours of the common law; another from 1414 made the breaking of truces and safe-conducts treason, with an official in every port to investigate alleged cases. It was not, however, always easy to invoke these procedures and in the meantime the situation tended to become more and more tangled and the missing goods harder and harder to track down. The goods of alien merchants were often involved, which added yet a further layer of complication. There are therefore copious records of cases of violence, robbery and general mayhem at sea.[39] Some of those involved were, at other times, in the king's service and were respected members of their communities. A prime example of the difficulty in drawing the line between legitimate reprisals and brigandage can be found in the careers of the two John Hawleys, father and son. The Hawleys were one of the leading families in Dartmouth. John Hawley senior was mayor of the town no fewer than fourteen times and also MP in at least two parliaments. In 1403 he was both nominated as a commissioner to inquire into a case of piracy and himself summoned before the Council to answer charges concerning an attack on a Spanish ship and the seizure of a cargo of olive oil valued at 'fifteen hundred gold scudi of France'. John junior had a very similar career, holding various positions under the crown, including being a JP for Cornwall in 1422–31. While he was still a magistrate he was apparently involved with an attack on a Scottish merchant and his ship off the coast of France at Oléron, seizing goods to the value of £220. There is no record, despite the case in Chancery, that Hawley either suffered any penalty for the attack or compensated the Scots merchant, John Lovell.[40]

Even more complex, and beset with serious political ramifications, was the capture of the entire Bay salt fleet in May 1449 by Robert Winnington.[41] He had been commissioned by indenture to keep the seas earlier in the year and may have encountered the fleet, largely composed of Hanseatic vessels, returning home to the Baltic from the Bay of Biscay, with salt supplies, indispensable for curing herring and other fish, by accident. As he told the story in a letter to Thomas Daniel, he went on board the leading ship and 'bade them strike in the name of the king of England and they bade me shit in the name of the king of England'.[42] Matters got heated after this exchange and fighting broke out between the two fleets, even though the English were greatly outnumbered. The next day, however, the entire Bay fleet surrendered to Winnington, who escorted them into Southampton Water. Some ships and their cargoes were later released but the majority were seized by the English. All this happened at a moment when relations between the Hanseatic cities and England were very bad, and there was a suspicion that the whole incident had been planned. The German merchants of the Steelyard in London later claimed that the salt taken out of the fleet had been brought up the Thames and stored in royal warehouses. Thomas Daniel himself was a royal councillor who had been negotiating fruitlessly with the Hanse for reciprocal privileges for English merchants in the Baltic.[43] Whatever the whole truth of the incident, it poisoned relations between the two parties for years. Eventually an open state of war existed between England and the League in the years 1470–74. This was conducted almost entirely at sea in the kind of attacks on merchant ships and their cargoes described above.

Piracy in northern waters therefore occupied a kind of no man's land between outright theft and semi-official or quietly winked at activity, a variety of low-level commercial warfare. It is hard to assess whether it had any real effect on trade; the number of cases in English records is quite significant but while the loss of a cargo and perhaps also a ship might be serious for an individual merchant, on a national level it might be hardly noticeable. In the years 1468–74, which include the war between the Hanse and England, the total number of cloths of assize exported from English ports by Hansards fell by 67 per cent but that of other aliens rose by very nearly the same amount.[44] A group like the so-called *Vitalienbrüder*, who were active as sea-robbers in the Baltic in the late fourteenth century, could cause disruption and infuriate their victims, but their activities did not prevent the rise of cities like Lübeck to economic dominance in the area. This group, based on the island of Gotland, were chased out of the Baltic at the end of the century and took refuge in Frisia, where again they had more nuisance value than real economic or maritime importance.[45]

The interest of the rulers of states bordering on the North Sea and the Channel, in naval matters, was intermittent at best. In certain political circumstances it could develop strongly and lead to the creation of something resembling a national naval force. This is evident in England in the time of Henry V and in France when the *Clos des galées* was set up, but no state could undertake the expense of a naval establishment with more than a temporary existence. Rulers were, however, aware of the way in which war at sea could be a powerful weapon against an enemy. Edward III's public rejoicing over his victory at Sluys in 1340 is evidence of this. Fortescue, as already noted, expressed the case for royal ships succinctly and powerfully in the 1470s. That both these reactions came from Englishmen is no surprise as, of all the states of northern Europe, England was the one with most to gain from war at sea. The others did not treat preparation for war at sea as a priority; low-level commerce raiding could be politically useful but did not require heavy investment by the ruler. The conditions in which Mahan's ideas of control of the seas could really flourish were still in the future. Did, however, these theories come closer to realisation in the Mediterranean?

The Mediterranean had long been the scene of sea battles and naval campaigns with considerable strategic significance. The Greeks in particular, in ancient times, had used fleets of galleys equipped with underwater bronze rams both to support land armies and in naval campaigns. Ancient writers like Herodotus and Polybius include descriptions of sea battles in their works. These imply that the Greeks had developed tactics which allowed galleys to use their rams against an enemy fleet in a very effective way.[46] Victory was gained by manoeuvring to destroy the enemy's vessels by ramming them, not by hand to hand fighting on the decks. From around the sixth century AD, Byzantium, the Roman Empire in the East, has been characterised as a thalassocracy; the sea (the eastern Mediterranean and the Black Sea) was the centre of its possessions not a frontier.[47] This did not change until the advance of Islam, with Moslem forces reaching the coast of the Mediterranean in the second half of the seventh century. The two powers then became locked in a continuing struggle for the domination of the seaways in the Levant, with the possession of strategic islands being of great importance. Both Crete (taken by Moslem forces in 826, recovered by the Byzantines in 963) and Sicily (under Moslem rule from 902 to 1060, then conquered by the Normans) served as naval bases for the galley fleets.

During this conflict the mysterious but undoubtedly effective weapon of 'Greek Fire', projected through a kind of siphon, was developed for use at sea by both the Byzantines and their opponents. Ships had to be specially equipped for this weapon: Anna Comnena describes how on the prow of each vessel, 'heads of lions and other land animals' were affixed; 'they were made of bronze or iron and the mouths were open: the thin layer of gold with which they were covered made the sight of them terrifying. The [Greek] fire to be hurled at the enemy through tubes was made to issue from the mouths of these figure-heads in such a way that they appeared to be belching fire.'[48] Apart from this there is little information about the way ships were employed at this period. Rams seem to have been replaced by above-water 'spurs' some time before the early sixth century; these were probably used to ride up over the oars of an enemy ship smashing them to pieces,[49] or to allow a boarding party easy access over the stern of their opponent, but there are no accounts of battles which clearly mention these tactics.

The arrival of the Crusaders in the region at the end of the eleventh century introduced new strategic considerations which had considerable influence on the way naval warfare developed. The 'Franks', as the crusaders were known in this area, had as their major preoccupation first the conquest and then the defence of *Outremer*, their territories 'beyond the sea'. The Byzantines wished to maintain their empire, and if possible regain lost lands, but were extremely suspicious of the 'Franks', whose aims did not always coincide with theirs. The Moslem rulers of the Levant undoubtedly wished to rid the region of Christian rulers and interlopers but were themselves threatened by a new Islamic power, the Turks. The most important Italian merchant cities, Pisa, Genoa and Venice, all saw the Levant as a source of riches and influence, for which they competed bitterly among themselves. In the western Mediterranean, Pisa and Genoa were also in competition with each other. Other major maritime powers were the rulers of Aragon and the Balearics, the Angevin family as rulers or would-be rulers of Sicily, and the Moslem emirs in the Maghreb and Andalusia. It is tempting to see the confrontation between Islam and Christianity as lying behind much of this conflict, and certainly religious and cultural differences were an element in some warfare, most notably, of course, the Crusades and the *Reconquista* in the Iberian peninsula. They were, however, far from being the only considerations of the various combatants. Issues of power, the possession of land, and the control of valuable trades and trade routes were at least as important. Just as in northern waters, the activities of pirates and corsairs, whether officially condoned or not, were also a constant problem for all those who travelled or consigned goods by sea.

In some ways it can be argued, however, that the geography of the Mediterranean made the application of Mahanian ideas of the control of the sea more plausible in southern, than in northern waters in our period. Seasonal wind patterns, the counter-clockwise current running along the coasts of the Mediterranean, the distribution of islands and the passages between them, all tended to force vessels onto much used 'standard' routes or sea lanes. Control of the narrows on these routes, for example the entrance to the Adriatic Sea or the Straits of Messina, was able, theoretically, to confer a strategic advantage on a combatant. Naval warfare in the Mediterranean in the period, however, was carried on almost exclusively by galleys. These vessels made effective and fearsome warships but could not stay at sea for more than a short period of time. It has been estimated that a galley oarsman required a minimum of four pints of water per day in the summer. This meant that a typical galley with a crew of 152 men would need 76 gallons of water a day. The absolute limit of the storage capacity of such a galley was around 1,520 gallons of water or twenty days' consumption. Normally a galley would carry other stores and would also face displacement problems if so much water was loaded; thus a galley could probably only stay at sea for a much shorter period than twenty days. This was acknowledged by a contemporary, the Venetian Marino Sanudo Torsello who said, 'in the summer time [galleys] are not able to stay at sea for many days without they frequently put into land to take on drinking water'.[50] Blockading was therefore only possible for short periods or with bases very near the disputed passage. As in northern waters, lack of good intelligence and the high cost of operating a galley fleet also made any sustained naval campaign very problematical. Here we will take a closer look at the way in which ships were used to support the Crusades, at the career of Robert of Luria, a Catalan nobleman in charge of the naval forces of Aragon during the war of the Sicilian Vespers, the conflict at sea between Venice and Genoa and finally the emergence of the Ottoman Turks as a major sea power at the end of our period.

During the First Crusade, the main body of the Frankish army made its way overland to the Holy Land. Ships brought much needed supplies to the siege of Antioch and to Jaffa, but there were no warlike encounters with the vessels of Moslem rulers. This logistical support proved itself essential to the establishment and continuation of the Crusader states of *Outremer*. (This very name, 'beyond the sea', implies the need for a long sea voyage.) Without the reinforcements, supplies and contacts with western Europe provided by the fleets coming not only from the ports on the northern shores of the Mediterranean and Byzantium, but also from as far away as Scandinavia,[51] these fragile states would have collapsed. By the time of the Third and later Crusades the expeditions were seen as essentially maritime in nature, unthinkable without the support of a fleet. Richard I of England ordered over a hundred vessels to be sent from England for the Third Crusade.[52] These were to meet the king at Marseille and then sail for Acre. Philip II of France hired ships from Genoa, the contract specifying that they should provide transport for 650 knights and 1,300 squires with their horses, provisions for both men and animals for eight months and wine for four months.[53] These very large demands illustrate the way in which setting up a major crusade could dominate the shipping market for a lengthy period. The pressing need for suitable horse transports seems also to have influenced ship design with the building of *huissiers*, vessels with doors in the hull not unlike those of a modern car ferry, which allowed the disembarking of horses onto the foreshore. In 1201, French noblemen contracted with the doge, Enrico Dandolo, for the Venetians to build ships and provide provisions for a total of thirty thousand Crusaders at a cost of 85,000 silver marks, for the Fourth Crusade. Their inability to raise this sum of money, and their wildly over-optimistic estimate of the numbers of Crusaders who would make their way to Venice, in effect gave them little alternative but to fall in with the doge's plans. This eventually led to the sack of Constantinople and the fall of the Greek Empire in 1204.[54]

If we move from consideration of the importance of the sea routes in the supply and reinforcement of *Outremer* to conflict at sea, our first consideration is, perhaps, the widespread belief that the Moslem states of the Levant from the eleventh century to the conquest of Egypt by the Ottomans in 1517 were reluctant to face their enemies at sea. The success of the Crusaders in maintaining their position in Syria and Palestine for nearly a hundred years has been attributed to this fact. It does perhaps ignore some incidents; in 1123 a Venetian fleet fought a bitter battle off the coast near Jaffa with the 'Saracens'. The chronicler describes how the Venetians managed to surround the enemy ships and block off their escape route. They then 'boarded their ships and cut their men to pieces'. Then 'after the corpses were cast out of the ships you could have seen the sea redden for four miles outward'. The Venetians then rowed on past Ascalon and captured ten other ships laden with long straight timbers for building war machines, and, what certainly pleased them even more than this, 'gold and silver coinage, pepper, cumin, and many kinds of aromatics'.[55]

Saladin made several attempts to use naval forces against the Crusaders, most notably after his victory at the battle of the Horns of Hattin had destroyed the kingdom of Jerusalem. In 1169, however, at the beginning of his rise to power, Saladin's position with regard to maritime matters was difficult. After the loss of Ascalon in 1153 the Moslems had no bases nearer Palestine than those on the Nile Delta. It was hard for them to protect their own coasts, let alone attack the Crusaders. Saladin did, however, take steps to build up a fleet. He even devised a scheme to carry boats in 'kit form' on camel back across the Sinai Peninsula to the Red Sea. These were used to launch a successful attack on the Crusader base at Ayla on the Gulf of Aqaba.[56] He also raised the pay of his mariners and used his few ships to take control not of Crusader held lands but of the coasts of North Africa to the west of Alexandria. Finally, he ordered in 1179 the building of what might indeed be called a war fleet, consisting of sixty galleys and twenty transports. This fleet began to raid the coast of Syria and even took and held Acre for two days in October 1179. All this was to the delight of Arab chroniclers and was followed up by administrative changes, improvement in the defences of Damietta and the successful capture of some large Frankish ships bringing supplies to *Outremer*.

After Hattin, however, when the remnants of the Frankish forces were clinging on to one or two coastal fortresses, an attack by Saladin's fleet on Tyre, in support of the armies besieging the town on the landward side, was a dismal failure. The ships blockading the harbour were taken by surprise and five were captured by the Christian forces. The remainder fled towards Beirut pursued by galleys from Tyre, now able to get out of the harbour. The wretched Egyptian crews made no attempt to stand and fight but abandoned their ships *en masse*, trying desperately to reach safety by swimming for the shore. An Arab commentator put the defeat down to the fact that Saladin found great difficulty in manning his fleet; the men were 'ignorant, without skill, experience or any fighting tradition so that whenever these men were faced by danger they were terrified and whenever it was imperative to obey, they disobeyed'.[57]

Saladin's ships were not able to prevent the disembarkation of the forces of the Third Crusade, led by Philip II of France and Richard I of England. The despondent and resigned tone of Imad al-Din the chronicler quoted above is echoed in the writing of later Mamluk writers. Sultan Baybars I again blamed the crews when disaster overtook his ships near Cyprus in 1270; they were 'peasants and rabble'. 'Anyone', he wrote, 'given an oar can row well, but not everyone can strike well if given a sword'. This disdain for the whole notion of seafaring among the upper echelons of Mamluk society has been blamed for the failure of their naval forces. Sailors cannot be compared to those 'who hunt on Arab steeds'; they are like 'those who hunt crows'.[58] There was, in fact, no permanent Mamluk naval force, but the same could be said of both England and France at the same period. Perhaps more significant is the fact that the distaste for maritime endeavour shown by their rulers was also present in lower levels of society. There were few, if any, Mamluk pirates in the eastern Mediterranean, despite the rich pickings offered by the vessels of the Venetians and Genoese, and the fact that virtually every other maritime community in the area regarded such activity as entirely normal. The rulers of Egypt and Syria prevented any fresh attempts by Crusaders to re-establish themselves in the old territories of *Outremer* by laying waste its coastal regions, so that an invading army would find no opportunities to forage or even obtain water. The harbours were totally destroyed, only Beirut and Tripoli recovering to some extent from the final campaign in the 1290s. From Sidon to al-Arish the coast was desolate. It has been said that, 'throughout the history of Islam, nowhere else in the Muslim world, from the Atlantic to the Pacific Ocean, was there destruction to equal in thoroughness, scale and gravity . . . the destruction of this coast by the Mamluks'.[59] Nevertheless, Italian merchants could and did trade freely with the Mamluks, largely through their *funduqs* in Alexandria. By the fifteenth century all that remained of Mamluk naval power was rotting ships and razed harbours.[60]

For the Franks in general, however, the period of the Crusades greatly stimulated the development of naval prowess. The need to sustain campaigns at a great distance from home undoubtedly encour-aged a better understanding of how this might be done by the careful use of shipping. Contact with Byzantine fleets in the early days of the Crusades had spread knowledge of their tactics, even though the West never obtained the formula for Greek Fire or learnt how to use it. The design of specialist horse transports probably owed much to these campaigns. Most notably, pilgrim traffic and the booming trade with all parts of the Levant set the Italian merchant cities, particularly the bitter rivals Genoa and Venice, on the path to their days of greatest prosperity.

In many ways these two cities were very similar. They both had a nominally republican form of government. They both lived by trade and both found that the greatest profits were to be made by trading with the Levant. In the markets and bazaars of Constantinople, Alexandria and Damascus were to be found all the spices and luxuries avidly desired in the West. It could well be argued that there was room for both of them in this commerce; that there was no pressing need for their rivalry for dominance to explode into war. Nevertheless from 1257, when the first Genoese–Venetian war started, until the ending of the war of Chioggia in 1381 these two city states fought each other, formally declaring war no fewer than four times. In between these major conflicts intermittent attacks by individual corsairs from each city on the other's shipping were always a possibility. There was, in fact, well over a hundred years of conflict, almost all of it at sea, between the rival merchants and fleets of these two cities.

To some extent the attacks by enterprising individuals always had an element of opportunism. There were, however, factors in the way seaborne trade between the markets in the Levant and the cities in the West was organised which reduced the need for luck for a profitable encounter and which could be used by a well-informed and experi-enced fleet commander to attempt to secure a decisive advantage over his enemy. These factors were the seasonal wind patterns and estab-lished trade routes already mentioned. In the case of Venice, the trading fleets or *mude* set forth and returned on a well-known schedule, so the time when a fleet laden with the results of a season's trading would approach the entrance to the Adriatic could be estimated with a fair chance of success. Genoese traders operated on a more individual basis but, even so, their movements conformed to a pattern. Thus in the first three wars between the cities, in 1257–68, 1295–99 and 1350–54, large-scale fleet actions and the most spectacular raids on commerce tended to take place either in the confined waters of straits or just off a harbour. They were not unlike many sea battles in northern waters, in support of land armies or connected with raids on coastal towns; these were encounters between rival fleets with the aim of asserting superiority over the enemy, seizing his assets, whether ships or valuables, and driving his forces from the area. Though round ships were occasionally involved, particularly if the action was against trading ships, these were most often galley battles fought between very similar vessels on each side, almost always under oars. The weapons used were very similar to those employed on land: javelins, crossbows, swords, and daggers. Vegetius, the Roman military theorist who included a section on naval warfare in his *Epitoma Rei Militaris*, mentions all kinds of slings and catapults being on board ships, but while stones and darts were certainly thrown at the enemy, particularly from the masthead castles of round ships, there is only a small amount of evidence of war engines being used.

Not surprisingly, because of the much more ordered and controlled nature of Venetian society, in these wars the Venetians tended to have greater success in galley actions and the Genoese in trapping and pillaging merchant fleets. What is clear, however, from all the accounts of battles, is that victory depended on the skill and determination in handling the fleet on the part of the commander, and the commitment and bravery of the crews. The strategy used in some campaigns gives every impression of being carefully worked out. A prime example of this is the campaign led by the Genoese commander Simone Grillo in 1264. To this point honours had been even between the combatants in the war, which had begun in 1257. Venice had had the better of galley fights in the harbour of Acre in 1258 and near Settepozzi in 1263. In the same year, the Genoese had successfully captured a large *nef* and three galleys near Abydos, laden with the proceeds of a whole year's trading by Venetians with the Black Sea ports. In the spring of 1264 the Genoese put together a large fleet; it may have included as many as 3,500 men, some mariners, others soldiers. Venice was also preparing its usual trading fleet for the Levant. This could not sail for Constantinople since, in 1261, with the help of the Genoese, the Greek emperor Michael Paleologus had regained the throne and removed all the privileges of the Venetians as prime supporters of the Latin conquerors of 1204. The *mude* were therefore primarily intended for Rhodes, Acre and Alexandria. Grillo set sail, announcing loudly at any port where his ships took on water that they were bound for Acre. He, in fact, put into Malta, sailing much further south than the route for Acre which was usually by Messina. The Venetians sent a galley fleet to cruise off Messina hoping to find the Genoese there, and also allowed trading vessels to leave for the Levant. Grillo then left Malta, sailing east; on the way he encountered a small trading vessel. At this point the sources diverge; the Genoese chronicle says that he learnt from the merchants that there was little point in continuing to *Outremer*; Venetian accounts claim that Grillo used the trader as bait to lure the Venetian galleys away from Messina towards Tyre, sending it north to meet the Venetian galleys and to give them misinformation regarding Grillo's plans. Whatever the truth of the matter, Grillo, after a further short delay, sailed north east towards the Gulf of Otranto where, on 14 August, he found the Venetian *mude* laden with rich cargoes. The Genoese went swiftly into the attack and overcame all the Venetian ships, except one very large round ship, the *Roccafortis*, which managed to escape. The Genoese then sailed home unhindered, loaded with spoils, to be greeted with 'rejoicing and triumph'.[61]

In 1266 the fortunes of war favoured the Venetians. What happened provided a good example of the importance of high morale among the galleymen in this kind of warfare. On this occasion a Venetian fleet, commanded by Jacopo Dandolo and Marco Gradenigo, sailed west hoping to encounter the Genoese, who were known to be in harbour at Bonifacio on Corsica. The Genoese were wary of the Venetians, who were thought to have a larger fleet than theirs, but their commander, Lanfranco Borbonino, decided to sail south towards Trapani to meet them. Borbonino found that his galley captains were reluctant to engage the Venetians and decided to adopt the cautious defensive strategy of keeping his fleet in the bay chained together with stems to shore. This meant that, while they might well be able to beat off an attack by boarders, it would be impossible to manoeuvre the vessels or put to sea quickly. When the Venetian fleet came into sight, the Genoese seamen panicked and made for the land in any way they could, abandoning their ships. With very little effort the Venetians took possession of the entire fleet, towing away the majority of the vessels in triumph.[62]

In the third war of 1350–55, the ostensible *casus belli* was the rivalry between Genoa and Venice for influence in Constantinople and the Black Sea, particularly the important trading outposts of Tana and Caffa. We are particularly well informed about the winter campaign of 1351–52 because not only do the Venetian Archives contain many of the orders sent to their commander Niccolo Pisani, but individual pursers' accounts survive in Genoa for two of their galleys which were under the overall command of Paganino Doria. That for the galley captained by Simone Leccavello allows us a glimpse of galley warfare at the level of an individual vessel. The war had begun with a Venetian attack on Genoese merchant ships, followed by a Genoese attack on the Venetian colony of Negroponte in 1350. In August of the following year, Leccavello's galley was ordered to sail east to join the Genoese squadron there and to bring them news of the entry of Catalonia into the war as an ally of Venice. It took him some time to assemble a crew and he probably left Genoa at the beginning of September. He sailed south down the coast, usually stopping at a convenient port every night. It took him a fortnight to reach Messina but from there he set a course straight for Crotone. Near this port the galley fell in with a Venetian vessel and took her as a prize. Their course then went via Zakinthos and Negroponte to Chios, which they reached on 7 October. While based here up to mid-November, the galley seems to have spent some time scouting for the enemy among the islands. Leccavello finally reached Pera where Doria's fleet was based, around 18 November. His galley remained near the Bosphorus, cruising for some of the time in the Sea of Marmara and the Black Sea until 7 May 1352. In this period he was also involved in the major engagement with the Venetians known as the Battle of the Bosphorus. The purser merely says, 'Monday at vespers, 13 February our galleys fought with the enemy and we took twenty-three galleys'. Two of Leccavello's crew later died of their wounds. Yet this was a hard-fought battle in the narrows of the Bosphorus, with heavy casualties according to the chroniclers. After this victory and a period of negotiation with the Greeks, Leccavello's men were finally homeward bound. They again spent some time in the waters off Chios and at last reached Genoa on 11 August after a voyage lasting a total of 343 days, of which 159 were spent at sea. Of the crew, 64 per cent seem to have returned safely, with the losses due to disease, incapacity, battle wounds and desertions.[63]

From this account we can see the scale of naval operations between Venice and Genoa at this time. Large numbers of ships were involved for lengthy periods of time. Navigation was not suspended during the winter months. While individual galley commanders had inevitably a degree of autonomy, there were also structures in place which allowed fleets to act in concert according to a plan. Most notably these were truly maritime campaigns, where the focus was on ship movements and encounters. On the other hand, in this whole series of wars, the outcome was curiously inconclusive. Galley actions and commerce raids could be dramatic but do not seem to have served to settle underlying problems. A temporary settlement might follow a victory but the rivalry between the two combatants and their allies remained and could surface again quickly.

The war of Chioggia (1378–81) developed in a rather different way from its predecessors. It began much as before in a quarrel over the control of Tenedos, an island at the entrance to the Dardanelles and therefore potentially able to control access to Constantinople and the Black Sea. This time, however, the Genoese concluded alliances with Padua, a rival to Venice on the mainland, and with Hungary, which wished to enforce its rule on the Dalmatian coast. These states could interrupt supplies reaching Venice despite its apparently impregnable position in the lagoon. The danger of a siege or blockade of the city became even more apparent when the Genoese fleet was able not only to sail up the Adriatic to Istria but also to defeat a Venetian fleet off Pola, capturing more than fifteen galleys. The Genoese established themselves in the lagoon at Chioggia, and Venice now indeed faced the real prospect of starvation and defeat.

Chinazzo's chronicle gives a vivid picture of the Venetians' response to this crisis.[64] The whole community threw itself into building defences along the Lido and putting together a new galley fleet to replace that lost at Pola. The crucial factor in saving Venice was probably the return of a second fleet under Carlo Zeno, who had been successfully raiding Genoese commerce, largely in the western Mediterranean, unaware of the desperate situation which had developed at home. The Genoese and their allies at Chioggia were now themselves besieged, with all the channels through the lagoon blocked by sunken ships or log barriers. They were finally forced to surrender in June 1380.[65] This time war had reached the heart of a state; commerce raiding like that of Zeno appeared almost as an irrelevance compared with the real disaster which threatened Venice. The need for galleys to patrol the Adriatic was emphasised, but at the same time much of Genoa's success was due to having land-based allies and troops to hold the islands and approach roads. A pointer to future developments was the use of cannon by both sides both on ships and fortifications. Another treaty at the end of the war again had little long-term effect, but this time not because of the continuing tensions between the two cities but because the whole strategic situation in the Levant was altered by the advance of the Ottoman Turks and their emergence in the course of the fifteenth century as a naval power.

This had consequences for the whole region, but before considering this we will move to the western Mediterranean to look at the conflict between the Aragonese and the Angevins and how this related to naval warfare. These two royal houses both laid claim to the island of Sicily. Peter III of Aragon wished to rule the island in right of his wife, daughter of the last Hohenstaufen king. Charles of Anjou had the backing of the pope for his claim. Aragon and Anjou (whose territory included Provence and the major port of Marseille) had also long been rivals in the western Mediterranean, each wishing to dominate the sea and its trade routes. The ensuing war, the War of the Sicilian Vespers, involved land armies and campaigns but, given the wide dispersal of each ruler's lands, the naval element in the conflict was important. The war also had a feature not seen in the other campaigns we have considered. One important aspect of these sea battles is that they are focused on the career of one brilliant commander, Roger of Lauria. He has been lauded as 'worthy of being ranked with Richard Coeur de Lion, the Black Prince and Nelson',[66] and not only as an audacious and courageous commander in battle but also 'as an administrator whose understanding of the changing strategic situations and possibilities . . . allowed him to use the fleet to maximum effect'.[67] His activities are recorded in a number of chronicles from Aragonese, Catalan, Italian and French sources and are also referred to in official administrative papers. His victories are generally seen as adding much to our understanding of galley battles at the time.[68] Is this reputation deserved? Or has the unusual amount of detail preserved about his activities served unduly to inflate it?

It must be said that there is very seldom agreement between the various chroniclers about the details of Roger's activities, while the numbers of vessels involved, for example, varies widely in the different accounts. Most of the writers also had little if any experience of the sea or galley warfare and often wrote to glorify the interests of their patron or their realm. One Catalan writer, Ramon Muntaner, unusually, seems to have been present at some of the fights described, but his chronicle was not written until his old age, at least thirty years after the events.[69] There is a suspicion that some of the writers at least were using conventional descriptions of sea battles derived from classical models rather than knowledge of actual events. The administrative papers, mainly account summaries, clearly indicate that Aragonese and Catalan fleets at the end of the thirteenth century were supported by a relatively efficient logistical system. The majority of the ships in Roger's fleets were royal property, with most of the finance coming from a variety of taxes. They also seem to have been well equipped with highly efficient crews. The fighting men on the Catalan galleys had a very high reputation. These *almugavars*, as they were called, were lightly armed, mainly with swords and daggers, but were clearly extremely effective in the hand to hand fighting of a boarding action. Their task was also eased by the skill of the Catalan crossbowmen, embarked on the galleys: in the preliminary 'missile exchange' phase of most naval battles of the period, these soldiers, either by virtue of superior training or by the possession of better crossbows and the quarrels fired by them, could disable a galley by the slaughter or wounding of many of its crew before boarding took place. Lauria was, in fact, involved in six major engagements at sea between 1283 and 1300: Malta (1283), Naples (1284), Las Hormigas or Rosas (1285), the battle of the Counts (1287), Cape Orlando (1299) and Ponza (1300). Also involved in raiding as far from his home waters as the Aegean, he was in general control of Aragonese naval forces from the time of his appointment as admiral in April 1283. This appointment ended only with his death in early 1305 (a grant for life of the office having been made in 1297).

A closer look at two of his battles, Malta and Naples, gives us some idea of the tactics Roger is associated with and enables us to make a better assessment of his skill as a commander. At the battle of Malta, the Angevin fleet was beached close under the protection of the Castel St Angelo in the Grand Harbour. Lauria's forces arrived off the harbour during the night; he then seems to have sent in a galley to reconnoitre the situation, creeping with muffled oars between the two guard ships at the harbour mouth. When he received the news that the enemy was beached, Lauria ordered a dawn attack. His next move caused consternation among the chroniclers. He did not attempt to surprise the enemy but sounded all his trumpets to rouse the enemy from their beds. The Angevin commander got his fleet into the water but, once there, they were comprehensively defeated by Lauria's forces. Since beached galleys were often thought to be unassailable in this position, Lauria's tactic of luring them out into the harbour, in an inevitable state of panic and disarray, had much to recommend it and may well reflect the audacity and drive of a very talented fleet commander.[70]

The battle of Naples in the following year involved the Aragonese fleet commanded by Lauria and the Angevins commanded by Charles of Salerno, the son of Charles of Anjou. Roger may have been anxious to attack the Angevin fleet based at Naples before it could receive reinforcements from Provence. He attacked and took the islands of Ischia and Capri; when this at first failed to lure the Angevins to sea he ordered a large section of his fleet to set sail for Sicily but, once out of sight of land, to double back and rejoin the remainder. This tactic worked. Charles of Salerno took his fleet to sea against the express orders of his father and, according to some accounts, with only the reluctant support of some galley captains and crews. Once at sea he found he was facing the whole Aragonese fleet and greatly outnumbered. Some of his ships fled and he himself with ten galleys was easily captured by Roger's forces. This again looks like a well-conceived and carefully planned operation. There are, however, some problems with this interpretation. First of all, the accounts of this battle in the various chronicles differ markedly; the story above is put together from several descriptions and there is no way of checking its accuracy. We can say that signalling systems at sea were little developed and naturally depended on 'line of sight'. To control a fleet of galleys performing a complex series of changes of course must have been extremely difficult. Luring Charles of Salerno to sea must always have been something of a gamble. Lauria would have had little if any intelligence of his intentions except perhaps gossip picked up from fishermen coming out from Naples. While his victory was undeniable, the course of the battle must remain uncertain in detail.[71]

Lauria's victories and the accounts of some other galley battles at this period raise another issue. This is the alleged practice of galley commanders when going into battle of lashing galleys together, sometimes using the oars in what is called, in the translations of chronicles into English, 'bridling' them together. The justification for doing this is usually said to have been to create a kind of floating fighting platform on which the hand to hand struggle could take place almost as if on land. It is possible to imagine this happening in a very sheltered harbour (as with the Genoese galleys in the harbour at Trapani) but it is very hard to see this being a viable tactic at sea. The effect of winds and currents on the vessels would have made controlling such a platform more or less impossible. It would also have made any form of manoeuvring very difficult and, in the last resort, would have removed the option of flight. It is possible that the existence of the tactic as described above is due to the mistranslation of an unfamiliar technical term in Catalan chronicles and other sources. If the terms used, mostly derived from the medieval Latin word *frenellum*, which normally means a bridle, are taken to mean a simple mechanism by which the galley oars were held out of the water but which could be released very quickly, a lot of the difficulties disappear.[72] Instead of a fighting platform, we can envisage each galley held on station by a bare minimum of oarsmen while the rest abandoned their oars to fight. The unused oars held out horizontally above the sea would make amidships boarding difficult but in emergency the galley could rapidly get under way.

There is, therefore, a degree of uncertainty about the details of Lauria's prowess as a naval commander. It is easier to see that, unlike the naval encounters between Venice and Genoa which were frequently of little ultimate consequence, Lauria's campaigns do seem to have been of importance in the outcome of the War of the Sicilian Vespers and to Angevin and Aragonese relations in the western Mediterranean. In this the support for the fleet of the Aragonese kings, Peter III and Alfonso III, was perhaps of as much importance as Lauria's leadership. By the beginning of the fourteenth century, when

Sicily had become an independent realm under Frederick III, the Aragonese kings were not willing to expend the enormous sums of money needed to keep a successful fleet in being on the scale of the previous years. The ability of Aragon to 'sustain a fleet and its support network on a continuous basis'[73] for as long as it did is perhaps as noteworthy as the achievements of Lauria.

The gradual spread of Ottoman power from the interior of Asia Minor to the coasts of the Levant, and eventually across the straits at the entrance to the Black Sea to the Balkans, introduced new strategic considerations into naval warfare in the Mediterranean. These dominated the second half of the fifteenth century. The Ottomans had had minimal experience of the sea and ships before their expansion into the Aegean and the Balkans. It seems that having Greek seamen and shipwrights among their newly conquered subjects allowed the Ottoman regime to begin the construction and operation of a naval force. This began in earnest after the fall of Constantinople in 1453. The Venetians soon became aware that the Ottomans were not only acquiring a fleet of galleys but were also building large round or cog type sailing vessels. The Ottoman use of cannon to attack galleys, a prominent feature of the siege of Constantinople, when guns on the Turkish fort in the Bosphorus had forced the Venetians from their anchorage in the Golden Horn, was also a new problem for Venetian commanders to face. Strategically, from the mid-fifteenth century, the Ottomans followed a policy of gradually driving the Venetians from their maritime bases, whether on the mainland or on the islands, denying their ships, whether merchant vessels, war galleys or corsairs, shelter and supplies and disrupting their trade routes. Tactically both sides faced the problem of how to deploy mixed fleets of galleys and round ships and to use cannon effectively at sea. The Ottomans enlarged their fleets; there were at least a hundred Turkish galleys at Negroponte in 1470, and around 250 ships at Zonchio in 1499, but they were almost always used in support of land armies.[74] The Ottoman aim was to extend their territory, and to eliminate Venetian and other Christian colonies, not to win fleet encounters. To answer this threat the Venetians relied on their fleets both of galleys and, increasingly, also of large round ships. Their aims were to some extent almost contradictory: they certainly wished to maintain their hold on their essential bases and colonies but, at the same time, also to maintain their valuable trade and cordial relations with areas in Ottoman control. Then, just at the moment when Venetian maritime supremacy in the Ionian and Aegean seas was most at risk, the attention of the *Signoria* was drawn away to the conflicts on the Italian mainland, particularly those resulting from the French invasions of the 1490s.

An attack on Negroponte had been feared by the Venetians ever since the fall of Constantinople. From the beginning of 1470 the *Signoria* took steps to reinforce the islands and direct galleys to its defence. The engagement which followed is described in unusual detail, coming from a letter from one of the Venetian galley commanders to his family. When his vessel, along with the rest of the fleet, reached the island, they found an enormous Turkish fleet including 108 galleys besieging the anchorage. The Venetians were outnumbered and retired to consider their best course of action. On their return they found that the Turks had thrown a bridge of boats across to Negroponte from the mainland and were using this to supply and reinforce their land forces. Either because of adverse winds and currents, or because they were intimidated by the Turkish artillery, or because the light was failing, no immediate attack was mounted on the bridge. In the morning the Venetians found that the town had fallen to the Turks in the night. Negroponte was irrevocably lost, causing uproar in Venice and the disgrace of the fleet commander.[75]

Despite this defeat, the Venetians and their allies the Knights of St John at Rhodes were able to contain Ottoman attempts to assert their dominion over the sea routes in the Levant with some success until 1499. The war of 1499–1502, however, led to the loss of Lepanto; Modon and Coron, once lauded as the two eyes of the Republic; as well as Zonchio and the island of Santa Maura (Levkas). These losses (which were extended in the sixteenth century, culminating in the Turkish conquest of Rhodes in 1523 and Cyprus in 1571) marked the beginning of Turkish domination of the area. The battle of Zonchio was the starting point of this process.[76] As at Negroponte, we are relatively well informed about the course of this engagement because of contemporary writings, principally Marino Sanuto's diaries, and also due to an account originally written by a galley commander present at the battle, Domenico Malipiero. There is even a near contemporary woodcut of the battle which does bear some relation to the action described in the written sources. The Venetians had had good advance intelligence that the Ottomans were intending to send a fleet to assist in the siege of Lepanto; in particular it would bring artillery, which was otherwise extremely difficult to transport over the mountainous interior of the Morea, to their land forces. The Venetian plan of attack was that it should be led by their large round ships backed up by the great galleys; the fast *gallie sottile* would join the fray once the Turkish fleet's centre (also large sailing ships) had been destroyed. In the event, things did not go according to plan; the round ships engaged each other with two Venetian vessels, including their mighty *Pandora*, grappling the Turkish flagship captained by a well-known corsair, Kemal Ali (or Camali to Europeans). Suddenly, for an unknown cause, his ship was engulfed in flames which soon spread to the other two ships, and all three sank. Only one of the Venetian great galleys attacked the enemy; the others withdrew, as did the light galleys. The fleets broke off contact but the remainder of the Turkish fleet eventually continued up the coast to Lepanto, which fell to the Turks with little further resistance from the Venetian garrison.[77] This outcome created another uproar in Venice. Antonio Grimani, the overall commander of the fleet, was imprisoned for a time but it is possible to feel some sympathy for him. He clearly did not have the full support of all his officers, while many of the galleys had inexperienced crews, unwilling to go into battle. An effective way to combine his mixed force of ships had not been devised. The battle of Zonchio, however, deprived the Venetians of their 'forward bases'. Without these it was hard to operate a fleet composed mainly of galleys in the eastern Mediterranean. The Turks gained not only territory but also access to recruiting grounds for crews and plentiful timber for ships. The possibility of their control of the sea lanes in this area was now a reality. This war of 1499–1502 between the Venetians and the Turks was not characterised by sea battles of tactical brilliance or innovation but did result in the emergence of a new dominant maritime power.

Did a similar shift occur in the fortunes of the *guerre de course*, that mixture of outright brigandage and semi-official reprisals which had long been a feature of maritime life in the Mediterranean as in other seas? As in northern Europe, the number of legal cases and reports of piratical attacks on shipping can give the impression that there was no security for traders at sea, and that every cargo shipped was at risk. The best antidote to this interpretation is knowledge of the insurance rates charged by Venetian or Genoese brokers on cargoes leaving the city. These were not high and many merchants apparently thought it unnecessary to insure cargoes carried in either galleys or carracks travelling in convoy. In Genoa, a table of insurance rates for cargoes to a variety of destinations shows that on voyages to England between 1449 and 1457 the average rate was around 8 per cent, the lowest being 5.5 per cent and the highest 12 per cent. 5 per cent was normally charged on the short route to Provençal ports. These rates do not imply a high level of risk.[78] Even the Venetians could not completely eliminate piracy in their sphere of influence. There were isolated communities among the islands of the Dalmatian coast, such as the Narentini of Omis, who had no other way of making a living in their bleak and unproductive homeland.[79] In general, however, their depredations could be kept within bounds. In the western Mediterranean, there was the added risk of attacks involving Moslem forces from the Maghreb, but, until the extension of the Ottoman empire along the coast of North Africa in the sixteenth century, this was not a serious problem but much on a par with attacks from other probably Christian sources.

The careers of some individual sea rovers can be traced, some at times being regarded with favour by the authorities and then attacked as public enemies. The Hawleys from Dartmouth, for instance, were simultaneously royal servants and suspected pirates. Others led adventurous lives by any standards but also exemplify the moral and legal ambiguities inherent in the 'profession' of corsair. The life of Don Pero Niño of Castile, recorded by his standard-bearer, illustrates this well. In 1404 Niño was commissioned by King Henry III of Castile to search for 'powerful corsairs of Castilian birth' who were plundering other Castilians as well as foreigners. Once at sea, Niño in fact spent some time searching unsuccessfully for Moorish shipping. When he did come across Castilian corsairs, he chased them into Marseille harbour, only to discover they were under papal protection and could not be touched. He was equally unable to take action against another group of corsair galleys which he found in the Sardinian port of Alguer (under Aragonese rule at the time). Here he was told by the town captain that the corsairs should be left in peace, as the town 'could not live without them since it was only they who guarded the harbours and brought them provisions'. Frustrated, Niño then sailed for Tunis, where he was involved in a bitter fight to take a Moorish galley and galleasse and much rich booty. Although wounded and very nearly losing his own galley which ran aground, he then returned to Cartagena to repair his vessels, rest his crews and load victuals for another voyage. His biographer lauds his determination to set out again on a similar expedition; the royal commission had clearly been forgotten as valuable booty was accumulated.[80]

The Genoese archives allow a similar close look at the career of Battista Aicardo de Portomaurizio, usually known as Scarincio. By 1454 he was based at Monaco and was accused of piratical attacks on the Ligurian coast against a Spanish ship (in Porto Pisano) and of robbing Venetians and Genoese. No action, however, was taken against him by Grimaldi, the local ruler, and in 1456 the Genoese authorities were happy to give him a safe-conduct despite the earlier accusations. The next year they wrote to the authorities at Beziers, which had authorised reprisals against a Genoese merchant because of losses suffered by one of their citizens apparently caused by Scarincio, calling him ' disobedient and a pirate'; similarly when writing to Florence he was described as a 'public enemy'. But only a year later the 'public enemy' was carrying despatches for the commune to Corsica and being addressed as *dilectus noster*. The rulers of Genoa were essentially pragmatic in their attitude to seamen like Scarincio, using them or disowning them as best suited the interests of the republic. Their justification was that, in the absence of any publicly funded form of naval defence, the commune had to seek help from any source available, without over much regard for legal niceties.[81]

Attacks on merchant ships and their cargoes were a source of considerable annoyance to the merchant community as a whole in the Mediterranean, but it would be unwise to over-emphasise their importance in the period up to the opening decades of the sixteenth century. There were mechanisms in place both legal and diplomatic to deal with the consequences, and the element of 'tit for tat' which undoubtedly existed tended to keep the problem within bounds. A more difficult question to answer is whether the spread of Ottoman power along the North African coast after their conquest of Mamluk Egypt in 1517 significantly worsened the problem of corsairs. The career of Khair-ad-Din or Barbarossa raises the possibility that this may indeed have been the case.[82]

Looking at the way in which warfare at sea developed across all the seaways of western Europe, some tentative conclusions can be drawn. First of all, until the introduction of cannon on board ship, a vessel which used oars as its principal means of movement in battle was preferable to one that used sails alone. Great galleys usually sailed on long passages but their oarsmen gave them vital manoeuvrability in an engagement. Certainly the ways in which fleets were deployed and the tactics in use in battle were more fully developed in southern waters, where galleys predominated in war, than in the north. The problems with cannon on board galleys were the practical ones of where to find room for them with little if any free deck space, and how to manoeuvre the vessel so that the guns could bear and be aimed. The development of gunports and moveable gun carriages, and changes in the sail plan and hull shape, solved these problems for sailing vessels. Galleys could only mount cannon on the poop deck and aim them by treating the whole ship as a gun turret; the poorly protected crew were also very vulnerable to the destructive effects of gunfire. Many of these developments lay in the future at the end of the fifteenth century, but naval power and its strengths and weaknesses were already better understood and better used in the Mediterranean than in northern waters. It was in this region that the insights of Admiral Mahan, the notions of control of the sea and the possibilities of sea power, were beginning to have some relevance.

People and Ports

Merchants formed one of the most prominent groups in medieval society. By the fifteenth century, there is copious documentation regarding their houses, their lifestyle and their ways of doing business. Private family letters and diaries, like those of the Celys or Datini, also provide intimate details of their lives. The richest merchants in Italy, in cities like Florence or Venice, lived like princes and became the leaders of their societies. In the Hanseatic ports the same could be said, while in London, Bruges or Ghent the most important merchants had both political influence and lived as well as any nobleman. Their portraits were painted by the best-known artists of the day, appearing first as donors in religious works intended for a church; later, as tastes changed, as individuals worthy of record. The whole Brömse family of Lübeck appears on the wings of an altarpiece in St Jacob's church in the city. On the left are the father and his six sons, all clad in fur-lined robes and with the canny expressions of good businessmen. On the right are the women of the family, richly attired except for a daughter who has taken the veil. The father was *burgomeister* of Lübeck, one son was an elder of the Steelyard in London, and another was involved in trade to Novgorod. The picture was painted in the late fifteenth century. In 1532, Hans Holbein the younger was commissioned to paint George Gisze from Cologne, a member of the London Steelyard. His luxurious clothing and elegant surroundings make plain his standing in society. It is less easy to gain an impression of the standard of living and lifestyle of shipmasters and seamen. The only well-known English 'Shipman' is Chaucer's fictional pilgrim. The wealth of those engaged in international trade may have depended on mariners' and shipmasters' skills, but little was recorded about the latter's individual lives. What we do know has to be largely extracted from legal and other administrative records.

The need for a law code which dealt with the problems of life at sea was realised as early as the twelfth century. The oldest codes are those drawn up at Rhodes (the *Lex Rhodia*) and the *Consolato del Mare*, best known in a copy from Barcelona. Both were the ancestors of the Laws of Oléron (originating on the west coast of France), a maritime law code which was used with only minor variations in all northern seafaring nations from the thirteenth century. The earliest copies in England, in a dialect of medieval French, are included in the *Liber Memorandum* and the *Liber Horn* of the City of London made about 1314, whilst that in German, now known as *Das Seebuch*, is from much the same date. Other versions can be found from Amalfi, from Visby and from Flanders. The Venetian codes are also similar in content. The way in which this law code spread across the seaways of western Europe is an eloquent demonstration of the way in which a community of seafarers and traders existed outside the divisions between states and rulers. The code is set out as a series of records of cases and the decisions made, presumably arising in the original court at Oléron, but later seen as having almost universal applicability. The working lives of mariners and shipmasters are, however, reflected in these decisions and they form one of the best contemporary sources for such information.

As portrayed in the code, the shipboard community of master and crew, in the earliest days, clearly had a strong cooperative aspect. In article 2 of the *Horn* book version it was decided:

A ship is in a harbour and stays to await her weather and when it comes to her departure the shipmaster must consult with his companions and say to them, 'Gentlemen, you have this weather'; there will be someone there who will say 'The weather is not good' and others who will say 'The weather is fair and good'. The shipmaster has to agree on this with the majority of his companions. And if he does otherwise, the shipmaster has to replace the ship and the cargo if they are lost. And that is the judgement in this case.[1]

The custom of consulting the crew in difficult circumstances continued into the fifteenth century. This happened during Don Pero Niño's corsair expedition in 1405. The vessel was off the North African coast and fast running out of water. They could not run for Spain because of adverse winds; in consultation with the crew, Niño rationed the remaining food and water and, in the end, with their consent, made a desperate raid on the Berber coast, getting away with full casks just as the Moors came up. The same evening he held a council of all the experienced sailors to discuss setting their next course. Sicily, Rhodes and the Aegean were all put forward as possible destinations with the wind in its current quarter, but in the end the wind changed overnight and they were able at last to sail home to Spain.[2] In the galleys of the Florentine fleet travelling to Flanders in 1429, the consultation was between the captain (the leader of the expedition), the patrons of the individual galleys and the *comiti* (mates or sailing masters) only; there was no say for ordinary galleymen.

In other articles the disciplinary powers of the shipmaster are asserted. The crew needed his permission to go ashore unless the ship was properly moored to the quay with four warps. A later compilation of reports of maritime cases, called *Les bones costumes de la Mer*, devotes a lot of space to crewmen who in effect 'jumped ship'. One can only presume that this was a recurrent problem which caused ships to leave harbour undermanned at times. A seaman could only break his terms of engagement, once he had shaken hands with the master or the ship's clerk, to get married, to go on pilgrimage, to keep a previously made vow, or, if 'a mariner before the mast' (an ordinary seaman), he was offered a position as mate or as 'mariner of the poop' (a skilled mariner able to navigate). If already engaged as a skilled man he could break the contract if offered a job as a *senyor* or shipmaster.[3] Once on board, a mariner was bound to carry out the directions of the master and could also be fined or punished for various other misdemeanours, including deliberately throwing food or wine away and undressing on board, unless overwintering in a port. The penalty for taking off one's clothes was to be dipped three times in the sea from the yardarm, with loss of wages and trade goods following the third offence.[4]

The shipmaster, however, had an obligation to provide at least a minimal amount of care for mariners who became ill while working on board. They would be put ashore with either a ship's boy, or a suitable woman, hired to look after them. They would still receive their usual shipboard rations (though the sick had to pay for any extras they might need). The ship would not wait in port for them to recover and if they died their family had no claim for the dead man's wages.[5] These wages could be hard to determine precisely, since seamen might be paid a wage by the day (sometimes with the addition of a weekly bonus known as a *regardum*; this was the custom in English royal ships). Or they might be paid by a combination of wages and the right to trade on their own account with a specified amount of goods. This right was much valued, particularly by the crews of Venetian galleys and Genoese carracks.[6] The laws and the later *Costumes* have much to say on these trading rights, which might possibly be in conflict with those of the merchants with freight on board. The Inquisition of Queenborough, a commission of inquiry into maritime legal matters in England, which sat between 1375 and 1403, sets out in detail the wages due to mariners on different passages, taking into account whether or not they also had a personal trading allowance. For example, between London and Lisbon the rate was twenty shillings and the trading allowance was a tun of wine. Between London and Calais, only five shillings in wages would be paid, with no trading rights. If sailing to Newcastle, a mariner could expect four shillings in wages and the right to transport two quarters of coal.[7]

There is no doubt that seamen, then as now, could at times be disorderly, drunk or riotous, especially on shore after a hard voyage. If at least two of the crew got into a drunken brawl on shore and were hurt, and were not on ship's business, the shipmaster had no obligation to offer them any assistance.[8] A study of cases in the town court in Southampton, involving the crews of ships from Venice, Florence and Genoa, which were frequent visitors to the port in the late fourteenth and fifteenth centuries, shows that the Italians were more often fined for assaulting each other than for getting into rows with the townsfolk. There were cases of petty theft; for example, the ostler of the Crown tavern in the town was fined for picking an Italian's pocket in 1492. The beadle of Godshouse was fined for a brawl in East Street with the black drummer off a Venetian galley, but the drummer and two oarsmen who joined in the fracas were also fined, so it is hard to be sure who started the trouble.[9] Fighting also broke out among the trumpeters of the Venetian fleet on one occasion while an oarsman called Giorgio was fined 9d. 'for pulling off another galyman by the hear'.[10]

When Luca di Maso degli Albizzi reached Southampton in January 1430 on his return voyage from Sluys to Florence as Captain of the Galleys, almost the first thing he did after his arrival in the port was to meet the mayor of Southampton in a church where he agreed certain principles governing the behaviour of the galleymen in the town. Only the officers of the galleys could carry arms; they would not go about at night without a light; and no-one would climb on the town walls or cause any damage to vegetable gardens or anything else. All this would be announced to the galley crews by Peter the trumpeter the next day.[11] London tended to be much less tolerant of foreigners whether seamen or merchants, with anti-alien feeling tending to explode into rioting at times of tension. For example, Flemings were attacked during the Peasants' Revolt of 1381 and Italians in 1451.

Reports of cases with maritime connections in the civil courts in England, mainly the court of Chancery, are another source which affords glimpses of the lives of seafaring men. Most refer either to commercial quarrels or to disputes arising out of the loss of goods at sea, usually to pirates or privateers. In one case, however, in 1408–09, a personal feud spilled over into violence at sea. A merchant who complained of his goods being robbed at sea also stated that one of his crew had been attacked and told that if the merchant himself had been on board he would have had 'his eyes beaten out of his head'. Another merchant's vessel was at anchor in St Ives Bay when it was spoiled of its cargo of wine, iron and saffron. The merchant could not get restitution because he feared for his life in the town, where the goods had been shared among 'misguided men of the town such as seamen and sea rovers of various nations'. In another incident, the crew of a ship called the *Isabell of Dantzig* were robbed of their sea chests with all their clothing and personal arms when in the port of Plymouth. These chests and their contents were valued at £17 13s. 4d., which suggests that the crew were relatively well off. Nevertheless, the overall impression is of a seagoing community with a good proportion of rough and often violent men.[12]

Controlling a group of men like these on a voyage which could last several months can never have been easy. The Laws of Oléron also placed heavy legal and commercial responsibilities on the master. Before about 1300, in northern waters, he was often also the sole owner of the vessel and also had responsibilities to the merchants whose goods he carried. After that date, ships were increasingly owned in shares, as in the Mediterranean. The success of the trading aspects of the voyage still rested on his shoulders, especially if the weather was unfavourable. It was his decision to change the 'advertised' destination in such circumstances, to put into an intermediate port or to delay departure. If caught in a storm, the question of whether or nor to jettison the cargo to lighten the ship was mainly in his hands. The Laws of Oléron suggest that the merchants on the ship were involved in the decision to take this drastic measure, but by the later fourteenth century, few travelled with their goods in this way.[13] Thus this would then, by default, have become the shipmaster's business. Once, in fact, the ship had cleared the harbour, its safety, the safety of the goods on board and that of the crew were in his hands. This was no light matter in view of the normal perils of the sea and the additional problems of pirates and raiders.

Food and accommodation on board were at best rough and ready. There were no set ration scales on northern ships, such as those laid down for Venetian galleys. The diet usually relied heavily on the staples of salt meat and salt fish, with carbohydrates provided by bread (for short voyages) and biscuit (for longer ones). For a voyage from Bayonne to England in the early fourteenth century, by two galleys and a galiot newly refitted for the English crown, along with unspecified victuals, 'twelve pigs and one small one' were provided. There were also large quantities of bread, mainly coming from women bakers; one supplied 500 loaves. This was apparently covered by a sail when at sea, so may have been hardly palatable by the time the ships reached England. Other supplies included napkins, dishes, platters, and saucers, 260 mackerel, and about twenty tuns of cider. Firewood was also loaded, which presupposes that there was some means of heating food; candles for the galley are also mentioned.[14] When the carvel *Edward Howard* was being victualled in Dunwich harbour in 1465, money was laid out upon '4 dozen bread', four barrels of beer, rye, herring, saltfish (probably cod), fresh fish, a cheese and the 'flesh of a whole beast'. More bread, beer, beef and salt and fresh fish was bought at Orwell and ale, for lack of beer at Walberswick. All this cost 36s. 2d., a not inconsiderable sum at the time. Twenty-six men and one 'child' were on the payroll, but it is not clear for how long the victuals were expected to last.[15] The impression is that, while, at sea, the diets of northern seamen were coarse and, to modern eyes, extremely dull, meals were, however, more regular than might have been the case ashore.

The beliefs and mindset of seamen are equally hard to determine. There is little evidence that they differed from those of other people at the time. It is hardly surprising that we know most about the religious observances on board pilgrim galleys and ships *en route* for the Holy Land.[16] Prayers were regularly said on these voyages but we should bear in mind that many of the accounts of these voyages were written by clerics and may reflect more their own practices than those of the crew. Undoubtedly sailors had their favourite saints. Virtually every port city had a church or chapel dedicated to St Nicholas, which was sometimes marked out as the seamen's church. In Venice, the church of San Niccoló on the Lido would have been both the last and first sight of their home city for a ship's crew. In Southampton, the chapel of St Nicholas lay behind St Mary's church outside the walls. This housed a splendid tomb erected in 1491 by the Scuola de Sclavonia (a guild of galleymen from Dalmatia and Istria, who formed part of the visiting galleys' crews) for those of their number who died at Southampton and never made the journey home.[17] When the future Henry IV, as earl of Derby, was crossing the Channel from Dover to Calais, on his way to Prussia to fight alongside the Teutonic Knights, he gave small sums as alms for 'St Nicholas's light'.[18] The bishop of Bangor came to Southampton to bless the *Gracedieu* at the time of her completion,[19] but other than that there are no records of formal religious ceremonies connected with ships and shipmen in England. Ser Stephano served as a chaplain on board Luca di Maso degli Albizzi's galley in 1429–30 but is not recorded as having any particular religious functions; he was, however, charged with the custody of the sealed bag of coins needed to pay the galleymen's wages when they reached Southampton. A mass was sung on the galley two days before they left Southampton on their homeward voyage, but this was more the prelude to a splendid farewell dinner with the mayor and other worthies in the town than connected directly with the galley's departure.[20]

The Captains of the Galleys in both Venice and Florence and those in charge of the largest Genoese carracks were in many ways from a different level of society than the shipmasters in northern waters.

Noblemen were involved at sea as the commanders of English naval expeditions; Thomas, duke of Exeter, led a patrol in 1418, and Hugh Courtney, earl of Devon, in the following two summers.[21] They were not, however, directly involved in or present on trading voyages. The murky semi-legal world of the privateer-pirate included men like Don Pero Niño whose biographer extols him as a 'most famous and illustrious knight . . . in arms a man of good fortune . . . in love very valiant and of good renown'.[22] John Hawley was mayor of Dartmouth and an MP as well as being involved in some more than legally dubious events at sea. Most northern shipmasters, however, were astute practical men with no claim to social eminence, being perhaps similar in status to the *comito* or first mate on the Florentine galleys. Luca di Maso degli Albizzi, the captain on the voyage of 1429–30, in contrast, was a member of a very prominent Florentine family; his father was captain of the people for over thirty years before ceding power to the first of the Medici. Luca was carefully educated, studying under some of the leading humanists of the Florentine Renaissance including Poggio Bracciolini. Before becoming Captain of the Galleys he had been on many diplomatic missions for his city and after his return he continued in this role, being a supporter of Cosimo de' Medici rather than his own brother Rinaldo degli Albizzi, Cosimo's opponent. Besides the diary of this voyage he was also the author of others relating to his diplomatic missions; his style is fluent and grammatical, showing the benefits of his humanist education. The patrons (or commanding officers) of the two galleys making up Luca's command were Piero di Simone Vespucci and Bernardo Carnesecchi. Piero had held various official positions in Florence before becoming a patron of a galley; Carnesecchi was a merchant, a partner in a trading firm with particular interests in Avignon. Neither had much practical experience at sea before this voyage and they had to rely extensively on the advice of their *comiti*. The diary shows that the advice of the *comiti* was anxiously sought, especially when the galleys ran into stormy weather.

Luca's responsibilities sometimes weighed heavily on him. He had to balance such factors as the concern of the pilots, hired to take the galleys past the Straits of Gibraltar, that his own galley was overloaded with cargo, with the desire of his patrons to maximise trading profits.[23] He conducted negotiations with the king of Portugal after an unexpected stop in Lisbon about opening trade between Florence and Portugal; these went well. The king sent fresh food to the galleys (four bullocks, ten dead pigs, four tuns of wine, honey and bread); Luca, in return, sent the king luxuries including dates, saffron, fine wine and cheeses from Tuscany.[24] He also had to deal with problems among the crew, pirates off the Galician coast and finally a potentially disastrous situation in Sluys where the duke of Burgundy threatened to requisition his galleys.

His worries over the crew feature prominently in the whole diary. In the fifteenth century, as has been said, the oarsmen of Mediterranean galleys were not slaves or convicts, nor were they chained to their benches. Most were paid volunteers willing to take on a strenuous job performed in harsh conditions because it offered adequate wages and regular meals and, most importantly, the chance to make good money from the crewman's allowance of trade goods. If men were being recruited for warships, some form of conscription might be used. In Venice in the twelfth and thirteenth centuries, each *contrada* or parish in the city enrolled all the adult males into groups of twelve. From this dozen, one, two or even three men would be chosen to serve in the defence of the city at sea, according to need. Those chosen could pay for a substitute, while the remainder of the group contributed to the wages of those serving the city.[25] The social status of galleymen tended to decline as it became more and more unusual for merchants to travel with their goods on trading voyages. To some extent the merchants had formed a useful social bridge between the captain and other officers and the galleymen. There was no question of crewmen being forced into their role until the sixteenth century. There was, however, continual concern about recruitment. In Venice itself this led to many crews consisting largely of men from the Venetian lands in Istria and Dalmatia, and from their island possessions, particularly Crete, rather than the city itself. The Genoese recruited from all along the Ligurian coast. When Simone Leccavello was on his way to join the Genoese fleet in the Bosphorus in 1351, eighteen of those originally recruited had either changed their minds or deserted by the time he reached Portovenere (only eighty kilometres distant from Genoa). Replacements were signed on at Messina and Chios.[26]

The usual system, followed in both Venice and Genoa when a galley was being manned, was for the patron or captain and his clerk to set up a table in a prominent place and wait for men to sign on. In Venice this was done in the Piazzetta outside the doge's palace. The popularity of the captain or of the expedition could make a considerable difference to the ease with which a crew could be recruited. This was clearly demonstrated in the dark days of the War of Chioggia, when Venice seemed on the verge of defeat. Vettor Pisani, a well-liked and experienced commander, was blamed by the Senate for the defeat of the Venetians at Pola in Istria which had allowed the Genoese to establish their siege of the city. He was imprisoned and many voices in the Senate called for his execution, as Venetian law required. When things were at their blackest, however, he was released in order to lead another expedition against the enemy with newly built galleys. When he appeared in the Piazzetta to recruit his crews the whole area was filled with

> the poorer citizens blowing trumpets . . . and all the people with great joy were shouting in the Piazzetta 'long live Miser Vetor, long live our father' . . . which didn't much please many Venetian gentlemen . . . but like a good and loyal citizen, he said, 'My children and friends we are all brave men and we will go together and have victory over our enemies, don't doubt it' . . . And the clerks could hardly write down fast enough the names of the oarsmen and crossbowmen and brave men who volunteered for Miser Vetor's galleys . . .[27]

Although on a commercial voyage, Luca di Maso noted very carefully in his diary changes in the crew. For example, one man was put ashore for theft. We can perhaps sympathise with the five who fled from the galley when she was held up by bad weather in Ribadeo. Luca recorded that they could not stand the cold (it was November) and the wet conditions in the galley (it was always raining). In his opinion, it was this that made them desert, not the hard work. When he was in port at Southampton on the return voyage, he tried hard to recruit some Englishmen to his crew but without success. They either wanted too much money or could not leave England because there was a need for seamen for royal ships at this date and they would have been unable to get a licence to leave the country.[28]

Since the muscles of a galley crew were its motive force when it was under oars, it is not surprising that ration scales were important. There are frequent references to the need for more supplies of *biscotti*, the basic carbohydrate in a galleyman's diet, in records and accounts in both Genoa and Venice. A scale for rations for galleymen included in a scheme for a crusade put forward by Marino Sanuto in 1320 suggests a diet of biscuit, wine, cheese, salt pork and beans. The pork and beans were used to make a soup; this was served out so that the crew had pieces of meat in their soup on three days, and broth only with vegetables on the remaining five, including Friday, a fast day.[29] There is unfortunately no way of knowing if this ration scale was ever implemented. A later document from the early fifteenth century suggests that '*ab antiquo*' each galleyman had had 18 ounces of *biscotti* or 24 ounces of fresh bread a day, together with wine, cheese and beans. He should also have had access to a barrel of water under his bench.[30] Victualling a large fleet, when the requirement per man was something in the region of 4,000 calories per day, was a formidable undertaking. If Paganino Doria's fleet off Constantinople in 1351 included around 11,500 men, rowers, 'marines' and officers, he would have needed nearly 16,500 kilograms of rations a day, including over 8,000 kilograms of biscuit. It is not surprising therefore to find him scouring the Genoese islands in the Aegean and Anatolia for provisions.[31]

In some ways the way of life at sea, the enforced intimacy in a confined space and the shared experience of alarms and danger, and the exhilaration felt on a vessel going well in good weather, created a community which was based on cooperation rather than hierarchy or coercion. This seems to be reflected in the tone of early examples of the sea laws in both southern and northern waters. The rise of long-distance trades, of voyages lasting several months, with cargoes of great value, so that the failure of a voyage could have repercussions for the authorities in a state, perhaps began to tilt the balance in favour of the investors in a ship and a voyage rather than the seamen. The position of Captain of the Galleys of Venice or Florence was one for a person of status and influence; he was the representative of many interlocking political, financial and economic interests going far beyond those of his squadron of galleys, perhaps clawing its way along the coast of Aragon in contrary winds. It is at least arguable that the development of 'galley lines' and regular sailings by large multi-owned carracks in the Mediterranean and the gradual extension of shipowning partnerships in northern waters both tended to lower the status of shipmasters and mariners in favour of that of the members of the largest merchant houses, the shipowners and their colleagues in official positions.

Did this community of seamen create a special and identifiable maritime society in ports in both northern and southern Europe? Any answer to this question must necessarily have a large speculative element because of the nature of the evidence, but certainly there were some common features. First, it was truly a community of seamen. Women, of course, went to sea as passengers or pilgrims but never as mariners. They might own ships, sometimes those bequeathed by their late husbands, but this would be as a form of investment. They might also be involved in the supply of victuals or other materials to ships and their crews. Bread for some royal ships was largely supplied by female bakers in Bayonne in the early fourteenth century.[32] Katerine Douchwoman of London and Isabella Roger of Southampton sold oakum to the office of the clerk of the king's ships in 1424.[33] There is no reason to think that these were the only women supplying victuals and chandlery to mariners. Extrapolating backwards from what is known of later fisheries, it is likely that women did much of the work involved in gutting and salting herrings and other fish on shore, but they did not go to sea.

Seamen did share common experiences of the dangers and pleasures of going to sea. They had something of a lingua franca covering the equipment of their vessels and the technical language of seafaring. The operation of trading vessels was covered, to a remarkable degree, by laws which were accepted in almost all European waters. These things bound the seafaring community together. How influential this community was in the society of their home port depended a great deal on the nature of that port and its economy and social composition.

In a small fishing village, the mariners might be, if not the most powerful, the most valuable members of the community, on whom the prosperity of the rest depended. There is little direct evidence of the methods used in the fishing industry in the Middle Ages, despite the fact that salted or dried fish of various kinds were some of the most important bulk goods traded internationally. We can, however, say something about English fishing villages which were part of the estates of a landowner for which some manorial records survive. This is the case with Walberswick, on the Suffolk coast, a little to the south of Southwold. It formed part of an estate inherited in 1430 by a certain John Hopton.[34] The village itself was situated where the rivers Blyth and Dunwich entered the sea. The surrounding lands were infertile, sandy and marshy, so the fishery was of great commercial importance to the village. From notes and entries in Hopton's account rolls some picture of Walberswick society emerges. From the point of view of the landlord the ferry across the river was the best source of income; there were also fees paid by fishing boats from other nearby places using the harbour, and fees for weighing salt and grain at the quayside. The total of all these was only about £3 6s. 8d. by 1490 but had risen steadily since Hopton inherited the place, indicating that the village was quietly prospering.[35] Boats were built on the foreshore at least occasionally;[36] there was also a mussel bed, commercially exploited. The career of Robin Dolfinby, one of the fishermen of Walberswick, saw his rise to the status of a comfortably situated leading man of the place. He first appeared in the accounts as selling fish to Hopton. By 1466 he part-owned a boat; two years later he had one of his own and by 1475 he owned the *Andrew*, a large off-shore herring boat. He was a churchwarden by 1479 and travelled beyond the village to London and Ipswich. In his will of 1489, he requested that his boat should be sold and the proceeds devoted to making statues for the church, St Andrew's, in the village, one of St John the Evangelist, the other of St John Baptist, both to be painted at his expense. His widow and daughter were also well provided for with property and household goods.[37] Other parishioners also donated generously to the church, which was built, decorated and furnished at this time. The herring and sprat boats provided a good living even if it had to be wrung from the stormy waters of the North Sea. In 1451, the villagers owned twenty-two sprat boats and thirteen of the larger herring boats. In such a place, it is no wonder if the sea bulked large in everyday concerns.[38]

Can the same be said of country towns of the order of Lynn or Southampton? Lynn's development as an important port on the North Sea, engaged in trade with Scandinavia, the Baltic and the Low Countries, depended largely on the success of works on a cut, the Brandon Creek, made in the thirteenth century. This joined the Great

Ouse to the Little Ouse south of Lynn, allowing the town much better access to its hinterland by water via the Great Ouse and the Nene and also serving to bypass Wisbech, which had been the more important trading settlement. Anchorages and staithes or wharves were also provided along the Fisherfleet (River Gay), the Purfleet, which led through the centre of the town, and the Millfleet. The royal customs accounts provide ample evidence of the success of the town as a trading centre dealing mainly in the English staple commodities of wool and cloth, with imports of fish and wine among other things. The way the town lies open to the broad waters of the Ouse with the wide skies of East Anglia arching above, to this day gives it a fresh open feeling with the smells and sights of a port still present. This would have been even more obvious in the Middle Ages especially when ships came up into the centre of the town along the various 'fleets'. The town records contain many mentions of these waterways and the need to keep them clear to prevent flooding and to allow the passage of ships. The merchants of Lynn petitioned Henry IV in 1411 that the passage of vessels in the Purfleet was being impeded by piles driven into the ditch and the disposing of animal guts and other waste in the water.[39] Casual mentions in deeds and other documents make clear that private individuals maintained their own staithes along these waterways, although there was also a common staithe on the river. The mayor had to make a grovelling apology to the duke of Exeter in 1426 for allowing the millrace from the town mill to damage the duke's quay adjacent to his house in the town.[40] The Great Gild or Trinity Gild also had a staithe off the Purfleet which formed a very profitable part of its assets. Tolls payable on goods unloaded there totalled £42 6s. 8d. in 1389.[41] The town was said to have been notable for the ease with which ships could be hired there. It was also possible to find pilots who were experienced not only in the local sea routes but in those across the North Sea in general. One of these pilots escaped a charge of theft in 1416 because he was said to be at sea on a ship of Danzig.[42]

It is hard to assess the number of people involved directly in shipping in the town as masters or mariners, though it is clear that overseas and inland trade by water was of great importance. The total population was about 9,000 at its height before the plague and population collapse of the later fourteenth century. It then stabilised at around 5,500, a level which did not to change greatly until the mid-sixteenth century. A detailed assessment of the chattels of the inhabitants of one ward of the town in the late thirteenth century includes a number listed as owning a share in a ship. Thomas of Newark had a half share worth £4 in one vessel and timber worth £2 as cargo. Henry the Iremonger, a much wealthier man (the total value of his goods was £95 15s. 16d. (sic)), had a fourth part (valued at 60s.) in a ship called *Blithe* and a half share in one called *Gozer* (valued at £6 13s. 4d.). Philip de Bekx, whose moveables were valued at the very large sum of £246 8s. 1½d., wholly owned a cogship valued at £40 and also a share in a hulk valued at £13 6s. 8d. The value of the cargoes in these ships was £43.[43] A fragmentary record of the 1379 poll tax for Bishop's Lynn lists twenty-eight individuals as either master mariners or mariners. The mariners normally are assessed at the minimum of 4d; the assessments of the five master mariners vary from 2s. to 6d. A similar fragment for the hundred of Freebridge in South Lynn includes only occasional mentions of the occupations of taxpayers; here one shipman can be found paying 2s., another paying 6d. and one shipwright also assessed at 6d.[44] Before, however, it is assumed that mariners were only an insignificant minority in Lynn, it must not be forgotten that a gild and fraternity specially for seamen was founded in 1386, something which presupposes that this group had a public presence in the town.

The tempo and excitement of life in Lynn was also increased by the number of foreigners, both merchants and seamen, who came to the town. Here the most important group were those who came from the Baltic, from cities which were members of the Hanseatic League, principally Lübeck and Danzig. Also known as Easterlings, this group were granted trading rights in Lynn in 1310. Their wares, including furs from Novgorod, beeswax, salt and dried fish, pitch, hemp for cordage and timber for shipbuilding, found a ready sale, while export cargoes consisted largely of wool. They were not, however, always welcome in the town. Lynn merchants found the fact that they were denied reciprocal rights in Danzig intensely irritating. Nineteen Lynn merchants had their goods arrested in Prussia in 1385.[45] Two merchants 'of Almayn of the town of Danske in Pruce', complained that their ship and its cargo had been arrested in Lynn in about 1460.[46] The Hanseatic League also eventually froze Lynn ships and merchants out of the profitable voyages to Bergen and Iceland. By 1475 relations were somewhat better and in this year the Hanseatic League built its warehouse and trading centre on a plot between St Margaret's church and the water, which still exists.[47]

Southampton was equally home to a prosperous foreign community, but in this case they were mainly Italians, principally from Genoa, a city with strong trading links with the town.[48] Seaborne trade had allowed the town to profit from its sheltered site at the head of Southampton Water and its deepwater anchorage which benefited from the double tides of the area. Foreign trade brought exotic merchandise to the town, and lively visitors including not only the Italians, but Frenchmen, Channel Islanders and Flemings. Most of the vessels at the quays,[49] however, were not engaged in cross-Channel or longer voyages but were fishing boats or other small craft, plying up and down the Solent, over to the Isle of Wight and along the south coast. The records of the town's local customs or port books make this clear.[50] The fortunes of the town were also more deeply affected by political considerations than was Lynn. The maritime aspects of this could be disastrous. In 1338, a force of French and Genoese galleys raided the town, putting it to the torch after rampaging through the town, raping and pillaging. The economic effects of the raid lasted for some years while, more practically, the raid galvanised the king and the town into action to wall the town with particularly strong fortifications along the waterfront.[51] For the remainder of the Middle Ages, rumours that another raid was imminent could cause alarm in the town. On a more positive note, in the fifteenth century, Southampton became for a brief period the centre of the administration of the royal ships of Henry V and the place where many of the most important were built. Many Southampton burgesses and their families must have crowded the quays and walls to watch when Henry V's expedition to France left the anchorage in 1415. Since, according to Henry's chaplain and biographer, fifteen hundred vessels were involved it would have been a brave sight to see them set out with a favourable wind on the morning of Sunday 11 August.[52] Southampton men were also involved in supplying the royal ships with timber, ironwork and other necessaries, and large numbers also found work at the temporary mud docks where several of them were built. The precise sites where this occurred are unknown but it may have been on the banks of the Itchen. Certainly the sums of money which fed into the local economy of Southampton were considerable. Between 1414 and 1416, William Soper received £1,873 4s. 2d. from the Exchequer for work on the refitting of the royal ship *Gabriel* and the rebuilding of the *St Clare of Spain* as the *Holyghost*. A further £1,000 or thereabouts came from the sale of surplus equipment and prize goods. Between 1416 and 1420 the larger project to build the enormous *Gracedieu* and her attendant barge and balinger, the *Valentine* and the *Falcon*, cost a total of £4,852 2s. 7d. of which only £300 did not come from the crown.[53] Thus, in about six years, over £6,000 of royal expenditure came into the town for this purpose alone; this at a time when the town farm was about £100 per year and the pay for a skilled carpenter was about 6d. per day worked. The number of men actually employed on shipbuilding for the crown naturally varied considerably as projects were ordered or completed. Between 1422 and 1427, when no major works were under way, thirteen smiths, thirty-one clenchers, twenty holders, twenty-eight unspecified carpenters, forty-six carters and twenty-three labourers worked on the royal ships for varying lengths of time.[54] Employment at this level in a small community must have had a noticeable effect on the local economy. The dismay when work on the royal ships disappeared in the 1430s was perhaps caused as much by worry over jobs as fears that commerce in the Channel would lack protection.

By the end of the fifteenth century, work on the king's ships was undertaken at Portsmouth. Maritime life in Southampton was concerned with commercial interests alone. The town was, however, prosperous. In 1530, John Leland described English Street, the main business thoroughfare, as 'one of the fairest streates that ys yn any town of al England . . . well buildid for timbre building'.[55] One of the houses he admired still stands, the Red Lion, now a public house, originally having a shop on the ground floor with a hall and other chambers running back from the street, a design which made very good use of the long narrow plots often found in towns. Elsewhere in the old town, often as the result of bombing in the Second World War, the substantial stone vaults and cellars where the merchants of the Middle Ages stored their goods have been revealed. Like Lynn, Southampton was a busy and successful trading centre and much of its wealth was due to the work of the mariners whose vessels lay alongside the quays.

In larger towns the role played by seafarers and the port in the overall prosperity of the place varied considerably. By the end of the fifteenth century, much of England's export trade, particularly in the vital commodities of wool and textiles, was concentrated in London, while provincial towns like Boston, Lynn and Bristol saw their share of the traffic in these goods fall considerably. Yet, although the quays along the Thames and the anchorages in the Pool of London were crowded and busy, London does not seem to have regarded itself primarily as a port town and often almost seemed to ignore its connection with the sea. In one of the London chronicles, there is plentiful news about political events in both England and abroad, but the 'local' items included relate either to public executions and burnings, or to oddities like the wax chandler of Fleet Street who diverted water from the conduit into his own cellar and as a punishment was forced to 'ride through the cite with a condit upon his hedde'.[56] The port and shipping are ignored.

The situation in Lübeck was somewhat different. Lübeck had been founded in the period 1143–59 and by 1181 was a free imperial city, a status which gave it a high degree of independence from the imperial or other authorities. Its position on an island formed by the confluence of the rivers Trave and Wakenitz was secure and defensible, and also highly suitable for the development of a port. There was easy access to the Baltic and to all the trading cities and posts to the east. It might be thought that it was a disadvantage for the city for its access by sea to the west, to Flanders and England, to entail a voyage through the Sound between Denmark and Scania and then via the Kattegat and the Skagerrak to the North Sea. This does not seem to have been the case. Although it was possible for goods to be transhipped at Lübeck to travel overland to Hamburg and then continue to the west by sea, there is plentiful evidence that vessels made the journey by sea, particularly with cargoes of bulk goods like salt fish.[57] Lübeck's relationship with the sea was in fact largely based on its access to salt from the Luneburg salt works used to preserve the herring caught in huge quantities off the coast of Scania. Barrels of salt herring were the foundation of Lübeck's prosperity. From what is known of the buildings and other facilities on Lübeck's waterfront along the River Trave in the thirteenth and fourteenth centuries, it is clear that the most prominent structures included a herring market and warehouses later converted to special salt stores, as well as shipyards and granaries for the storage of grain. Ships from different home ports used different quays which have also been identified.[58]

The all-important herring fishery off the coast of Scania was in the hands of Danish fishermen, but the processing of the fish was largely done at Skanör south of Malmö. Here merchants established concessions called *vitte* where the fish were prepared and salted largely by local women. The Lübeck *vitte* included some sort of housing for the workers, a church and a cemetery, all under the supervision of the city. In 1368 some 250 ships from Lübeck came to the *vitte* or the fairs at Skanör or Falsterbo where the salt fish was sold. By 1400 550 vessels from Lübeck were involved in the traffic. Totals gradually declined form this high point as the herring shoals migrated to the North Sea.

The port of Lübeck itself gained considerably from this traffic and by the fifteenth century, apart from the warehouses along the Trave, probably also had a crane like those shown in paintings of Bruges and Hamburg. The miniature of the port of Hamburg, which comes from the 1497 *Book of Rights of the Town*, shows clearly the operations of the port, which was very similar to that of Lübeck. Large three-masted ships are anchored off the quay. They have discharged their cargo into smaller oared vessels, and the barrels are being raised by the crane from these onto the wharf. The crane is operated by a treadmill. In a large building nearby, wealthy and well-dressed merchants are concluding their bargains and paying dues.[59]

Shipowning was clearly an important and profitable form of investment in Lübeck, especially as the power of the Hanseatic League grew and the town was accepted as the leading city within the League. From the beginning of the fourteenth century ships were commonly owned in shares. This helped spread risks (better to own a quarter of each of four ships than to lose one's whole investment when one wholly owned vessel was sunk), helping to raise the capital to build new ships, especially as the size of these tended to increase and they became more expensive. One shipowner, Herman Mesman, at the end of the fifteenth century, estimated his own wealth as amounting to 3,900 marks. This included the values of three whole ships and fractions, from one-half to an eighth, of six others.[60] Shipmasters were regarded with great respect and were usually also shareholders in their vessel. It was the custom that they should be married, as this was thought to be some sort of guarantee that they would return to their home port. Some became, in their own right, important members of the merchant patriciate of the town. Their status in Lübeck is well illustrated by the mariners' guild of St Nicholas, founded in December 1400 with the purpose of providing help and shelter for all sea-going persons. A particular duty of the members was to pray for the souls of those who had been lost at sea without the benefit of the rites of the church. In 1497 a guild under the patronage of St Anne was founded for shipbuilders grouped around a chapel in St Jacob's church. After the Reformation the two came together and their surviving guild house, the Schiffergesellschaft, dating from 1535, can still be seen in the town. The Great Hall of the building has much of its original furnishings, including carvings of the arms of those trading to Bergen, Rival and Riga and tables made from ships' timbers.[61]

Lübeck's overland trade was always of importance, as is symbolised by the magnificence of the Holstentor gate set at the exit through the city walls of the road leading to Hamburg. The town also had considerable political power until the middle of the sixteenth century as the centre of the Hanseatic League, but its seaborne trade and the role of ships and mariners in its success was as important here as in a fishing village like Walberswick or a much smaller town like Southampton. In the Mediterranean, in very different circumstances, are similar conclusions likely?

Venice was a much older settlement than Lübeck, the original inhabitants of the islands in the lagoon being refugees from the Lombard invaders of Italy in the mid-fifth century. By AD 1000 a sea-going nation had coalesced from these small groups of boatmen and traders. Certainly Venice, a city with no walls except the waters of the lagoon, and no parade ground for patriotic display except the Bacino San Marco, was the supreme example of a community whose living came from the sea in one way or another. By 1000 the structure of the city with which we are familiar was visible. Parishes were grouped around their church and an open space or *campo*. They were linked by waterways and bridges to neighbouring parishes and to the centre of the city. Here lay the Piazza San Marco, the Duomo, the Doge's Palace, the Piazzetta, the Bacino San Marco where the larger vessels were at anchor, and the Riva degli Schiavoni where othere were moored. Vessels up to 200 tons capacity could make the journey up the Grand Canal as far as the Rialto, but the majority would deal with their cargo in the Bacino, where the Customs House, on the island of San Giorgio, was nearly opposite the landing stages at the end of the Piazzetta.[62] The resulting scene of large and small vessels at anchor, or moving slowly through the throng, with gondolas, ferries and market boats of all kinds adding to the confusion, is familiar from paintings and engravings of Venice. It would hardly have been possible to pass more than a very short space of time in Venice without entering a boat, whether to move about the city, attend some ceremony, a wedding or a funeral, or perhaps visit the *Terra Firma*, as the lands beyond the lagoon were, revealingly, known. But does this everyday use of small boats equate with the Venetians being a true sea people?

As far as the upper echelons of Venetian society are concerned – the nobles who had the right to sit on the various governing councils of the city, and who held the highest positions in its administration – it seems hard to deny this assertion. Venetian nobles were not wild, romantic sea rovers or inspired navigators or explorers; they were cautious, careful men of business, sober and reserved in many ways, but they did understand the origins of the wealth of the city and of their own families and how this could only be maintained by careful oversight and protection of sea routes and ships. Reading the registers of the council of Rogati for the fourteenth century and the series called Senato Mar for the fifteenth century leaves one in no doubt of the concern for both trading galleys and those engaged in warlike operations. In January 1349, because there was a problem recruiting crews the Senate suggested that the diet on the galleys could be improved. There would be four meals a day, with good quality bread, vegetables every lunchtime and meat on Sundays, Tuesdays and Thursdays. Cheese with vegetables would be offered on other days along with more cheese for supper, served with onions, garlic and sardines. There is no mention of *biscotti*, the usual staple of the galleyman's diet.[63] At the end of the fifteenth century, in May 1493, orders went from Venice to Alvisto Justiniani about how to deal with the corsair Martin de la Zusta, *byscanio*, who was attacking Venetian shipping off Cape Otranto. In June, there was further trouble with pirates near Amalfi, and at the end of the month directions went to Antonio Quirino to negotiate with the rulers of Tunis or Tripoli the return of goods taken off a Venetian bark by a Turkish corsair. There are also many orders concerning the manning of ships, the pay of the crews, their destinations and any repairs needed in the Arsenale.[64]

The way in which the appointed Captain of the galleys on a particular voyage combined the roles of a diplomat, an admiral and merchant, in a manner copied by Florence for its aristocrats in similar positions,[65] is made clear in the instructions set out for the Captain of the galleys for Romania in the same year. The galleys would leave between 1 and 8 August, and those going to Cyprus or Alexandria would take on extra cargo at Modon, Coron or Negroponte as seemed best. Once at Constantinople the Captain was to assess the situation regarding relations with the Genoese and, if recent damage had been done to Venetian interests, demand compensation, by force if necessary. If this was not the case, the galleys could proceed to Tana but should stay there no more than eight days. There were then further instructions regarding the return cargoes. The final order was that 'in omnibus cum omni bona cautela et diligentia procedatur', something which could almost be a motto for Venetian attitudes to both business and politics.[66]

The occupation of positions like this, and service on the various committees of the Republic concerned with the sea and ships, ensured that the nobility of Venice did not lose sight of the importance of the sea in the city's affairs. The fact that many of these positions were in fact only open to members of the nobility served to maintain their prestige even if it cut the Republic off from useful sources of talent. The public life of the Republic also laid great emphasis on the city's connection with the sea. The most striking ceremony was, of course, the doge's symbolic marriage to the sea, which took place on Ascension Day every year. This ceremony dated back to the last years of the tenth century but attained the format of a marriage, with a ring thrown into the water by the doge from his ceremonial barge in front of a large crowd of Venetians, following the visit of the Emperor Frederick Barbarossa and Pope Alexander III to Venice in 1177. At that meeting the pope gave the doge a ring as a sign of Venetian supremacy at sea, a symbol which was then absorbed into the Ascension Day festival.

Other events, such as races between teams of oarsmen (the origins of the regattas of today), had the effect of turning the rivalry between different districts of the city or different trades into a means of promoting the skills of boatmen, vital for the crews of the galleys. The number of Venetian artisans and workmen whose livelihood depended directly or indirectly on maritime activity is impossible to estimate with any accuracy. It was, however, considerable. The *Arsenalotti* have already been mentioned as a distinct group within the population, inhabiting their own quarter and with their own organisation. There were also the employees of other shipyards, building small boats or round ships, ships' crews, boatmen and the fishermen on the lagoon. This was undoubtedly the pre-eminent maritime city of the Middle Ages. Other cities in Italy and elsewhere in the Mediterranean had a similar deep interest in seaborne trade, prime examples being Genoa or Barcelona, but none had quite such a close and general relationship with maritime matters as Venice.

Those whose lives were spent at sea, whether in northern or southern waters, shared certain characteristics. Life at sea had similar dangers and delights in the Channel and in the Adriatic Sea. At the level of the ordinary seaman, there was perhaps little to choose between the life of a mariner on a ship putting out from Southampton and one based in Marseille. There were, however, considerable differences between the prestige and status of the Captains of the galleys, and the masters of individual vessels in the Mediterranean and those in northern waters. In the north, the profession of merchant attracted men of talent and enterprise who could exert considerable power both economically and politically in the right circumstances. The merchant elites of Bruges and Ghent, for example, or the richest citizens of London, were a powerful group in society. Even though much of their wealth came from seaborne trade, they were only intermittently directly concerned about maritime matters, usually at times when the seaways seemed to be particularly at the mercy of pirates or privateers. These men did not themselves go to sea. They might own ships or shares in ships, like William Cannynges of Bristol, but this was largely as a form of investment. In contrast, at Genoa or Venice service at sea was honourable and desirable, being potentially a route to the highest honours in the state. The change in the social prestige of seamen, which became very noticeable in Elizabethan England, was of lasting significance. Men like Richard Grenville and Francis Drake were not only skilled and experienced seamen but also courtiers, welcome at the side of the queen and instruments of her policies. They attained this status because maritime affairs in general, and ocean navigation in particular, had ceased to be of concern only to professionals in the field and had entered the calculations of European rulers anxious to maintain or extend their power and their realm.

7

The New World

Over the course of the medieval period, the design of sailing craft radically improved. Sailing ships became more seaworthy, more stable, able to sail closer to the wind and easier to handle. They required smaller crews, offered much better shelter on board for all those who went to sea in them and more capacious and useful cargo space. The design of the three-masted caravel of the Portuguese in the late fifteenth century offered many opportunities for improvement. In contrast, although the galleys of the great Mediterranean maritime powers were successful and well proven in both trade and war, theirs was a design which had very nearly reached the end of its useful life. Navigation, the essential skill of those who wished to go on lengthy voyages, had become more robust mathematically and scientifically. The experience of an old 'seadog' was still highly useful but by the end of the fifteenth century was no longer enough on its own. The makers of maps and charts, and instruments like magnetic compasses, quadrants and cross-staffs, began to develop greater expertise as the demand for their products increased. The more homely pilot books or rutters likewise improved in quality and reliability and were produced in larger numbers.

Going to sea was still a chancy business. Few hazards on dangerous coasts were marked by buoys or lights; only the most frequented channels or notorious shifting sandbanks were buoyed or had other markers in the shallow water. By the end of the fifteenth century, however, seafaring had become a more organised and professional business than it had been in earlier times. Merchants could still suffer devastating losses on single voyages, yet the calculation of risk by those offering to insure ships and cargoes did not result in unaffordable premiums.

More general speculation about the nature of the world and about the disposition of land masses on its surface had, of course, been indulged in by both philosophers and geographers of the ancient world and intermittently in later periods. There were, however, particular reasons why this kind of speculation gathered pace at the end of the Middle Ages. Perhaps by an interaction between the world of scholars and that of more practical travellers and seafarers, maps which had been devotional objects designed to present an image of the world centred on the Holy City of Jerusalem became more realistic representations in graphic form of the state of knowledge of the world.[1] The maps of the eastern Mediterranean, which accompanied Marino Sanudo's project for a new crusade, were surprisingly accurate being drawn by Petrus Vesconte, the maker of the first dated portalan.[2] The Catalan Atlas is enlivened by pictures of exotic animals and foreign rulers but presents as good a picture of the lands included as was possible at the time.[3] Mapmakers like Andrea Bianco took pains to include as much information as possible about the 'new' islands in the Atlantic: in his 1448 map the Azores as well as the Canaries are shown.[4] He included some mythical islands as well, a fact which perhaps demonstrates not so much that people at this time were unduly credulous but that there was a real hunger for knowledge about the lands and oceans of the world. The truth regarding new-found lands really was no stranger than fiction.

This interest in other lands and other peoples was also fed by a mixture of fictional and factual writing. It should not be forgotten that, in its various versions in Latin, French, English and German, the *Travels of Sir John Mandeville* was one of the most popular books in the fourteenth and fifteenth centuries. Whether it was seen as fantasy or as a factual account of actual travels in some ways hardly matters. It fed into the widespread desire to widen horizons. Given the descriptions of the city of Kinsay (Hanchow), for example, in Marco Polo's book of his travels, who at the time could say that this was more likely to be true than Mandeville's description of Susa, the city of Prester John?[5] It is known that Columbus owned and annotated a copy of Polo's *Travels*, but it is perhaps more significant that this was a very widely distributed book which helped create the belief that there were all manner of unknown or unvisited places in the world. Maps of the known world made before the end of the fifteenth century usually showed an enclosed land mass with Africa extending eastwards across the Indian Ocean, thought of as an inland sea, to join with more land in the east. This had been the usual view of ancient geographers, including Ptolemy, and was a discouraging one for those who saw the sea as a highway to new lands. The early navigators who first reached the Canaries (about 1339–40) Madeira (colonised 1419–20), the Azores (occupied 1427–39) and the Cape Verde islands (reached 1444), and clawed their way painfully south along the coast of Africa, began the process of showing that this was not so. The voyages of Diaz (1488), da Gama (1497–99) and Columbus (1492) completed the process, showing that 'all the seas of the world are one'. The fact that a ship could, in theory, sail to any country in the world which had a sea coast, and then return home, was an immensely liberating idea.[6] The sea, especially the Atlantic Ocean on the western shores of Europe, was no longer the abode of darkness, as it had been to the Arabs of the Maghreb, but a possible highway to untold riches and unknown lands. This realisation did not of course, become widespread in a sudden revelation. It was more a question of gradual absorption, with its implications being slowly internalised by individuals. The closely knit world of familiar routes with familiar ports and coastlines began to look rather dull and confined; English sailors could still find voyaging to Iceland a challenge or find adventure in the Mediterranean but the lure of open waters was becoming greater and greater.

It is easy to romanticise the European navigators who undertook these pioneering voyages, but more useful to assess the physical and mental equipment that was needed before these journeys could be successfully completed. We have already said something about the growing conviction of the possibility of much longer sea journeys than those routinely attempted at the time. This conviction, as well as being rooted in the confirmation of the existence of formerly unknown islands in the Atlantic, was strengthened by the work of several scholarly writers and commentators. The translation of Ptolemy's Geography into Latin from Greek at the beginning of the fifteenth century rekindled a great deal of interest in the whole area among scholars and helped spread his system of the use of coordinates (degrees of latitude and longitude) to fix a position accurately. Another ancient geographical text, that of Strabo, was in circulation in humanist circles from 1423, giving authority to the idea that a large land mass, the Antipodes, must exist on the far side of the world. The letter of Paolo Toscanelli written in 1474 shows how far ideas about the size and spherical nature of the globe and the use of mathematical navigation had spread in erudite circles. He mentions that he has sent to the king of Portugal:

> A chart, made by my hands, wherein your shores are shown, and the islands from which you may begin to make a voyage continually westwards, and the places whereunto you ought to come and how much you must decline from the pole or from the equinoctial line and through how much space you ought to arrive at the places most fertile in all spices and gems.[7]

While ordinary seamen were certainly not aware of writings like this, they did help create an intellectual climate and the existence of an inclination among patrons to take the idea of such a voyage seriously.

We should also remember that, particularly in the Mediterranean, there were men, some of good social standing, who were well educated and had maritime experience. Some of this speculation filtered down into the minds of these men and began to stimulate their imaginations with thoughts of voyages away from familiar routes and destinations. Here there seems to be an important difference between the Venetians and the Genoese, the two principal maritime nations of the south. The Venetians had established a sophisticated and well-organised system of trading galleys on regular routes whose operation was normally extremely profitable. Despite the rougher conditions on the voyage to Flanders, losses from shipwreck were relatively rare, while the better timekeeping and security of the *gallie grosse* offered advantages to merchants, especially those trading in luxury goods. An honourable and profitable career could be made in the service of the Serenissima whether in the trading or the war fleets. Individual adventures were not greatly encouraged.

The Genoese, coming from an organisationally much weaker state, were used to a more individualistic approach to trade and ship-owning. By the fifteenth century galleys were only used for warlike purposes, while carracks carried both bulk and high-value cargoes all over the Mediterranean and to Flanders and England. The Genoese had also established themselves in most of the ports in the western Mediterranean. They had particularly close ties with North African ports through which came basic information regarding Africa south of the Sahara. The Genoese were also involved in some of the earliest exploratory voyages. The fate of the expedition of the Vivaldi brothers, Ugolino and Vadino, who passed through the Straits of Gibraltar in 1291 with the intention of finding a sea route to India, is unknown. One can only presume that at some point on the long journey south they came to grief; perhaps they failed to find water, foundered or were attacked by local people when foraging on land. Lancelotto Malocello, the first known European since Classical times to visit the Canary Islands, is remembered in the name of the island of Lanzarote. He himself was Genoese but on this occasion he was in the service of the Portuguese crown.[8] Catalans and Majorcans also took part in these and other early expeditions, so that it is not fanciful to suggest that in Iberia, among the seamen on the waterfront or attached as courtiers to the households of noblemen, there was a shifting group of men with some experience of navigation and the sea. These men had their own dreams and plans for new voyages or were happy to be involved in those of others.

The only sign of a similar kind of interest further north was at Bristol. A description of the town includes a casual mention of a voyage in the 1480s to the west, said to be in search of the island of Brazil.[9] An even more enigmatic record of an Exchequer inquisition in 1481 records that a Bristol merchant accused of illegal trading defended himself by claiming that he had had shares in two ships which had left Bristol to 'th'intent to search and fynde a certain isle called the isle of Brasil'.[10] It was from this port that John Cabot, one of the few Venetians interested in this kind of matter, set sail in 1497 on the voyage which resulted in the discovery of Newfoundland. Interest in voyages of discovery, if indeed any really existed in Bristol, soon evaporated after the disaster of Cabot's second voyage in 1498, when all the ships were lost. Even the exploitation of the cod fishery on the Grand Banks, which has been suggested as the motivation of the early voyages, was left to Portuguese and French mariners.[11] The initiative for voyages to the west, and southwards along the coast of Africa, lay firmly in the hands of seamen from southern ports until the second or third decade of the sixteenth century.

If the speculations of scholars and the work of mathematicians and astronomers had created the intellectual climate in which an interest in voyages of exploration was respected and understood, had developments in ship design and construction produced vessels which made such voyages practicable? There are many uncertainties in this field which make drawing firm conclusions difficult. Ironically we know most about the design of the class of vessels, the galleys, which had no involvement in these new voyages. Even if the Atlantic is routinely crossed by rowing boats nowadays, this was not a practical route for the *galie grosse*, with their low freeboard, large crews and constant need for supplies. The sailing craft of the late Middle Ages, those seen in the Beauchamp pageant drawings and elsewhere, were well-found ships. Once the Atlantic crossing was shown to be possible, it was not a particularly dangerous voyage. Later in the sixteenth century, when a great many ships were involved on the route from Seville or San Lucar to the Spanish Caribbean ports, wrecks or losses due to adverse weather occurred most frequently off the Spanish coast itself. A calculation of all the losses due to adverse weather conditions on the routes between Seville and the Caribbean in the sixteenth century, including vessels that were sunk and those that ran aground or were wrecked on shore, produced a total of only four between 1515 and 1550 on the outward journey. On the inward journey to Seville nineteen ships were lost in this way. The totals increased in the second half of the century but this was because so many more ships were making the Atlantic crossing.[12] Neither the *Santa Maria* (the best known of Columbus's ships) nor the *Matthew* (Cabot's ship on the 1497 voyage) was a specially designed or modified vessel. They were run-of-the-mill trading sailing ships of the day but fit, as events were to prove, for an Atlantic crossing. The changes in ship design from the somewhat ponderous cogs of northern waters to the more effective caravels of the late fifteenth century occurred probably between 1440 and 1460, a period for which there is, unfortunately, little detailed evidence. What seems to have happened is that the longer and more slender carvel-built hulls of the south were adopted by northern shipbuilders, with a three- or four-masted rig becoming the norm. The result was a ship which could sail much closer to the wind than earlier northern vessels; not unduly affected by leeway, it could also cope well with heavy seas. It needed a smaller crew than earlier ships but had enough capacity in the hull to carry a profitable cargo.

A further advantage of this design and its later adaptations was that it could be developed into an effective and manoeuvrable gun-platform. In the Beauchamp Pageant pictures the cannon are placed on deck firing over the rail. This solution of the problem of where to locate guns must have had disadvantages, not least in that the recoil of the gun would have sent it crashing into other vital equipment located on deck. The development of gun decks and gun ports in the early sixteenth century opened the way to the ability to fire a broadside with all that this meant for the development of naval tactics in battle. In galleys, the main guns were fixed firmly on the fore deck so that the whole vessel had to alter course for them to be aimed. The large crew needed to perform this kind of manoeuvre were also extremely vulnerable to the weapons of the enemy, with very little shelter from gunfire or other missiles.

If a contemporary had been asked in the late 1490s which was the leading maritime nation of Europe, and which nation showed the most understanding of the sea and its ways and was most able to profit from its exploitation, he or she might have pointed to Venice, as pre-eminent in seaborne trade and successful in keeping its colonies bound to the motherland by the strength and organisation of its galley fleets. The result of the battle of Zonchio, with the consequent loss of important Venetian colonies on the coast of the Morea, perhaps demonstrated the growing weakness of Venice and the importance of the emergence of the Ottomans as a sea as well as a land power.[13] The impact of the results of Columbus's first voyage was also still largely confined to the Spanish court at this date. Within ten years, however, the answer would have been different. Either Spain or Portugal would by this time have been seen as leading the way in maritime affairs. The development of Spanish knowledge of the new world in the Americas and the rapid settlement of Spanish colonies in the Caribbean was now common knowledge. The direct Portuguese route to the East, especially India, promised access to immense wealth. All this directed attention to these two kingdoms bordering on the Atlantic, away from those nations now seen as confined within the Mediterranean. The day of the more northern states, particularly England and the Low Countries, as pioneers, adventurers and dominators of the sea was, however, yet to come. It is notable that sixteenth-century English literature is not full of those images of the sea that are such a feature of Anglo-Saxon and Norse writing. Little, in fact, was published with a

nautical content in England until the very end of the century, when
Richard Hakluyt's *Principal Navigation, Voiages, Traffiques and
Discoveries of the English Nation* brought to wider attention the
achievements of the mariners of past years.[14] The glorification of
activity at sea – which was a result of the war against Spain, the
exploits of Drake and the defeat of the Armada – was a new thing.
The only previous victory at sea which had been treated as a national
triumph was the battle of Sluys over two hundred years before. In the
same way Dutch maritime domination, like the very existence of a
Dutch nation, lay in the future.

In 1500, Iberia was the home of the most skilled navigators and
mariners, and those most influenced by new ways of thinking in
Europe. The idea of the open seas, stretching around the globe, was
stimulating and exciting. Those states with an Atlantic seaboard
would be the greatest beneficiaries of this idea, but, as the sixteenth
century began, those in the south-west corner of Europe seemed
poised to take most advantage of this great opportunity.

Notes

Chapter 1

1 All quotations from the Exeter Book poem, *The Seafarer*, are from E. Treharne, ed., *Old and Middle English, c. 890–1400: An Anthology* (Oxford, 2000), pp. 17–23.

2 *Beowulf*, trans. K. Crossley-Holland (London, 1973), p. 20.

3 *Beowulf*, pp. 78–79.

4 A. F. Scott, ed., *The Saxon Age: Commentaries of an Era* (London, 1979), p. 69.

5 H. T. M. Buckhurst, 'Terms and Phrases for the Sea in Old English Poetry', in K. Malone and M. B. Rund, eds, *Studies in English Philology* (Minneapolis, 1929), pp. 104–15.

6 Buckhurst, 'Terms and Phrases for the Sea', p. 117.

7 J. Jesch, *Ships and Men in the Late Viking Age: The Vocabulary of Runic Inscriptions and Skaldic Verses* (Woodbridge, 2001).

8 C. Villain-Gandossi, 'La mer et la navigation maritime à travers quelques textes de la littérature française du XIIe au XIVe siècle', in *La Mediterranée aux XIIe–XVIe siècles* (London, 1983), pp. 181–87.

9 Villain-Gandossi, 'La mer et la navigation maritime', p. 157.

10 A. Navarro Gonzales, *El Mar en la literatura medieval castellana* (La Laguna, 1962), pp. 478–80.

11 C. Hillenbrand, *The Crusades: Islamic Perspectives* (Edinburgh, 1999), p. 557.

12 C. Picard, *L'Océan Atlantique musulman: de la conquête arabe à l'épopée almohade: navigation et mise en valeur des côtes d'al-Andalus et du Maghreb occidental* (Paris, 1997), p. 31.

13 Hillenbrand, *The Crusades*, p. 559.

14 T. Carmi, ed. and trans., *The Penguin Book of Hebrew Verse* (London, 1981), pp. 349–50.

15 *The Depositional and Landscape Histories of Dungeness Foreland and the Port of Rye: Understanding Past Environments and Coastal Change* (London, n.d.), p. 5.

16 I. Pomian, 'Water or Land?', in *Down the River to the Sea*, ed. J. Litwin (Gdansk, 1997), p. 35.

17 A. M. Lambert, *The Making of the Dutch Landscape: An Historical Geography of the Netherlands* (London and New York, 1971), p. 86.

18 S. Rose, 'Shipping in Southampton in the Fifteenth Century', *Hampshire Studies*, 61, 2006, pp. 174–81.

19 P. Dollinger, *La Hanse, XIIe–XVIIe siècles* (Paris, 1964), p. 182.

20 J. H. Pryor, *Geography, Technology and War* (Cambridge, 1988), p. 20.

21 P. Horden and N. Purcell, *The Corrupting Sea: A Study of Mediterranean History* (Oxford, 2000), p. 139.

22 B. Sandahl, *Middle English Sea Terms*, ii, *Masts Spars and Sails* (Uppsala, 1958), entry for 'mizzen', pp. 73–78. Jal is quoted on p. 76.

23 Sandahl, *Middle English Sea Terms*, iii, *Standing and Running Rigging*, pp. 3–4.

24 H. and R. Kahane, *The Lingua Franca in the Levant: Turkish Nautical Terms of Italian and Greek Origin* (Urbana, Illinois, 1958), pp. 7, 152, 801, 826, 868.

Chapter 2

 1 I. Friel, *The Good Ship: Ships, Shipbuilding and Technology in England, 1200–1520* (London, 1995), p. 39.

 2 Even at the end of our period there are gaps in the evidence; the earliest shipbuilding plans and manuals exist for ships built under Venetian auspices in the fifteenth century. There is nothing similar in the north.

 3 J. Bernard, *Navires et gens de mer à Bordeaux vers 1400 à vers 1550* (Paris, 1968), i, p. 240.

 4 Both images can be found in Friel, *The Good Ship*, plates 4.5 and 1.5.

 5 L. R. Martin, *The Art and Archaeology of Venetian Ships and Boats* (London, 2001).

 6 Martin, *The Art and Archaeology of Venetian Ships and Boats*, p. 114.

 7 Expeditions have tended to concentrate more on warm, clear Mediterranean waters than the somewhat murky and chilly Channel and North Sea.

 8 G. Hutchinson, *Medieval Ships and Shipbuilding* (London, 1994), p. 16.

 9 Hutchinson, *Medieval Ships and Shipbuilding*, p. 19.

10 J. H. Pryor, 'The Naval Architecture of Crusader Transport Ships: part 1', *Mariner's Mirror*, 70 (1984), p. 175.

11 Martin, *The Art and Archaeology of Venetian Ships and Boats*, pp. 148–57.

12 The Dibner Institute which organised the conference has now transferred its library to the Huntington Library at Pasadena. The publication of a facsimile edition of the whole text is forthcoming as P. O. Long, D. McGee and A. M. Stahl, eds, *The Book of Michael of Rhodes: A fifteenth century maritime manuscript* (MIT Press, Cambridge, MA).

13 This MS is fully discussed and partially translated in R. C. Anderson, 'Italian Naval Architecture about 1445', *Mariner's Mirror*, 11 (1925).

14 Anderson, 'Italian Naval Architecture', p. 163.

15 This manuscript is held in the Pepys Library at Magdalene College,

Cambridge. The Ark illustration is Pepys MS 2820, p. 1.

16 This material is in the National Archives, PRO, Kew; in the pipe roll series until the reign of Richard II and then in the series of foreign accounts of the lord treasurer's remembrancer to the 1450s. The records from the reign of Henry VII are in the series of Exchequer Accounts Various and have been published in M. Oppenheim, *Naval Accounts and Inventories of the Reign of Henry VII, 1485–8 and 1495–7* (London, 1896). Some accounts for the reign of Henry VI are in S. Rose, ed., *The Navy of the Lancastrian Kings* (London, 1982).

17 These records have been published in A. Merlin-Chazelas, *Documents rélatifs au clos des galées de Rouen*, 2 vols (Paris, 1977–78), and in Charles Bréard, ed., 'Le compte du clos des galées de Rouen au XIVe siècle, 1382–1384', in Blanquart et al., eds, *Documents, Deuxième série* (Rouen, 1893).

18 Hutchinson, *Medieval Ships and Shipbuilding*, p. 8.

19 I. Bill, 'Ships and Seamanship', in P. Sawyer, ed., *The Oxford Illustrated History of the Vikings* (Oxford, 1997), p. 194.

20 S. McGrail, *Ancient Boats in North-West Europe: The Archaeology of Water Transport to AD 1500* (London, 1998), has a full discussion of the techniques used in wooden ship building in chapter 8. See p. 100 for an illustration of a boat ell.

21 R. W. Unger, *The Ship in the Medieval Economy* (London, 1980), pp. 83–94, gives a full description of Viking ships.

22 Frame 37 and 38 in the Folio Society edition. Lewis Thorpe, ed., *The Bayeux Tapestry and the Norman Invasion* (London, 1973).

23 McGrail, *Ancient Boats*, p. 150.

24 Hutchinson, *Medieval Ships and Shipbuilding*, pp. 10–11.

25 D. Burwash, *English Merchant Shipping, 1460–1540* (Newton Abbot, 1969), pp. 192–93.

26 P. Spufford, *Power and Profit: The Merchant in Medieval Europe* (London, 2002), p. 398.

27 Hutchinson, *Medieval Ships and Shipbuilding*, p. 16.

28 Unger, *The Ship in the Medieval Economy*, p. 164.

29 Hutchinson, *Medieval Ships and Shipbuilding*, p. 44.

30 R. Clarke et al., 'Recent Work on the River Hamble Wreck near Bursledon, Hampshire', *International Journal of Nautical Archaeology*, 22 (1993), pp. 21–44.

31 A. Sinclair, ed., *The Beauchamp Pageant* (Donnington, 2003), p. 122, plate 36 (fol. 8v).

32 A. Crawford, ed., *The Household Books of John Howard*, i (Stroud, 1992), p. 489.

33 C. S. Knighton and D. M. Loades, eds, *The Anthony Roll* (London, 2000), pp. 73, 93–106.

34 This is the explanation put forward in *OED* linking the word to the Old

French *baleinier*, a whaling ship.

35 D. McWhannell, 'Campbell of Breadalbane and Campbell of Argyll Boat-building Accounts, 1600–1700', *Mariner's Mirror*, 89 (2003).

36 W. Sayers, 'Fourteenth-Century English Balingers: Whence the Name?', *Mariner's Mirror* (2006).

37 J. B. Hattendorf et al., eds, *British Naval Documents, 1204–1960* (Aldershot, 1993), pp. 43–44.

38 S. Rose, ed., *The Navy of the Lancastrian Kings* (London, 1982), pp. 250–51.

39 Hattendorf et al., eds, *British Naval Documents, 1204–1960*, p. 13.

40 Rose, *The Navy of the Lancastrian Kings*, p. 49.

41 It is hoped that further investigations of the wreck will produce more details of her construction.

42 M. L'Hour and E. Veyrat, 'A Mid-Fifteenth Century Clinker Boat off the North Coast of France, the Aber Wrac'h I Wreck: A Preliminary Report', *International Journal of Nautical Archaeology and Underwater Exploration*, 18 (1989), pp. 285–98.

43 The best source for details of the Newport ship is the web site: full details of her construction are not yet available but it seems that she was a 'shell first' clinker-built vessel, http://www.thenewportship.com.

44 J. H. Pryor, 'From Dromon to Galea: Mediterranean Bireme Galleys AD 500–1300', in R. Gardiner, ed., *The Age of the Galley: Mediterranean Oared Vessels since Pre-classical Times* (London, 1995), p. 110.

45 N. Fourquin, 'Galères du moyen âge', in *Quand voguaient les galères* (Paris, 1990), pp. 67–68.

46 Pryor, 'From Dromon to Galea', pp. 110–11.

47 Pryor, 'From Dromon to Galea', p. 112.

48 Pryor, 'From Dromon to Galea', pp. 115–16.

49 Fourquin, 'Galères du moyen âge', p. 73, gives the date of 6 August 1290 for the first occurrence of this innovation, but it seems more likely that it spread in the first half of the fourteenth century to all the galley fleets in the Mediterranean.

50 The mechanics of rowing in medieval galleys is discussed in detail in 'Oar Mechanics and Oar Power in Medieval and Later Galleys', by M. Bondioli, R. Burlet and A. Aysberg in Gardiner, *The Age of the Galley*, pp. 172–205.

51 http://www.diveturkey.com/inaturkey/serce/hull.htm visited on 15/11/04. Article 'Reconstructing the Hull', by J. R. Steffy. The design process has been described as an 'early example of modern forms of naval architecture where simple geometric projections are used to predetermine the rising of the bottom and narrowing of the hull sides'.

52 U. Alertz, 'The Naval Architecture and Oar Systems of Medieval and Later Galleys', in Gardiner, *The Age of the Galley*, p. 144. Alertz points out that this system would strike a modern shipbuilder as ideal for computer aided design.

53 Alertz, 'The Naval Architecture and Oar Systems', pp. 145–46.

54 Alertz, 'The Naval Architecture and Oar Systems', pp. 157–58.

55 The most detailed study of Mediterranean round ships is that by John Pryor in a series of articles in *Mariner's Mirror* for 1984. Pryor also discusses Mediterranean round ships in his chapter of that name in R. Gardiner, ed., *Cogs, Caravels and Galleons* (London, 1994), pp. 59–76.

56 J. H. Pryor, 'The Naval Architecture of Crusader Transport Ships; Part II', *Mariner's Mirror*, 70 (1984), p. 279.

57 The model is now in the Maritime Museum in Rotterdam. It came originally from Mataro near Barcelona.

58 The towns were Bristol, Newcastle upon Tyne, Southampton, Ipswich and Gosford, London, Dunwich and Orford, Winchelsea, Yarmouth, Grimsby, Ravenser and Hull, Lyme and Weymouth, Lynn, Romney and Hythe, Shoreham and Seaford, Dartmouth and Plymouth, Sandwich and Dover, York, and Scarborough. Only eight were, as far as we know, built.

59 R. J. Whitwell and C. Johnson, 'The Newcastle Galley, AD 1294', *Archaeologia Aeliana*, fourth series (1926), pp. 150–51.

60 C. Johnson, 'London Shipbuilding, AD 1295', *Antiquaries Journal* (1927), p. 427.

61 Rose, *The Navy of the Lancastrian Kings*, p. 39.

62 L. A. Burgess, ed., *The Southampton Terrier of 1454* (London, 1976), p. 85.

63 N. A. M. Rodger, *The Safeguard of the Sea* (London, 1997), p. 71.

64 Merlin-Chazelas, *Clos des galées de Rouen*.

65 F. C. Lane, *Venice, A Maritime Republic* (Baltimore, Maryland and London, 1973), pp. 163–64.

66 Rose, *The Navy of the Lancastrian Kings*, p. 101.

67 A. Merlin-Chazelas, *Clos des Galées de Rouen*, p. 183.

68 S. Rose, 'The Bayonne Galleys', in M. Duffy, ed., *The Naval Miscellany* (Aldershot, 2003), p. 28.

69 Rose, *The Navy of the Lancastrian Kings*, p. 31.

70 Rose, *The Navy of the Lancastrian Kings*, p. 202.

71 A. Tenenti and U. Tucci, eds, *Storia di Venezia: temi. Il mare* (Rome, 1991).

72 Lane, *Venice*, p. 318.

Chapter 3

1 G. J. Marcus, *The Conquest of the North Atlantic* (Woodbridge, 1980), p. 102.

2 E. G. R. Taylor, *The Haven-Finding Art: A History of Navigation from Odysseus to Captain Cook* (London, 1956), p. 9.

3 Taylor, *The Haven-Finding Art*, pp. 43–44.

4 This is a genealogical work setting out the stories of the first settlers in Iceland written originally by Ari Thorgilsson the Learned, probably in the early twelfth century.

5 Marcus, *The Conquest of the North Atlantic*, pp. 55–56.

6 S. McGrail, *Ancient Boats in North-West Europe: The Archaeology of Water Transport to AD 1500* (London, 1998), p. 266.

7 Marcus, *The Conquest of the North Atlantic*, p. 104.

8 This translation of the *Flateyarbok* comes from C. L. Vebaek and S. Thirslund, *The Viking Compass: Guided Norsemen First to America* (1992), p. 11.

9 B. E. Gelsinger, 'Lodestone and Sunstone in Medieval Iceland', *Mariner's Mirror*, 56 (1970), p. 222.

10 G. J. Marcus, 'The Navigation of the Norsemen', *Mariner's Mirror*, 39 (1953), pp. 112–31, argues strongly for the use of a form of latitude sailing by the Norsemen. The *Landnamabók* and the *Hauksbók* have been edited by G. Jónsson (Copenhagen, 1900, and 1892).

11 McGrail, *Ancient Boats*, p. 284.

12 G. Chaucer, *The General Prologue to the Canterbury Tales*, lines 401–10.

13 Chaucer was writing *The Treatise of the Astrolabe* at the same time as finishing the *Canterbury Tales*.

14 Taylor, *The Haven-Finding Art*, p. 95.

15 A. D. Aczel, *The Riddle of the Compass* (New York, 2001), pp. 30–31.

16 Aczel, *The Riddle of the Compass*, p. 36.

17 A. Moore, 'Accounts and Inventories of John Starlyng', *Mariner's Mirror*, 4 (1914), p. 168.

18 G. P. B. Naish, 'The 'Dyoll' and the Bearing-Dial', *Journal of the Institute of Navigation*, 7 (1954), pp. 205–7.

19 S. Rose, ed., *The Navy of the Lancastrian Kings: Accounts and Inventories of William Soper, Keeper of the King's Ships, 1422–7* (London, 1982), pp. 136, 157, 163, 164, 169, 173, 177, 192, 206.

20 Sir G. Warner, ed., *The Libelle of Englyshe Polycye* (Oxford, 1926), p. 41. The mention of a 'stone' may be more for poetic reasons than to indicate that the most primitive form of direction-finding device is meant.

21 G. L. Marcus, 'The Mariner's Compass: Its Influence upon Navigation in the Later Middle Ages', *History*, 41 (1956), p. 21.

22 All the material on these manuscripts comes from R. Ward, 'The Earliest Known Sailing Directions in English', *Deutsches Shiffahrtsarchiv* 27: 2004, pp. 49–90. Dr Ward includes a full transcription of the Hastings MS version of this rutter in appendix 1 of the article. This is section 7; the modernisation of language and spelling is my own. *Stepilhord* has not been identified but is probably a hill on the north Somerset coast.

23 C. O. Frake, 'Cognitive Maps of Time and Tide among Medieval Seafarers', *Mind*, new series, 20 (1985), pp. 254–70, discusses this issue in detail.

24 Taylor, *The Haven-Finding Art*, p. 132.

25 Ward, 'The Earliest Known Sailing Directions in English', Appendix 1, p. 83. The modernisation of the text is my own.

26 Tidal currents are mentioned, however, in directions for voyages in the Arabian Sea.

27 Taylor, *The Haven-Finding Art*, pp. 49–53.

28 Taylor, *The Haven-Finding Art*, p. 59.

29 P. G. Dalché, *Carte Marine et Portulan au XIIe siècle* (Rome, 1995), pp. 21, 103, 166. No unit of distance is given.

30 B. R. Motzo, ed., *Il Compasso da Navigare* (Cagliari, 1947), p. 112.

31 Taylor, *The Haven-Finding Art*, pp. 107–8.

32 R. Ward, 'The Mystery of the Medieval Shipmaster: The English Shipmaster at Law in Business and at Sea between the Mid-Fourteenth and Mid-Fifteenth Centuries' (London, unpublished PhD, 2000), p. 128.

33 Taylor, *The Haven-Finding Art*, pp. 117–21.

34 J. R. S. Phillips, *The Medieval Expansion of Europe* (Oxford, 1998), pp. 149, 207–8.

35 Phillips, *The Medieval Expansion of Europe*, p. 208.

36 A new Christian and master of nautical chart making (Ribes). From Genoa, a painter of nautical charts (Becaria). R. A. Skelton, 'A Contract for World Maps at Barcelona, 1399–1400', *Imago Mundi*, 22 (1968), p. 107.

37 J. Evans, ed. and trans., *The Unconquered Knight: A Chronicle of the Deeds of Don Pedro Niño, Count of Buelna by his Standard-Bearer Gutierre de Gamez* (London, 1928), pp. 97–98. The translation has been slightly adapted.

38 I am grateful to Robin Ward for this suggestion.

39 Taylor, *The Haven-Finding Art*, p. 159.

40 Taylor, *The Haven-Finding Art*, p. 166.

41 Quoted in S. Rose, 'Mathematics and the Art of Navigation: The Advance of Scientific Seamanship in Elizabethan England', *Transactions of the Royal Historical Society* (2004), p. 176. The 'cardes and plattes' referred to are charts; the 'boord' is a traverse board, on which a compass rose was drawn, the points of which could be linked by pegs and cords to a series of pegholes at the bottom of the board. It allowed a record to be kept of the time sailed on each rhumb of the wind.

42 Taylor, *The Haven-Finding Art*, p. 194.

43 Quoted from the *Mu'allim* in Taylor, *The Haven-Finding Art*, p. 85.

44 F. C. Lane, 'The Economic Meaning of the Invention of the Compass', *American Historical Review*, 68 (1963), pp. 606–13.

Chapter 4

1 Aelfric later became abbot of Eynsham and wrote a series of over eighty homilies, some of the most important surviving Anglo-Saxon prose works.

2 A. F. Scott, *The Saxon Age: Commentaries of an Era* (London, 1979), p. 87.

3 Scott, *The Saxon Age*, p. 142.

4 J. L. Bolton, *The Medieval English Economy, 1150–1500* (London, 1980), pp. 194–201, 290–94. A full discussion of all aspects of the English trade in raw wool can be found in E. Power, *The Wool Trade in English Medieval History* (Oxford, 1941), and T. H. Lloyd, *The English Wool Trade in the Middle Ages* (Cambridge, 1977).

5 The originals of the papers can be found in TNA, PRO Ancient Correspondence SC1/53 and 59, and in Chancery Miscellanea C47/37, files 10–16. A selection was first printed in 1900, edited by H. E. Malden (Camden Society, third series, 1). The modern edition of the letters is *The Cely Letters 1472–88*, ed. A. Hanham, Early English Text Society, 273 (Oxford, 1975).

6 'Cots' or wool from the Cotswolds was the most commonly bought and sold; finer wool came from Herefordshire (Leominsters) or Shropshire (March wool). All wools were graded as good, middle, good young or middle young. Dirty wool from the hindquarters of sheep was known as 'clift wool' and kept separate from the rest.

7 Hanham, *The Cely Letters*, no. 132, p. 119.

8 A. Hanham, *The Celys and their World: An English Merchant Family of the Fifteenth Century* (Cambridge, 1985), p. 130.

9 Hanham, *The Celys and their World*, p. 367.

10 A. R. Myers, ed., *English Historical Documents*, iv, *1327–1485* (London, 1969), p. 1028.

11 Hanham, *The Celys and their World*, p. 129.

12 Hanham, *The Cely Letters*, no. 234, p. 233–34.

13 The Johnson letters have been transcribed in an unpublished London PhD thesis, B. Winchester, 'The Johnson Letters, 1542–1552' (1953). Much of their content was summarised in B. Winchester, *Tudor Family Portrait* (London, 1955).

14 Hanham, *The Celys and their World*, chapter 7, 'Monetary Matters', discusses the finances of the wool trade in detail. The example transaction can be found on p. 179.

15 M. K. James, *Studies in the Medieval Wine Trade* (Oxford, 1971), pp. 121–22.

16 TNA, PRO E364/54, Catton's account for 1413–16; foreign receipts section.

17 Southampton City Record Office port books for 1469–70 and 1494–95.

18 The figures on which the chart is based come from James, *Studies in the Medieval Wine Trade*, appendix 16, pp. 107–16.

19 E. M. Carus-Wilson, 'The Overseas Trade of Bristol in the Fifteenth Century', in *Medieval Merchant Venturers* (London, 1967), pp. 4–9.

20 Carus-Wilson, 'The Overseas Trade of Bristol', pp. 84–90.

21 Hanham, *The Celys and their World*, pp. 361–97. This chapter includes detailed extracts from the accounts of the *Margaret Cely*.

22 W. R. Childs, *Anglo-Castilian Trade in the Later Middle Ages* (Manchester, 1978), p. 110.

23 E. M. Carus-Wilson, 'The Iceland Venture', in *Medieval Merchant Venturers*, p. 108.

24 This reference has been used to argue that English sailors still used a very primitive form of compass with a needle magnetised by rubbing it on a lodestone. A compass with a wind rose enclosed in a binnacle was known at this date in England and the reference is probably no more than poetic licence.

25 W. R. Childs, 'England's Iceland Trade in the Fifteenth Century: The Role of the Port of Hull', *Northern Seas Yearbook*, 5 (1995), p. 22.

26 P. Dollinger, *La Hanse (XII–XVII siècles)* (Paris, 1964), pp. 211–12.

27 R. Hammel-Kiesow, 'Lübeck and the Baltic Trade in Bulk Goods for the North Sea Region, 1150–1400', in L. Berggren, N. Hybel and A. Landen, eds, *Cogs, Cargoes and Commerce: Maritime Bulk Trade in Northern Europe, 1150–1400* (Toronto, 2002), pp. 54–55. The cog excavated at Bremen is described above, pp. 21–22.

28 J. W. Tonkin, 'Two Hanseatic Houses in the Shetlands', *Hansische Geschichtsblatter*, 93–95 (1975–77), pp. 81–82 (1976).

29 Carus-Wilson, 'The Iceland Venture', p. 108.

30 Dollinger, *La Hanse*, p. 179.

31 These figures come from P. Spufford, 'The Relative Scale of Medieval Hanseatic Trade', *Hansische Studien XII* (Trier, 2002), pp. 153–61.

32 S. D. Goitein, *A Mediterranean Society* (Berkeley and London, 1967 and 1999), i, pp. 44–46.

33 A. O. Citarella, 'A Puzzling Question Concerning the Relations between the Jewish Communities of Christian Europe and Those Represented in the Geniza Documents', *Journal of the American Oriental Society*, 91 (1971), pp. 390–97.

34 Goitein, *A Mediterranean Society*, p. 153.

35 Goitein, *A Mediterranean Society*, p. 296.

36 Goitein, *A Mediterranean Society*, p. 303.

37 Goitein, *A Mediterranean Society*, pp. 320–21.

38 Goitein, *A Mediterranean Society*, p. 322.

39 Goitein, *A Mediterranean Society*, pp. 332–46, which discusses the question of shipping and packing costs in detail.

40 P. Spufford, *The Merchant in Medieval Europe* (London, 2002), p. 133.

41 I. Origo, *The Merchant of Prato* (London, 1963), p. 89.

42 See above, chapter 3, for the contracts for the maps. Origo, *The Merchant of Prato*, p. 92.

43 F. C. Lane, 'Venetian Merchant Galleys, 1300–1334: Private and Communal Operation', *Speculum*, 38 (1963), p. 194.

44 Lane, 'Venetian Merchant Galleys', p. 180.

45 ASV Senato Misti, *Regeste 1349–1354*, fos 108v–109v.

46 In A. Tenenti and C. Vivanti, 'Le film d'un grand système de navigation: les galères marchandes vénitiennes XIV–XVe siècles', *Annales E.S.C.*, 16 (1961), a complete list of all recorded Venetian galley voyages is illustrated with dated maps of the routes followed.

47 ASV Senato Mar, registro 9 1469–70, fol. 36v et seq.

48 H. S. Cobb, *The Local Port Book of Southampton for 1439–40* (Southampton, 1961), pp. 77–82.

49 J. Sottas, *Les messageries maritimes de Venise aux XIVe et XVe siècles* (Paris, 1938), p. 95.

50 F. C. Lane, 'Diet and Wages of Seamen in the Early Fourteenth Century', in *Venice and History: The Collected Papers of F.C. Lane* (Baltimore, 1966), pp. 263–68.

51 Sottas, *Les messageries maritimes*, pp. 90–94.

52 Sottas, *Les messageries maritimes*, pp. 120–23.

53 H. G. Rawlinson, 'The Flanders Galleys: Some Notes on Seaborne Trade between Venice and England, 1327–1532 AD', *Mariner's Mirror*, 12 (1926), pp. 148–49.

54 B. Doumerc, 'La crise structurelle de la marine Vénitienne au XV siècle: le problème des *Mude*', *Annales E.S.C.*, 40 (1985), pp. 605–20.

55 Sottas, *Les messageries maritimes*, pp. 99–102.

56 S. Epstein, *Genoa and the Genoese, 958–1528* (Chapel Hill and London, 1996), pp. 22–23.

57 R. S. Lopez has pointed out that there are thousands of documents concerning Genoese trade with Majorca alone, dating from the second half of the thirteenth century. 'Majorcans and Genoese on the North Sea Route in the Thirteenth Century', *Revue Belge de Philologie et d'Histoire*, 29 (1951), p. 1175.

58 R. Doehaerd, 'Les Galères gènoises dans la Manche et la Mer du Nord à la fin du XIIe siècle et au debut du XIVe', *Bulletin de l'Institut Belge de Rome*, 19 (1938), pp. 33–35.

59 E. H. Byrne, *Genoese Shipping in the Twelfth and Thirteenth Centuries* (Cambridge, Massachusetts, 1930), pp. 24–25.

60 Byrne, *Genoese Shipping in the Twelfth and Thirteenth Centuries*, pp. 29–42.

61 Byrne, *Genoese Shipping in the Twelfth and Thirteenth Centuries*, pp. 134–39

62 B. Foster, *The Local Port Book of Southampton for 1435–6* (Southampton, 1963), pp. 92–119. The references to the elephant tooth and the golden clasp are on p. 95 and p. 103.

63 Epstein, *Genoa and the Genoese, 958–1528*, pp. 150–66, 193–230. Tables on pp. 97, 142 and 231 show how the main foci of Genoese overseas trade shifted between 1191 and 1376. In 1376 the most important sources of goods imported by Genoese merchants were Alexandria, Spain, Flanders and Provence. Only 0.2 per cent came from Chios by this date.

64 G. Forcheri, ed., *Nave navigazione a Genova nel trecento: il libro Gazarie* (Genoa, 1974), prints the text of this important work. Aspects of the regulations are discussed in J. E. Dotson, 'Safety Regulations for Galleys in Mid-Fourteenth Century Genoa: Some Thoughts on Medieval Risk Management', *Journal of Medieval History*, 20 (1994), pp. 327–36.

65 J. H. Pryor, *The Voyage of Jacques de Vitry from Genoa to Acre 1216: Juridical and Economic Problems in Medieval Navigation* (Madrid, 1988).

66 The details of this voyage will be found in M. Jones, 'Le voyage de Pierre de Lesnac en Navarre, 1386', *Mémoires de la Société d'Histoire et d'Archéologie de Bretagne*, 61 (1984), pp. 81–99.

67 TNA, PRO, Accounts Various E101/44/12, particulars of account of John Elmeton, clerk of the king's ships.

68 L. T. Smith, *Expeditions to Prussia and the Holy Land Made by Henry, Earl of Derby, Afterwards Henry IV in 1390–1 and 1392–3* (London, 1894), pp. 36–37, 157.

69 'The Diary of Felice di Michele Brancacci Going to Cairo as Ambassador to the Sultan', *Archivio Storico Italiano*, 4th series, VII (1881), pp. 160–88.

70 Henry of Lancaster, the future Henry IV of England, made arrangements like this in Venice in 1392–93 for his pilgrimage to the Holy Land at a cost of £5,000. The Beauchamp Pageant, an illustrated roll which includes the story of Richard Beauchamp, earl of Warwick's pilgrimage to Jerusalem in 1408–9 has little information about his journeys by sea, except for some detailed and accurate pictures of sailing ships *c.* 1480, the probable date of the creation of the Pageant. For good modern reproductions see A. Sinclair, ed., *The Beauchamp Pageant* (Donington, 2003).

71 'The Pilgrimage of William Wey', in D. Englander, D. Normand et al., eds, *Culture and Belief in Europe, 1450–1600: An Anthology of Sources* (Oxford, 1990), pp. 18–20.

72 Margery Kemp, a visionary and mystic from King's Lynn, dictated her memoirs to a priest at the beginning of the fifteenth century. Her incessant weeping made her a trying travelling companion. Her journey to Compostela is *The Book of Margery Kemp*, ii, pt 2, lines 2586–603, http://lib.rochester.edu/camelot/teams/kemptxt2.htm.

73 F. J. Furnivall, ed., *The Stacions of Rome and the Pilgrim's Sea Voyage* (EETS, London, 1867). The original manuscript is at Trinity College Cambridge.

74 The pilgrimage of 1458 is fully described in R. J. Mitchell, *The Spring Voyage: The Jerusalem Pilgrimage in 1458* (London, 1964). Sanseverino's *Viaggio in Terra Santa* has been edited by G. Maruffi (Bologna, 1888), and M. Cavaglia (Alessandria, 1999). S. Brasca has edited Capodilista's work (Milan, 1966). Wey's *Itineraries* have been edited by G. Williams (Roxburghe Club, London, 1857).

75 From the opening of the Wanderings; quoted and translated in H. F. M. Prescott, *Jerusalem Journey* (London, 1954), p. 14. The complete text can be found in *Evagatorium in Terra Sancta Arabiae et Egypti peregrinationem*, ed. C. D. Hassler (Stuttgart, 1843).

76 M. C. Seymour, ed., *Mandeville's Travels* (Oxford, 1967). The foot was so large it could act like a sunshade when lying down. The gravelly sea ebbed and flowed like water and was full of fish, even though there was not a drop of water present.

77 *The Book of Margery Kemp*, lines 1530–47.

78 Prescott, *Jerusalem Journey*, p. 59.

79 Mitchell, *The Spring Voyage*, p. 51.

80 A mass without wine or a host; this was for fear of accidents with the consecrated elements.

81 Prescott, *Jerusalem Journey*, pp. 59–62.

82 Mitchell, *The Spring Voyage*, p. 63.

83 D. James-Rauol, 'La mer Mediterranée dans les récits de pèlinerages et les récits de croisades', in H. Akkari, ed., *La Mediterranée Médiévale* (Paris, 2002), p. 73

84 James-Rauol, 'La mer Mediterranée', p. 78. The translation from French is mine.

85 Prescott, *Jerusalem Journey*, p. 68.

86 Mitchell, *The Spring Voyage*, pp. 70, 168.

Chapter 5

1 Admiral Mahan's book, *The Influence of Sea Power on History, 1660–1783* (London, 1889), has influenced the thinking of all later historians on these matters.

2 R. I. Burns, 'Piracy as an Islamic–Christian Interface in the Thirteenth Century', *Viator*, 11 (1980), pp. 165–66.

3 E. Monsen, ed., *Heimskringla: or The Lives of the Norse Kings by Snorre Sturlason* (Cambridge, 1932).

4 *Heimskringla*, p. 55.

5 *Heimskringla*, p. 145.

6 *Heimskringla*, pp. 496–97.

7 G. N. Garmonsway, ed. and trans., *The Anglo-Saxon Chronicle* (London, 1972), p. 63.

8 *The Anglo-Saxon Chronicle*, p. 108.

9 *The Anglo-Saxon Chronicle*, pp. 90–91.

10 *The Anglo-Saxon Chronicle*, p. 199.

11 J. Fortescue, ed. S. Lockwood, *On the Laws and Governance of England* (Cambridge, 1997), p. 89.

12 J. B. Hattendorf et al., eds, *British Naval Documents, 1204–1960* (Aldershot, 1993), pp. 42–43.

13 Details of the administration of the king's ships in the late medieval period in England can be found in S. Rose, ed., *The Navy of the Lancastrian Kings* (London, 1982), and in S. Rose, 'Dockyards and Administration', in *Medieval Naval Warfare 1000–1500* (London, 2002).

14 The accounts of the *Clos des galées*, which give a clear view of the condition of the ships based there and the amount of activity in the yard, have been edited by A. Merlin-Chazelas, *Documents rélatifs au clos des galées de Rouen et aux armées de mer du roi de France de 1293 à 1418* (Paris, 1977–78). A smaller collection of similar documents can be found in C. Bréard, ed., 'Le compte du clos de galées de Rouen au XIVe siècle 1382–1384', in Blanquart et al., eds, *Documents, Deuxième série* (Rouen, 1893).

15 There are several poems and romances about his exploits including that edited by D. S. Brewer, *Two Medieval Outlaws: Eustace the Monk and Fouke Fitz Waryn* (Woodbridge, 1997).

16 F. W. Brooks, 'The Battle of Damme', *Mariner's Mirror*, 16 (1930), pp. 264–71, gives a full account of that battle. The adventures of Eustace the Monk are chronicled in D. J. Conlon, ed., *Li romans de Wistasse le Moine, roman du trezième siécle* (Chapel Hill, North Carolina, 1972). His career is also discussed in 'The Battle of Sandwich and Eustace the Monk', *English Historical Review*, 27 (1912), pp. 649–70. Mathew Paris's version of the Battle of Dover is in his *Chronica Majora*, ed. H. Luard (London, 1964), p. 26, and his *Historia Anglorum*, ed. F. Madden (London, 1866), pp. 217–21.

17 The poem (written between 1304 and 1307) was published in *Recueil des historiens des Gaules et de la France*, vol. xxii (Paris, 1865). The commentary mentioned is by Legrand d'Aussy, 'Notice sur l'étât de la marine en France au commencement du quartorzième siècle: et sur la tactique navale usitée alors dans les combats de mer', *Mémoires de l'Institut de France, Classe des Sciences Morales et Politiques*, 2, year VII (1798), pp. 302–75.

18 The Spanish at sea.

19 G. Brereton, ed. and trans., *Froissart Chronicles* (Harmondsworth, 1968), pp. 113–19. TNA, PRO, E101/24/14, the expenses of William Clewere, clerk of the king's ships, 18–32 Edward III.

20 J. Bill, 'Scandinavian Warships and Naval Power in the Thirteenth and Fourteenth Centuries', in J. B. Hattendorf and R. W. Unger, eds, *War at Sea in the Middle Ages and Reniassance* (Woodbridge, 2003), p. 47.

21 M. Hughes, 'The Fourteenth-Century French Raids on Hampshire and the Isle of Wight', in A. Curry and M. Hughes, eds, *Arms, Armies and Fortifications in the Hundred Years War* (Woodbridge, 1994), p. 129.

22 *Froissart Chronicles*, p. 60.

23 *The Parliament Rolls of Medieval England*, ed. C. Given-Wilson (Leicester, 2005), ii, p. 105, 1339; p. 314, 1372; iii, p. 162, 1383.

24 The biography is *El Victorial: A Chronicle of the Deeds of Don Pero Niño*, ed. J. de Mata Carriaga (Madrid, 1940). This episode can be found in *British Naval Documents, 1204–1960*, pp. 26–29.

25 F. Taylor and J. S. Roskell, eds, *Gesta Henrici Quinti* (Oxford, 1975), p. 21.

26 *British Naval Documents, 1204–1960*, pp. 29–30.

27 A. Giustiniani, *Annali della republica di Genova* (Genova, 1854), pp. 278–79.

28 *British Naval Documents, 1204–1960*, p. 44.

29 S. Rose, *The Navy of the Lancastrian Kings: Accounts and Inventories of William Soper, Keeper of the King's Ships, 1422–27* (London, 1982), pp. 48–51. This gives a full account of naval activity in the Channel at this time, including the near mutiny on the *Gracedieu* when an attempt was made to take the muster of her crew.

30 Rose, *The Navy of the Lancastrian Kings*, pp. 52–55.

31 M. Oppenheim, *Naval Accounts and Inventories of the Reign of Henry VII 1485–8 and 1495–7* (London, 1906), includes details of Henry VII's ships and the costs associated with their building and maintenance.

32 *British Naval Documents, 1204–1960*, pp. 11–13.

33 *British Naval Documents, 1204–1960*, p. 13.

34 A. R. Myers, ed., *English Historical Documents, 1327–1485* (London, 1969), pp. 516–22, Lord Cromwell's estimates of royal revenue and expenditure, 1433.

35 TNA, PRO, E/101/54/14.

36 J. Gairdner, ed., *The Paston Letters, 1422–1509* (London, 1900), i, letter 317, pp. 428–29.

37 C. Richmond, 'The Earl of Warwick's Domination of the Channel and the Naval Dimension to the Wars of the Roses, 1456–1460', in *Southern History*, 20/21 (1998–99), pp. 1–19, gives a full account of the earl of Warwick's activities at sea.

38 *British Naval Documents, 1204–1960*, p. 15.

39 C. L. Kingsford, 'West Country Piracy: The School of English Seamen', in *Prejudice and Promise in Fifteenth-Century England* (Oxford, 1925), discusses many incidents. Details of Chancery cases often involving piracy can be found in D. M. Gardiner, *A Calendar of Early Chancery Proceedings Relating to West Country Shipping, 1388–1493* (Torquay, 1976).

40 Details of the lives of both Hawleys can be found in the *Oxford Dictionary of National Biography* (Oxford, 2005). The Lovell case is calendared in Gardiner, *A Calendar of Early Chancery Proceedings Relating to West Country Shipping, 1388–1493*, pp. 25–26.

41 The name is spelt Wenyngton in the Paston Letters; in German sources he appears as Robert de Cane.

42 *British Naval Documents, 1204–1960*, pp. 30–31.

43 T. H. Lloyd, *England and the German Hanse, 1157–1611: A Study of Their Trade and Commercial Diplomacy* (Cambridge, 1991), pp. 182–83.

44 Lloyd, *England and the German Hanse*, table p. 218.

45 U. Scheurlen, 'La course et la piraterie aux XIVe et XVe siècles sur les côtes de la Frise', in *Course et piraterie*, i (San Francisco, 1975).

46 The method of fighting of ancient Greek galleys is fully described in J. Morrison, 'The Trireme', in R. Gardiner, ed., *The Age of the Galley* (London, 1995), pp. 59–62.

47 H. Ahrweiler, *Byzance et la Mer* (Paris, 1966), sees the Byzantine fleet as the tool by which Byzantium hoped to reconquer all the lost lands in the west, p. 395.

48 E. R. A. Sewter, ed. and trans., *The Alexiad of Anna Comnena* (London, 1969), p. 360.

49 J. H. Pryor, 'From Dromon to Galea: Mediterranean Bireme Galleys AD 500–1300', in Gardiner, *The Age of the Galley*, p. 102.

50 J. H. Pryor, 'The Geographical Conditions of Galley Navigation in the Mediterranean', in Gardiner, *The Age of the Galley*, p. 210.

51 Sigurd, the king of Norway, brought a fleet to Sidon to assist Baldwin I, king of Jerusalem, in 1110. H. E. Mayer, *The Crusades* (Oxford, 1988), p. 69.

52 The chronicle record of the building of these ships mentions that they were equipped with 'spurs' in the Byzantine manner. M. Mollat, 'Problèmes navales de l'histoire des Croissades', *Cahiers de Civilisation Médievale*, 10 (1967), p. 353.

53 Mayer, *The Crusades*, p. 145.

54 Mayer, *The Crusades*, p. 198.

55 Fulcher of Chartres, trans. F. R. Ryan, *A History of the Expedition to Jerusalem* (Knoxville, Tennessee, 1969), pp. 244–45.

56 Reynald of Chatillon, the Crusader lord based at Kerak in Moab, did something rather similar in 1182–83 when he launched a squadron of ships on the Red Sea to attack Moslem shipping and attempt raids on settlements.

57 A full discussion of Saladin's attitude to naval power can be found in A. H. Ehrenkreutz, 'The Place of Saladin in the Naval History of the Mediterranean Sea in the Middle Ages', *Journal of the American Oriental Society*, 75 (1955), pp. 100–16. The quotation from Imad ad-Din is on p. 111.

58 D. Ayalon, 'The Mamluks and Naval Power: A Phase of the Struggle between Islam and Christian Europe', *Proceedings of the Israel Academy of Sciences and Humanities*, I (1965), pp. 5–6.

59 Ayalon, 'The Mamluks and Naval Power', p. 12.

60 A. Fuess, 'Rotting Ships and Razed Harbors: The Naval Policy of the Mamluks', *Mamluk Studies Review*, 6 (2001), pp. 45–71, makes this point very forcefully.

61 J. E. Dotson, 'Fleet Operations in the First Genoese–Venetian War, 1264–1266', *Viator*, 30 (1999), pp. 168–76. The Venetian galley fleet continued to Tyre, finding only one Genoese galley there.

62 Dotson 'Fleet Operations in the First Genoese–Venetian war', pp. 176–79.

63 J. E. Dotson, 'The Voyage of Simone Leccavello: A Genoese Naval Expedition of 1351', *Saggi e Documenti*, 6 (Genoa, 1985), pp. 269–82.

64 Daniele di Chinazzo, *Cronica de la Guerra da Veniciani a Zenovesi*, ed. V. Lazzarini (Venice, 1958).

65 F. C. Lane, *Venice: A Maritime Republic* (Baltimore, Maryland, 1973), pp. 189–96.

66 J. H. Pryor, 'The Naval Battles of Roger of Lauria', *Journal of Medieval History*, 9 (1983), p. 179.

67 L. V. Mott, *Sea Power in the Medieval Mediterranean: The Catalan-Aragonese Fleet in the War of the Sicilian Vespers* (Gainesville, Florida, 2003), p. 265.

68 Mott, *Sea Power in the Medieval Mediterranean*; L. V. Mott, 'The Battle of Malta', in D. J. Kagay and L. J. A. Villalon, *The Circle of War in the Middle Ages: Essays on Medieval Military and Naval History* (Woodbridge, 1999); Pryor, 'The Naval Battles of Roger of Lauria'.

69 Lady Goodenough, *The Chronicle of Muntaner* (Hakluyt Society, London, 1920–21)

70 Mott, 'The Battle of Malta', discusses the battle and the sources for it at length.

71 Rose, *Medieval Naval Warfare*, pp. 48–49.

72 W. Sawyer, 'The Lexis of Naval Tactics in Muntaner's *Cronica*', *Catalan Review*, 17 (2003), discusses the linguistic elements of this puzzle in full.

73 Mott, *Sea Power in the Medieval Mediterranean*, p. 265.

74 J. H. Pryor, *Geography, Technology and War: Studies in the Maritime History of the Mediterranean, 649–1571* (Cambidge, 1988), p. 180.

75 The letter is printed in *Dannali Veneti del 1457 al 1500 del Senatore Domenico Malipiero*, ed. F. Longo (Florence, 1843), i, p. 50. The battle is also discussed in Rose, *Medieval Naval Warfare*, pp. 111–13.

76 See the article by L. Fincati, 'La deplorabile battaglia del Zonchio', *Rivista marittima* (1883).

77 Rose, *Medieval Naval Warfare*, pp. 113–15. The contemporary accounts are in *Dannali Veneti del 1457 al 1500 del Senatore Domenico Malipiero*, and in *I diarii di Marino Sanuto* (Bologna, 1969–70), pp. 1122–26 and 1130–38. The woodcut is in the collection of the Print Room of the British Museum.

78 J. Heers, *Gênes au XVe siècle: activité économique et problèmes sociaux* (Paris, 1961), table 11, pp. 635–38.

79 B. Kreki, 'Piracy on the Dalmatian Coast, Seventh to Thirteenth Centuries', in *Course et piraterie*, i, pp. 30–35.

80 The great majority of Dom Pero Niño's biography by Gutierre Diaz de Gamez has been translated by J. Evans, in *The Unconquered Knight* (London, 1928). These events are on pp. 51–78.

81 L. Balletto, 'A travers la Méditerranée avec le pirate-corsaire Scarincio', in H. Akkari, ed., *La Méditerranée médiévale: perceptions et représentations* (Paris and Tunis), pp. 153–69.

82 J. Mitchell, trans., *The History of the Maritime Wars of the Turks* (London, 1831), p. 47.

Chapter 6

1 All quotations from and references to the Laws of Oléron come from the transcription and translation in appendix 1 of R. Ward, 'The Mystery of the Medieval Shipmaster: The English Shipmaster at Law, in Business and at Sea between the Mid-Fourteenth and Mid-Fifteenth Centuries', unpublished PhD thesis (London, 2000).

2 J. Evans, ed., *The Unconquered Knight* (London, 1928), pp. 93–97.

3 Sir T. Travers Twiss, *The Black Book of the Admiralty*, iii (London, 1874), p. 221. The *Costumes* were originally written in Catalan.

4 Travers Twiss, *The Black Book*, iii, pp. 231, 233.

5 Ward, 'The Mystery of the Medieval Shipmaster', appendix 1, article 7.

6 See above, pp. 87–8.

7 Travers Twiss, *The Black Book*, i, pp. 139–40.

8 Ward, 'The Mystery of the Medieval Shipmaster', appendix 1, article 6.

9 Godshouse or the hospital of St Julian was situated near the Watergate and the Customs House in Southampton; it cared for the old and sick.

10 A. A. Ruddock, *Italian Merchants and Shipping in Southampton, 1270–1600* (Southampton, 1951), pp. 150–51. The quotation is from the steward's book for 1456–57.

11 M. E. Mallett, *The Florentine Galleys in the Fifteenth Century* (Oxford, 1967), p. 256, from Albizzi's diary of his voyage.

12 D. M. Gardiner, *A Calendar of Early Chancery Proceedings Relating to West Country Shipping, 1388–1493* (Torquay, 1976), pp. 12, 46, 84–85.

13 Travers Twiss, *The Black Book*, i, p. 99.

14 S. Rose, ed., 'The Bayonne Galleys', in M. Duffy, ed., *Naval Miscellany*, VI (London, 2003), pp. 21–26.

15 A. Crawford, ed., *The Household Books of John Howard, Duke of Norfolk, 1462–71, 1481–3* (Stroud, 1992), pp. 200–1.

16 These are described in Chapter 4, above.

17 Ruddock, *Italian Merchants and Shipping*, pp. 132–33. In 1951 the tombstone was visible in the church at North Stoneham to which it was removed when St Nicholas's chapel was demolished in the seventeenth century. The position of the chapel may have some relation to the use of the spire of St Mary's church as a navigation mark.

18 L. Toulmin-Smith, *The Expedition to Prussia and the Holy Land Made*

by Henry Earl of Derby in the Years 1390–1 and 1392–3 (London, 1894), p. 37.

19 F. Devon, *Issues of the Exchequer* (London, 1837), p. 356.

20 Mallett, *The Florentine Galleys*, pp. 210, 262.

21 Rose, *The Navy of the Lancastrian Kings*, p. 50.

22 Evans, *The Unconquered Knight*, pp. 13–15.

23 Mallett, *The Florentine Galleys*, p. 224. 175 cases of raisins had to be shifted to the second galley in his group.

24 Mallett, *The Florentine Galleys*, p. 226.

25 F. C. Lane, 'Venetian Seamen in the Nautical Revolution', in B. G. Kohl and R. C. Mueller, eds, *Studies in Venetian Social and Economic History* (London, 1987), p. 405.

26 J. E. Dotson, 'The Voyage of Simone Leccavello: A Genoese Naval Expedition of 1351', *Saggi e Documenti*, 6 (Genoa, 1985), pp. 273–75.

27 D. di Chinazzo, *Cronica de la Guerra da Veniciani a Zenovesi*, ed. V. Lazzarini (Venice, 1958), pp. 60–61. The translation from the Venetian dialect is by the author.

28 Mallett, *The Florentine Galleys*, pp. 218, 234, 263–64.

29 F. C. Lane, 'Diet and Wages of Seamen in the Early Fourteenth Century', in *Venice and History: The Collected Papers of Frederick C. Lane* (Baltimore, Maryland, 1966), pp. 263–68.

30 L. Greco, ed., *Quaderno di Bordo di Giovanni Manzini, prete-notaio cancelliere, 1471–84* (Venice, 1997), p. 96.

31 J. E. Dotson, 'Economics and Logistics of Galley Warfare', in R. Gardiner, ed., *The Age of the Galley* (London, 1995), p. 222.

32 See above.

33 Rose, *The Navy of the Lancastrian Kings*, pp. 112, 116.

34 C. Richmond, *John Hopton: A Fifteenth-Century Suffolk Gentleman* (Cambridge, 1981), p. 25.

35 Richmond, *John Hopton*, pp. 41–42.

36 Richmond, *John Hopton*, p. 50.

37 Richmond, *John Hopton*, pp. 171–73.

38 Richmond, *John Hopton*, pp. 173–74. Walberswick creek eventually suffered from silting up, so that the fishing boats largely moved to Southwold.

39 D. M. Owen, *The Making of King's Lynn: A Documentary Survey* (London, 1984), pp. 193–94.

40 Owen, *The Making of King's Lynn*, p. 205.

41 Owen, *The Making of King's Lynn*, p. 62.

42 Owen, *The Making of King's Lynn*, p. 285.

43 Owen, *The Making of King's Lynn*, pp. 235–49.

44 Owen, *The Making of King's Lynn*, pp. 221–34.

45 Owen, *The Making of King's Lynn*, p. 332.

46 Owen, *The Making of King's Lynn*, p. 334.

47　P. Richards, *King's Lynn* (Chichester, 1997), p. 6. The warehouse lies behind a Georgian façade added to the building in the eighteenth century.

48　Some Italians settled in the town and took out letters of denizenship; others rented some of the largest and most impressive houses in the town. The properties which were in Italian hands can be traced through the *Terrier of 1454–5*, ed. L. A. Burgess (London, 1976).

49　The quays were outside the Watergate, and also the West Hithe or galleys quay, stretching between Westgate street and Pilgrims gate, outside the walls.

50　Port books for Southampton exist for quite a large number of years in the fifteenth century. Some have been edited in the Southampton Record Series, notably H. A. Cobb, ed., *The Local Port Book of Southampton for 1439–40*, which includes a full introduction and a glossary.

51　C. Platt, *Medieval Southampton: The Port and Trading Community*, AD *1000–1600* (London, 1973), pp. 107–16.

52　F. Taylor and J. S. Roskell, *Gesta Henrici Quinti: The Deeds of Henry V* (Oxford, 1975), p. 21.

53　W. J. Carpenter-Turner, 'The Building of the *Gracedieu, Valentine* and *Falconer* at Southampton 1416–20', and 'The Building of the *Holy Ghost of the Tower*, 1414–16, and her subsequent history', in *Mariner's Mirror*, 40 (1954), pp. 59–74, 271–81.

54　S. Rose, *Southampton and the Navy in the Age of Henry V* (Hampshire, 1998), p. 11.

55　Platt, *Medieval Southampton*, p. 182.

56　*A Chronicle of London from 1089–1483 Written in the Fifteenth Century* (Felinfach, 1995), p. 146.

57　R. Hammel-Kiesow, 'Lübeck and the Baltic Trade in Bulk Goods for the North Sea Region 1150–1400', in L. Berggren, N. Hybel and A. Landen, eds, *Cogs, Cargoes and Commerce: Maritime Bulk Trade in Northern Europe, 1150–1400* (Toronto, 2002), pp. 53–55.

58　Hammel-Kiesow, 'Lübeck and the Baltic Trade in Bulk Goods'. See maps of Lübeck waterfront on pp. 60–61.

59　A. d'Haenens, *Europe of the North Sea and the Baltic: The World of the Hanse* (Antwerp, 1984), p. 146.

60　P. Dollinger, *La Hanse XIIe–XVIIe siècles* (Paris, 1964), p. 189.

61　Haenens, *Europe of the North Sea and the Baltic*, pp. 300–3.

62　The early days of Venice are fully described by F. C. Lane in *Venice: A Maritime Republic* (Baltimore and London, 1973), pp. 1–12.

63　ASV, Senato Misti, 1439, pp. 56v–57.

64　ASV, Senato Mar, Regeste 14, 1493–99, pp. 10v, 13, 14v and passim.

65　Luca di Maso degli Albizzi, as we have seen above, had a very similar brief on his voyage as captain in 1429–30.

66　ASV, Senato Misti, 1439, p. 65. The order translates as 'Act in all things with all good caution and care'.

Chapter 7

1 A typical example of this kind of map is the Hereford *Mappa Mundi*.

2 J. R. S. Phillips, *The Medieval Expansion of Europe* (Oxford, 1998), p. 207.

3 Some leaves of the Atlas can be found at http://expositions.bnf.fr/ciel/catalan

4 F. Fernandez-Armesto, *Before Columbus: Exploration and Colonization from the Mediterranean to the Atlantic, 1229–1492* (Philadelphia, 1987), pp. 247–48.

5 http://www.fordham.edu/halsall/source/polo-kinsay.html includes an extract from Polo's text.

6 J. H. Parry, *The Discovery of the Sea* (London, 1974), p. vii.

7 C. W. Hollister et al., eds, *Medieval Europe: A Short Sourcebook* (New York, 1982), p. 261.

8 Phillips, *The Medieval Expansion of Europe*, pp. 146–49.

9 The mention occurs in the *Itineraries* of William of Worcester; these have been edited in J. H. Harvey, ed., *William Worcestre Itineraries* (Oxford, 1969).

10 D. B. Quinn, 'Edward IV and Exploration', *Mariner's Mirror*, 21 (1935), pp. 280–81.

11 A full discussion of the Bristol voyages and of Cabot's expedition can be found in S. Rose, 'English Seamanship and the Atlantic Crossing, c. 1450–1500', *Journal for Maritime Research* (2002), http://www.jmr.nmm.ac.uk.

12 P. and H. Chaunu, *Séville et l'Atlantique* (Paris, 1955–60), vi, pt 3, tables 616, 617.

13 See pp. 142–3. Although the battle itself had no outright victor, the Venetians suffered the loss of Lepanto, Modon and Coron in the immediate aftermath.

14 This work was first published in 1600.

Bibliography

This is not a complete bibliography of all the works consulted in the writing of this book but a list of those books which will help a reader pursue further the subjects discussed and the issues raised. Included are all those studies which I have found most useful myself.

Akkari, H., *La Méditerranée médiévale: perceptions et représentations* (Paris and Tunis, 2002).

Berggren, L., Hybel, N. and Landen, A., *Cogs, Cargoes and Commerce: Maritime Bulk Trade in Northern Europe 1150–1400* (Toronto, 2002).

Brooks, F. W., *The English Naval Forces, 1199–1272* (London, n.d.).

Burwash, D., *English Merchant Shipping, 1460–1540* (Newton Abbot, 1969).

Byrne, E. H., *Genoese Shipping in the Twelfth and Thirteenth Centuries* (Cambridge, Massachusetts, 1938).

Carus-Wilson, E. M., *Medieval Merchant Venturers* (London, 1954).

Childs, W. R., *Anglo-Castilian Trade in the Later Middle Ages* (Manchester, 1978).

Course et piraterie: études présentés à la commission internationale d'histoire maritime à l'occasion de son XVe colloque internationale pendant le XIV Congrès des Sciences Historiques, San Francisco (Paris, 1975).

Curry, A. and Hughes, M., eds, *Arms, Armies and Fortifications in the Hundred Years War* (Woodbridge, 1994).

D'Haenens, A., *Europe of the North Sea and the Baltic* (Antwerp, 1984).

Dollinger, P., *La Hanse XIIe–XVIIe siècles* (Paris, 1964).

Epstein, S., *Genoa and the Genoese: 958–1528* (Chapel Hill, North Carolina, 1996).

Evans, J., *The Unconquered Knight: A Chronicle of the Deeds of Don Pero Niño by his Standard Bearer Gutierre Diaz de Gamez* (London, 1928).

Fernandez Duro, C., *La marina de Castilla desde su origin y pugna con la de Inglaterra hasta la refundicion en la Armada Española* (Madrid, 1894).

Fernandez-Armesto, F., *Before Columbus: Exploration and Colonization from the Mediterranean to the Atlantic, 1229–1492* (Philadelphia, 1987).

Friel, I., *The Good Ship: Ships, Shipbuilding and Technology in England, 1200–1520* (London, 1995).

Fudge, J. D., *Cargoes, Embargoes and Emissaries: The Commercial and*

Political Interaction of England and the German Hanse, 1450–1510 (Toronto, 1995).

Gardiner, R., ed., *The Age of the Galley: Mediterranean Oared Vessels since Pre-Classical Times* (London, 1995).

Gardiner, R., ed., *Cogs, Caravels and Galleons: The Sailing Ship, 1000–1650* (London, 1994).

Hanham, A., *The Celys and their World: An English Merchant Family of the Fifteenth Century* (Cambridge, 1985).

Hattendorf, J. B. et al., *British Naval Documents, 1204–1960* (London, 1993).

Hattendorf, J. B. and Unger, R. W., *War at Sea in the Middle Ages and Renaissance* (Woodbridge, 2003).

Haywood, J., *Dark Age Naval Power: A Reassessment of Frankish and Anglo-Saxon Seafaring Activity* (London, 1991).

Heers, J., *Gênes au XVe siècle: activité économique et problèmes sociaux* (Paris 1961).

Heers, J., *Société et Économie a Gênes* (London, 1979).

Hewitt, H. J., *The Organisation of War under Edward III* (Manchester, 1966).

Hillenbrand, C., *The Crusades: Islamic Perspectives* (Edinburgh, 1999).

Hutchinson, G., *Medieval Ships and Shipping* (London, 1994).

Kagay, D. J. and Villalon, L. J. A., eds, *The Circle of War in the Middle Ages: Essays on Medieval Military and Naval History* (Woodbridge, 1999).

Knighton, C. S. and Loades, D. M., *The Anthony Roll of Henry VIII's Navy* (Aldershot, 2000).

Lane, F. C., 'Naval Actions and Fleet Organisation, 1499–1502', in J. Hale, ed., *Renaissance Venice* (London, 1973).

Lane, F. C., *Venice: A Maritime Republic* (Baltimore and London, 1973).

Lane, F. C., *Venice and History: The Collected Papers of Frederic C. Lane* (Baltimore, 1966).

Lloyd, T. H., *England and the German Hanse 1157–1611: A Study of their Trade and Commercial Diplomacy* (Cambridge, 1991).

Lloyd, T. H., *The English Wool Trade in the Middle Ages* (Cambridge, 1977).

Marcus, G. J., *The Conquest of the North Atlantic* (Woodbridge, 1980).

Martin, L. M., *The Art and Archaeology of Venetian Ships and Boats* (London and College Station, 2001).

McGrail, S., *Ancient Boats in North-West Europe: The Archaeology of Water Transport to AD 1500* (London and New York, 1998).

Miskimin, H. A., *The Economy of Early Renaissance Europe, 1300–1460* (Cambridge, 1975).

Mott, L. V., *Sea Power in the Medieval Mediterranean: The Catalan-Aragonese Fleet in the War of the Sicilian Vespers* (Florida, 2003).

Navigation et gens de mer en Méditerranée de la prehistoire à nos jours (Paris, 1980).

Oppenheim, M., *A History of the Administration of the Royal Navy and of Merchant Shipping in Relation to the Navy from MDIX to MDCLX with an Introduction Treating of the Preceding Period* (London, 1896).

Parry, J. H., *The Discovery of the Sea* (London, 1974).

Pertusi, A., ed., *Venezia e il Levante fino al secolo XV* (Florence, 1973).

Phillips, J. R. S., *The Medieval Expansion of Europe* (Oxford, 1998).

Power, E. and Postan, M. M., *Studies in English Trade in the Fifteenth Century* (London, 1933).

Pryor, J. H., *Geography, Technology and War: Studies in the Maritime History of the Mediterranean, 649–1571* (Cambridge, 1992).

Ragosta, R., *Le genti del Mare Mediterraneo* (Naples, 1981).

Rodger, N. A. M., *The Safeguard of the Sea: A Naval History of Britain, 660–1649* (London, 1997).

Rodgers, W. L., *Naval Warfare Under Oars 4th to 16th Centuries: A Study of Strategy Tactics and Ship Design* (Annapolis, 1940).

Rose, S., *Medieval Naval Warfare, 1000–1500* (London, 2002).

Rose, S., *The Navy of the Lancastrian Kings: Accounts and Inventories of William Soper, Keeper of the King's Ships, 1422–1427* (London, 1982).

Rose, S., *Southampton and the Navy in the Age of Henry V* (Winchester, 1998).

Ruddock, A. A., *Italian Merchants and Shipping in Southampton, 1270–1600* (Southampton, 1951).

Sottas, J., *Les messageries maritimes de Venise aux XIVe et XVe siècles* (Paris, 1938).

Spufford, P., *Power and Profit: The Merchant in Medieval Europe* (London, 2002).

Tangheroni, M., *Commercio e navigazione nel medioevo* (Rome, 1996).

Taylor, E. G. R., *The Haven-Finding Art: A History of Navigation from Odysseus to Captain Cook* (London, 1956).

Unger, R. W., *The Ship in the Medieval Economy, 600–1600* (London and Montreal, 1980).

Unwin, G., ed., *Finance and Trade under Edward III* (London, 1962).

Villain-Gandossi, C. et al., *Medieval Ships and the Birth of Technological Societies* (Valetta, 1989).

Waters, D. W., *The Art of Navigation in Elizabethan and Early Stuart Times* (Greenwich, 1978).

Index